ईशोपनिषद्

Īśopaniṣad

The Secret Teaching on the Lord

Śrī Gaṇeśāya namaḥ

ईशोपनिषद्
(ईशा-उपनिषद्)

Īśā Upaniṣad

The Secret Teaching on the Lord

(Grammatically and semantically analyzed word by word)

शङ्करमध्वभाष्यसहिता

With the commentaries of
Śaṅkara (Non-dualism) and Madhva (Dualism)

Edited, translated, analyzed, and annotated
by
Neal Delmonico and Lloyd W. Pflueger

Blazing Sapphire Press
715 E. McPherson
Kirksville, Missouri 63501
2017

ISBN 978-1-936135-09-7 (1-936135-09-4))

Library of Congress Control Number: 2017937559

Published by:
Blazing Sapphire Press
715 E. McPherson
Kirksville, Missouri 63501

Available at:
Nitai's Bookstore
715 E. McPherson
Kirksville, Missouri, 63501
Phone: (660) 665-0273
http://www.nitaisbookstore.com
http://www.naciketas-press.com
Email: neal@blazing-sapphire-press.com

Contents

Acknowledgments

I (Delmonico) would first like to recognize my partner in this endeavor, Dr. Lloyd W. Pflueger, who came up with the idea of translating this Upaniṣad as a way of teaching the fundamentals of Vedānta and Indian philosophy while also introducing students to the beauty and depth of the Sanskrit language. We have spent uncountable hours together discussing, debating, disagreeing, agreeing, compromising, writing and re-writing. It has been a tremendous experience for me and a valuable one for us both, I think, in terms of learning to negotiate the murky waters of an ancient text and its interconnections with other ancient texts without being unduly influenced by the anachronistic views of later commentators (Śaṅkara, Madhva, and a slough of others more modern). This is not to say that these later views are not important. They are certainly valuable in understanding how later members of the tradition read and understood the text.

An enormous aid in our endeavor has been the work of Dr. Mislav Ježić of the Department of Indology and Far Eastern Studies at Zagreb University. Dr. Ježić wrote a cutting-edge paper on the structure, development, and connections with other Upaniṣads of the *Īśopaniṣad*. He also gave liberally of his time to answer our questions, encourage us in our efforts, and express his views on various theories of interpretation relating to the text. Dr. Ježić has even allowed us to include his paper in this book as Appendix A. We are thrilled to share the work of such an extraordinary scholar with the rest of the world through the publication of this book.

Finally, Delmonico would like to recognize his wife Betsy for reading through this work twice (except for the Devanāgarī parts) and making improvements in its language and logic. Because of her this is a much finer piece of work than it would otherwise have been.

I (Pflueger) wish to acknowledge my deep gratitude to the Department of Philosophy and Religion and the School of Social and Cultural Studies of Truman State University for the year-long sabbatical that made this book possible. I am also grateful to friends, students, and colleagues for their feedback and support along the way. In particular, this book would not have been possible without the indefatigable efforts of my partner in crime (*traduttore traditori*) Neal Delmonico, with his perspicacious grasp of Pāṇini's grammar, the wiles of Sanskrit commentaries, and the ins and outs of the florid jungle of Indian philosophy and religion. Reading the Upaniṣads and relevant indological work with Neal on a regular basis over the last years of this project has been a significant chapter of my ongoing education and intellectual enrichment—thanks for your patience and friendship! Most of all I wish to express my enduring gratitude to my earliest Sanskrit professors at the University of California, Santa Barbara, Gerald James Larson and Nandini Ayer, as well as all my teachers both spiritual and academic, starting with my parents: सर्वेभ्यो गुरुभ्यो नमः, *sarvebhyo gurubhyo namaḥ*.

Photographic Credits

The following people and museums are responsible for the photographs and images found scattered throughout the text:

Cosmovitrol Botanical Garden, Toluca, Mexico: p.106 (Sun Man, https://unsplash.com/, 1223424).
Melinda Delmonico: p. 101 (Golden Disc of the Sun).
Jagdish and Kamla Mittal Museum of Indian Art: Back cover image (Vishwarupa).
Ivars Krutainis: p. 88 (https://unsplash.com/, 153526).
Kalyan Kumar: p. 80 (https://unsplash.com/, 28795).

The Los Angeles County Museum of Art: p. 28 (Shiva as the Lord of Dance, M.75.1); p. 36 (The Heavenly Audience of Shiva and Parvati, M.85.283.3); p. 56 (The Maharshi Agastya, M.90.117.1); p. 71 (Eclipse, ?); p. 84 (The Hindu Goddess Kali, M.83.48).

Lloyd W. Pflueger: Front cover image (Naṭarāja), frontispiece (Śrī Gaṇeśa); p. 20 (Red Tree); p. 24 (Manifestation); p. 46 (Hilo-Falls); p. 52 (Cave of the Heart); p. 60 (Chicago Temple); p. 64 (Mountain Top, Garden of the Gods, CO); p. 76 (Chipmunk Trail); p. 94 (Water and Ice); p. 110 (Bonfire); p. 114 (Sacrificial Fire).

NASA: p. 42 (Moon, https://unsplash.com/).

Introduction

General Remarks on the Upaniṣads (Pflueger)

The *Īśā Upaniṣad* (ĪU),[1] The Secret Teaching on the Lord, is usually the first Upaniṣad in traditional collections. Despite this place of honor, modern scholars do not place it chronologically first or even among the earliest Upaniṣads, which are prose. Rather, as a verse Upaniṣad the ĪU is thought to be closer in time with other middle Upaniṣads also written in verse. These are dated to between 400 and 200 BCE, though there is considerable imprecision in dating any of these ancient documents exactly. Certainly the ĪU is closely linked with the prose *Bṛhad-āraṇyaka Upaniṣad* (It quotes from Ch. 4.) which, along with the *Chāndogya Upaniṣad*, is considered to be the earliest of Upaniṣadic texts. Authorship of the ĪU is unknown. Its place of honor in traditional collections marks its importance; perhaps it was seen as a short summary of ideas in the earliest Upaniṣads, with particular reference to the concept of god as Īś, the one Lord, the Divine Ruler. As such, the ĪU can serve, dense and ambiguous, as an extremely concise introduction to the ideas and problems in dealing with Upaniṣadic thought. To deal with the Lord's Upaniṣad is to deal at once with the phenomenology and meaning of mystical experience and the most important philosophical and theological issues in Indic culture, Vedic literature, and Hinduism as a whole. We hope that this intellectual wrestling match might begin for the interested student with the reading of this short but complete Upaniṣad in depth, with commentary: Vedic mysticism in miniature.

In India the earliest revealed (*śruti*) literature, for which the Upaniṣads are the capstone, is simply known as Knowledge, Veda. This knowledge pertains to human interaction with invisible powers which underlie the visible realm. This invisible network of powers is understood to respond to particular sacrificial rituals and chants. Veda, per se, begins with the *saṃhitā* (collection) of chants or hymns (ca. 1500 BCE). These are poetic invocations and praise of the shining, subtle, supernatural powers (*devas*) understood to rule the natural world and respond to human supplications as allies against the powers of darkness and chaos. The very sound of the verses, the metrical *mantras* of the Vedic hymns, downloaded, as it were, from the cosmic ether by the intuition of the earliest sages, *ṛṣis*, was understood to vibrate with sacred power, *brahman*. In their understanding, this holy power could then be channeled through ritual offerings to balance the powers of nature and grant human votaries and their society everything they needed—wealth and fertility[2] here, and pleasant heavenly worlds after death.

This religion of sonorous sacrifice to the shining powers of nature makes up the earliest documented strata of Indic religion, and is certainly a contender for the earliest religious literature known on the planet (ca. 1700-1500 BCE). These poetic hymns in Vedic Sanskrit expanded from the original hymns to include four collections divided for different priestly purposes (Ṛg, Sāma, Yajur, and Atharva Vedas). Each collection was memorized and passed down orally in priestly families comprising branches (*śākhās*) of the vedic corpus, often with their own version of the texts. The ritual use and meaning of these basic hymns, which are often elliptical and difficult to interpret, are further elaborated in appended priestly liturgical manuals called *Brāhmaṇas* (ca. 900 BCE). Later, the higher symbolic meanings of the texts are brought out in further appended literature for contemplation outside the village in forest retreats (*Āraṇyakas*, Forest Books, ca. 800 BCE.). The final crown of this exploration of the highest meaning of the Vedic hymns, understood as the last portion of the Veda itself, or Vedānta (*veda* + *anta*, Veda-end or Veda-

[1] More phonetically, *Īśopaniṣat*, also called *Īśāvāsya Upaniṣad*, using its first phrase as its name.

[2] Especially important was the desire for male offspring to continue the family line and provide for proper funeral rituals which ensure auspicious afterlife.

goal) is the literature known also as Upaniṣads (ca. 800-200 BCE). Many have explained the term (*upa-ni-ṣad*) as "sitting-down-near-[the teacher-]doctrines," meaning "special hidden teachings revealed only to close disciples sitting down next to their spiritual teacher or *guru*." However, it may be that the term, according to the native usage in the texts themselves is best translated simply as "secret equivalences" or "esoteric connections" (between Veda verses and words and their ritual use) which build to an ultimate understanding of the very core or essence of life, spiritual enlightenment. Thus we may translate *Īśopaniṣad* as "The Secret Teaching Concerning the Lord (Īś)."

The final revelations, or keys to perfected understanding, were originally simply appended to the oral versions of the corpus of Vedic hymns and ritual instructions passed down verbatim in priestly families through scrupulous memory training. The ĪU for example comprises Chapter Forty of the *Vājasaneyī Saṃhitā* also known as the Śukla (White) Yajur Veda, a collection of hymns used in performing the Vedic sacrifices, geographically linked to the area of Kosala and Videha (a little east of ancient north-central India). Eventually the "secret equivalences" were extracted out of their ritual explanatory contexts at the end of such family collections of Vedic hymns, *Brāhmaṇas*, and *Āraṇyakas* into collections of Upaniṣads only, (ca. 1000-1500 CE). In their new context, the teachings of various *gurus* in various families could be easily read side by side to support and strengthen an understanding of total esoteric wisdom—the early subject of Indian philosophical schools which would debate the meanings and a possible overarching philosophical system to integrate them all.

Philosophical thought was formulated in six systems of orthodox Vedic schools of thought, the six *darśanas*, of which the last and most famous is the *Vedānta-sūtras* (*Brahma-sūtras*) of Bādarāyaṇa (ca. 400 CE). which attempts to systematize the thinking of the *Chāndogya* and other principal Upaniṣads. These *Vedānta-sūtras* (VS), establish what becomes later the single most important source for Indian theology, establishing the "correct orthodox viewpoint" on the meaning of the Upaniṣads vis-a-vis their philosophical rivals in Indian systems such as Sāṃkhya-Yoga (the strongest) and Nyāya-Vaiśeṣika schools. Significantly, there was also vigorous debate countering the views of the competing non-orthodox religious schools, those not based on the Veda, such as Buddhism and Jainism. The *Vedānta-sūtras*, too brief and ambiguous to be read without accompanying explanations, were commented on by India's most illustrious thinkers, most famously by Śaṅkara (ca. 700 CE) according to his Non-Dual (Advaita) Vedānta philosophy, and then by Rāmānuja (b. 1017 CE) through his Qualified Non-Dual Philosophy (Viśiṣṭādvaita), and later by Madhva (b. 1199 CE), a Dualist, (Dvaita Vedānta), among many others.

Notwithstanding the efforts of the VS and its many great commentators, *the distillation and defense of one consistent underlying logical viewpoint therein is perhaps a doomed task.* The Upaniṣads are after all a gathering of insights from a wide range of spiritual teachers over the Indian subcontinent over centuries. Not only are we dealing with an interpretation of poetic insights of vedic seers of many times and periods, we are also dealing with an intellectual culture which prized polysemy and ambiguity. The struggle for just one and only one correct, logical, and absolute doctrine of existence seems, indeed, antithetical to the cultural and religious variety of the subcontinent. Indeed, the early vedic seers embrace both unity and multiplicity in mystery: *ekaṃ sat*, "the Truth is One", *viprāḥ bahudhā vadanti* "[but] seers speak of it in a variety of ways" (Ṛg Veda 1.164.46). And as the *Aitareya Upaniṣad* states: *parokṣapriyā iva hi devāḥ* the gods seem to love what is mysterious" (AU 1.3.14).

Many literal as well as metaphorical meanings are possible for most Sanskrit words—and Sanskrit syntax, the way words are linked together either grammatically or in compounds which do away with obvious grammatical endings, as well as the rules for combining sounds when words follow one another, (*saṃdhi*) give tremendous license for a multiplicity of interpretations. In this literature there is both a goad to find the ultimate meaning and to raise one's awareness to see the relativity and artificiality of any rigid viewpoint. The Upaniṣads work as a kind of "jawbreaker" to the inflexible intellect. Perfect material for cutting the teeth of scholars of religion.

We offer the *Īśā Upaniṣad* with Śaṅkara's uncompromising Non-Dual interpretation along with Madhva's uncompromising Dualism and our own comments and notes, complete with Sanskrit vocabulary and grammatical explanations so that the determined student *can work with the primary text and get a sense of the mind-expanding possibilities of Vedic revelation and Indian philosophy in miniature*: an Upaniṣad in a mere eighteen verses, the understanding of which could take a lifetime, or more. It is our hope that these eighteen verses will unfold a vision of unlimited possibilities for the Western student—a nutshell to explore, giving a vision of the infinite space which is Vedic literature and philosophy.

Some Historical Background: Ritual and Revolution

It must be emphasized that unlike the widely published texts of major world religions today, the Upaniṣads and the philosophical/theological literature commenting on them and systematizing them was essentially *an esoteric priestly knowledge, composed for priests, by priests, memorized, edited, and preserved by priests.* The Upaniṣads themselves make it clear that the insights and formulae delivered are not even for all of the elite priestly class, but only for the oldest son, or closest disciples among them. It was never imagined that these texts would be heard or read by anyone outside the closest inner circle of highly trained students, qualified by family, character, culture, and life circumstance. It was not imagined that they would or could be read, and understood as we do today, around the world, whether by Hindu, or non-Hindu, essentially out of context!

In what context did the secret formulations of Upaniṣadic truth develop? Though authorship and exact times of origin are still uncertain, the cultural soil in which the esoteric literature developed is widely known. Human habitation and civilization in India is quite ancient, and archeological exploration only in early stages. As with most ancient cultures, evidence is relatively sparse. Much of its interpretation is still controversial. Stone age civilization goes back some 500,000 years in the subcontinent. The earliest civilization, whose writing remains undeciphered, is associated with the Indus and Sarasvatī rivers in NW India, and goes back to ca. 2500-2000 BCE, declining apparently due to climatic change. Vedic civilization rises in its place and spreads east and south, integrating various elements of the stone age culture and the Indus civilization culture(s) (which may have been largely Dravidian) with a nomadic culture of horse-drawn chariots and Sanskrit language. This nomadic culture referred to itself as *ārya*, or noble (cognate with Ireland, and Iran). Though tribal and wandering early on, the new cultural synthesis becomes more complex and settled over time. Small-scale, tribal, village culture grows to city culture, with trade, kingdoms, armies, and complex social and religious differentiation (ca. 1000—400 BCE.) This momentous social transformation results in religious revolution as well.

The Upaniṣads mark this religious and social upheaval. We see a movement from small scale informal religious sacrifice and chant to highly elaborate seasonal sacrifices, from one sacred fire to three, from one Veda to four collections of hymns, etc. Likewise the elaboration of sacrifice necessitated new ritual texts which taught priests the meaning of sacrificial actions and words, the links which made vedic sacrifice a model of the cosmos harmonizing humans and the deities at all levels, the texts of the *Brāhmaṇas*, *Āraṇyakas*, and finally the Upaniṣads. With the new high level esoteric teachings in the *Āraṇyakas* and Upaniṣads (sometimes they are indistinguishable) we see something new. A new set of religious questions arise—whereas the earlier rites focus on, "How can one gain wealth, heavenly worlds after death, and excellent progeny to maintain the family now and herafter?"—the Upaniṣads focus more inwardly, mystically. In the breakdown of the village culture and the rise of kingdoms and the elaboration of both the ritual performance and its cost, a palpable sense of skepticism arose: with society changing so radically, and everything changing—maybe the results of ritual are temporary as well. Is there anything that really lasts? Ideas of reincarnation and the return of souls from heavenly rewards back to the earth in endless recycling and resuffering arise. The new religious question was for an identity which was beyond this cycle of change—is there anything known within a human being which is beyond the vicissitudes of change? Or more simply stated, "Who am I?"

Just as the ancient sages intuited the sacred chants and rituals which linked humans and the beings of light, the *gurus* of the Upaniṣads, each in their own way, with their own vocabulary and angle, intuited in their deepest inner contemplation a revolutionary new answer, the secret of secrets, which had the power, if known through direct experience, to transform darkness and turmoil and ceaseless change to the inner light of certain knowledge and eternal peace.

Though it may be best in the case of ĪU for the student to explore the text without too many expectations, the material is difficult enough and foreign enough to profit from an introduction to the general themes in the Upaniṣads which precede it. To be a priest meant to learn the revealed texts of the Veda, *Brāhmaṇas*, *Āraṇyakas*, and Upaniṣads by heart, including their use in the performance of the chief daily, monthly, and seasonal rituals. Thus, as we have already discovered, *the emphasis was on elucidating the hidden connections between human being, cosmic and divine beings, and the holy rituals.* If the connections were obvious, there would be no need for this knowledge. The presupposition was that rituals themselves gained immeasurably in power when the performer knew the hidden connections and meanings of the sounds and actions. Like a strong thread which links the various beads of a necklace, the Upaniṣads assert an underlying unity that penetrates and unites the vast diversity of the world of human experience. This uniting thread is understood as both the most fundamental and the hierarchically highest principle, the ultimate Absolute. Knowing it experientially, one knows all, and attains salvation from the changing world of inevitable suffering. This all-important Absolute is known as the be-all and end-all of life: both the objective material universe in all its infinite complexity, energy, and scale, as well as the subjective, variegated inner life, the mental, emotional, and psychological aspect of living beings, from the creator god to a blade of grass—all arise, grow, and dissolve back into this primal Absolute. It is the source, the course, and the final end of all. What is it? Here various Upaniṣadic seers, each understood as valid in their revealed personal vision, speak of it in a great variety of ways: Fire, Wind, Water, Space, Life-energy, Pure Consciousness, Primordial Man, Being, Non-Being, the Unmanifest, the Indestructible One, the Inner Regulator, the Expansive Power (Brahman), the True Self (*ātman*), and the Lord God (Īś).[3]

The *Īśā Upaniṣad* represents one expression of the puzzle, both concise and mysterious, original and traditional. It draws a great deal on early traditions both Upaniṣadic and ritualistic. But what is it trying to say? What is the Lord and how is he related to the creation, the Absolute and the True Self? Your challenge is to puzzle over each word and phrase and like a vast number of Hindu students and modern students of religion beyond the Hindu fold, contemplate the keys, the clues, and the connections it offers.

Tools

We offer the following tools for your research:

1. Text in Sanskrit.
2. Text in Sanskrit broken down into words.
3. Translations of the original text both literal and poetic.
4. Vocabulary and grammar notes to help you understand both the range of meanings of the Sanskrit words, which often hold many levels of meaning, and the patterns of syntax and grammar which specify their possible relationships.
5. Traditional commentaries on each verse by both Śaṅkara (the most famous of the non-dualist commentators) and Madhva (the most famous of the dualist commentators) with Sanskrit texts as well as translation.
6. Scholarly notes on the suggested corrections (emendations) and analysis by modern scholars, including links to other Upaniṣads and vedic literature (*Brāhmaṇas*, *Bhagavad-gītā*, Vedic *Saṃhitā*, *Purāṇas*, etc).
7. Bibliography: texts consulted and useful texts for further research.
8. General vocabulary of Sanskrit words found in the ĪU.
9. Questions (to guide your inquiry and serve as seeds for possible analysis. For example:
   (a) After reading this introduction what problems can you imagine will present themselves in your reading and understanding of the text?
   (b) What might you do about each problem?
   (c) How can you use the resources and tools to help?

In reading this text in terms of its original contexts in priestly families, their worship, and contemplation of the revealed mysteries which they believed bestow salvation itself, we should tread lightly and cautiously. We are not religious tourists, but intellectual pilgrims, seeking with the Vedic seers and their spiritual heirs the hidden connections that illuminate and pervade the surfaces as well as the depths of our lives.

[3]Nakamura (1990), 104-5.

The Scholarship on the Īśā (Delmonico)

The Upaniṣad translated here is perhaps the most translated and commented upon of all the major or principal Upaniṣads which number either ten, twelve, thirteen, or eighteen according to different authorities.[4] Eventually, the tradition recognized the number of Upaniṣads to be one hundred and eight, which is a magical number in Hindu religious worldview, but there are many more Upaniṣads than that.[5] Nevertheless, this Upaniṣad, the *Īśā Upaniṣad,* stands out not only as ancient but also as exerting a powerful influence on the later Hindu tradition.

But first, let's raise the question: what does *upaniṣad* mean? The honest answer is that we do not really know for sure. We know for certain that the term is applied to certain parts of the vast corpus of ancient Vedic texts, usually to the last or most recently composed sections of those texts. But what does the word mean? Perhaps the best suggestion so far for what the word meant to those who wrote the texts or who were members of the intended audience of those texts is that given by Olivelle in the introduction to his recent translation (footnotes are mine):

> In the early vedic literature the term most commonly used for "connection" is *bandhu*, a term derived from a verb meaning "to bind," "to connect." *Bandhu* commonly means kin, but when one thing is said to be a *bandhu* of another, the meaning is that the former is connected to or is a counterpart of the latter. The earliest usage of the term *upaniṣad* indicates that it too carried a similar meaning: *upaniṣad* means "connection" or "equivalence." In addition, the term implies hierarchy; the Upaniṣadic connections are hierarchically arranged, and the quest is to discover the reality that stands at the summit of this hierarchically interconnected universe. It is, however, assumed that such connections are always hidden. We see the term used with this meaning in the Upaniṣads themselves, for example, at CU [Chāndogya Upaniṣad] 1.1.10 and 1.13.4.[6] Because of the hidden nature of these connections, the term *upaniṣad* also came to mean a secret, especially secret knowledge or doctrine. It is probably as an extension of this meaning that the term came finally to be used with reference to entire texts containing such secret doctrines, that is, our Upaniṣads.[7]

In one of his footnotes connected with this passage, Olivelle writes: "On this meaning of *upaniṣad,* see Renou 1946;[8] and Falk, 1986b.[9] In the light of these studies, the older view (Deussen 1966 [1906], 13) that the term derives from "sitting near" a teacher and refers to a group of disciples at the feet of a teacher imbibing esoteric knowledge is clearly untenable.[10]" Sadly, it is this last meaning, the untenable one in Olivelle's view, that is the one most often encountered even today in discussions of the meaning of the term.

The great logician and Indologist, Frits Staal, in his last book, *Discovering the Vedas*, criticized Olivelle's view:

> The term *upa-ni-ṣad* is derived from *sad-*, *ni* and *upa* which mean 'sit,' down' and 'close' ... , respectively. Most modern scholars have interpreted its changing meanings as referring to mystical hidden connections. But these were already a favoured topic of the Brāhmaṇas and Āraṇyakas, referred to by the Sanskrit term *bandhu*, which was widely used. I accept the traditional interpretation: 'sitting close (to the teacher)' and therefore secret (*rahasya*).[11] It is a one-to-one relationship.

[4]Hume thought there were thirteen principal Upanisads: *Bṛhad-āraṇyaka*, *Chāndogya*, *Taittirīya*, *Aitareya*, *Kauṣītakī*, *Kena*, *Kaṭha*, *Īśā*, *Muṇḍaka*, *Paśna*, *Māṇḍukya*, *Śvetāśvata*, and *Maitrī*. See his classic translation, *The Thirteen Principal Upaniṣads* (Oxford: Oxford University Press, [repr.] 1977). Radhakrishnan adds the *Subāla*, *Jābāla*, *Paiṅgala*, *Kaivalya*, and *Vajrasūcikā*, making the principal Upaniṣads eighteen. See his *The Priṇcipal Upaniṣads* (New Delhi, India: Indus [HarperCollins India], [repr.] 1994) . Olivelle's recent translation includes twelve Upaniṣads, dropping the *Maitrī* which Hume and Radhakrishnan include. See his *Upaniṣads* (Oxford, New York: Oxford University Press, 1996.

[5]Most of these additional Upaniṣads are later compositions. The twelve or thirteen that are usually included in translation collections are generally dated to the period between the 6th century and the 2nd century BCE.

[6]These passages claim that one who knows the hidden connections (*upaniṣad*) gains special advantages: the rites performed are more powerful according to the first passage, and the knower comes to own and eat food.

[7]Olivelle, ibid., lii-liii.

[8]Renou, L. (1946), '"Connexion" en védique, "cause" en bouddhique,' in *Dr C. Kunhan Raja Presentation Volume*. (Madras: Adyar Library)

[9]"Vedisch *upaniṣád*." *ZDMG* (*Zeitschrift der Deutschen Morgenländischen Gesellschaft*) 136: 80-97.

[10]ibid., lii.

[11]It is not clear what Staal means by "traditional" here. The only proponents of the "sitting close" interpretation of Upaniṣad are Western

> There are several reasons for this interpretation. The Upaniṣads are full of stories of students looking for teachers. Sitting is venerable, auspicious even, a topic on which I shall expatiate in Chapter 13. Secrecy is the last remnant of the originally secret oral traditions of families and clans. There is one paradox: the Upaniṣads became the most famous part of the Vedas. Does it mean that if one keeps something secret, it will eventually become public? Given the obsession with exposing secrets (or scandals), the answer must be, yes.[12]

Though the original meaning of the term *upaniṣad* may have been "hidden connection," by the time of Śaṅkara (700-750 CE), who wrote his commentaries some twelve hundred years after the composition of the earliest Upaniṣads (6th-2nd cents. BCE), that meaning either had been lost or had been replaced by others. Śaṅkara was the earliest commentator on the Upaniṣads whose commentaries have survived. (Certainly there were other commentators before him whose commentaries have not been preserved for us.) In his independent work, the *Thousand Teachings* (*Upadeśa-sāhasrī*), he defines the term *upaniṣad* in a different way:

> The word *upaniṣad* comes from the root *sad* preceded by the verbal prefixes *upa* and *ni* and followed by the primary suffix *kvip* because [they, the Upaniṣads,] cause birth and the rest[13] to weaken and be destroyed.[14]

For Śaṅkara one of the meanings of the term *upaniṣad* was salvific knowledge. This is not contradictory to the idea that the Upaniṣads teach "hidden connections." This merely emphasizes the idea that by understanding the connections and hierarchies ordinarily hidden from our view one becomes freed from the forces that bind us to cycles of this world. We find in the *Īśā Upaniṣad* precisely this kind of presentation of hidden connections and hierarchies with similar implications for those who properly understand these connections.

In other places in his commentaries, Śaṅkara understands the root $\sqrt{sad}$, which is at the core of the word *upaniṣad*, to mean three things: destroy, go, and mitigate. Thus, he takes the word *upaniṣad* to mean: "destroy the seeds of transmigratory existence such as nescience," "make seekers after final release go to the highest Brahman," and "mitigate a multitude of miseries such as living in the womb, birth, old age, and so on."[15]

This definition of *upaniṣad* of Śaṅkara's demonstrates the importance of knowing Sanskrit well in order to properly understand the subtleties of these texts and their interpretations. This is one of the major reasons we have chosen to translate the *Īśā* in the way we have, with each word given its various most common root meanings and grammatically identified and analysed. Śaṅkara breaks the word *upa-ni-ṣad* down into its three component parts and then on the basis of that presents the three most likely and meaningful interpretations of it. The two parts, *upa* ("near to," "under") and *ni* ("in") are technically called *upasargas* in Sanskrit grammar. They are verbal prefixes or prepositions that bring out or narrow down the broad meaning of a verbal root to convey a restricted, specific sense. *Sad* is the verbal root itself which conveys a range of possible meanings such as those Śaṅkara pointed to above.[16]

The important message here is that grammar matters. Without knowing the grammar just about anything goes. The grammar provides the best tool for discovering what the author of a text really had in mind. Grammar also provides a powerful means of determining which interpretation among several possible interpretations is the most likely. Therefore, understanding Sanskrit grammar is essential for understanding what a Sanskrit text really means.

---

scholars beginning with Deussen. There appears to be no "traditional" source for that interpretation. Those who belong to the tradition, like Śaṅkara, give different interpretations of the meaning of the word. For him the *sad* of Upaniṣad didn't mean "to sit;" it meant "to destroy," "to go, to reach," or "to mitigate." Finding or sitting at the feet of a teacher was what every male of the upper three castes was expected to do after the age of seven. It may be true that the Brāhmaṇas and Āraṇyakas were already concerned with drawing connections between diverse things or discovering *bandhus*, but those pointed out in the Upaniṣads were believed to have some special power, a power to bring salvific knowledge.

[12]Staal, Frits, *Discovering the Vedas*, 160. (Gurgaon, India: Penguin Books, 2008)

[13]Birth, old age, disease, and death.

[14]Śaṅkara, *Upadeśa-sāhasrī*, 2.1.26:

> *saderupanipūrvasya kvipi copaniṣadbhavet|*
> *mandīkaraṇabhāvācca garbhādeḥ śātanāttathā||*

[15]Mayeda, Sengaku, *A Thousand Teachings: the Upadeśasāhasrī of Śaṅkara*, 106-7, fn.18. (Albany: State University of New York Press, 1992)

[16]The *kvip* affix is a primary suffix, called a *kṛt* suffix, which when added to verbal roots makes nouns out of them. In Sanskrit, nouns can be made out of verbal roots and sometimes verbal roots are made out of nouns. The *kvip* primary affix is an unusual one in that it is always deleted. Even though it is deleted and even though the verbal root looks unchanged in any way, the effect of the *kvip* suffix is still present in that the verbal root has been changed into a noun and can be declined like any other noun.

The Sanskrit language is an extraordinarily complex and yet flexible language. The name Sanskrit means "made whole or complete" or "refined." The name Sanskrit refers specifically to an ancient language belonging to the Indo-Aryan sub-group of the Indo-European family of languages which includes Greek, Latin, German, Celtic and other related languages. Sanskrit refers to the form of the language of the Vedas that was "refined" or "purified" by the grammatical analyses and descriptions of it created by the great grammarian Pāṇini (4th cent. BCE) and his predecessors. This *Īśā Upaniṣad* may be dated to roughly the same period as Pāṇini. Thus, the language of this text is quite close to the language Pāṇini had before him when he was describing the language and forming his rules for the formation of its words. The earlier language, the language of the Vedic hymns (Saṃhitās) and their ritual and mythological elucidations (Brāhmaṇas) are in an older, pre-Pāṇinian form of the Sanskrit language that operated somewhat differently. For a more detailed account of the Sanskrit language and how it operates, see our introductory discussion of the language in the appendices.

However, even with a good understanding of Sanskrit grammar, the *Īśā* is not easy to translate. To give some sense of the variety found in the English translations of this Upaniṣad, here are a few of the available translations by various scholars, arranged chronologically, of the first *mantra* of the text:

> ॐ *īśāvāsyam idaṃ sarvaṃ*
> *yat kiṃca jagatyāṃ jagat|*
> *tena tyaktena bhuñjīthā*
> *mā gṛdhaḥ kasya svid dhanam|| 1||*

> In the Lord [*īśā*] is to be veiled all this—whatsoever moves on earth. Through such renunciation do thou save (thyself); be not greedy, for whose is wealth?[17]

> All this is for habitation by the Lord, whatsoever is individual universe of movement in the universal motion. By that renounced thou shouldst enjoy; lust not after any man's possession.[18]

> By the Lord (*īśā*) enveloped must this all be—
> Whatever moving thing there is in the moving world.
> With this renounced, thou mayest enjoy.
> Covet not the wealth of anyone at all.[19]

> (Know that) all this, whatever moves in this moving world, is enveloped by God. Therefore find your enjoyment in renunciation; do not covet what belongs to others.[20]

> *Oṁ.* All this—whatsoever moves on the earth—should be covered by the Lord. Protect (your Self) through that detachment. Do not covet anybody's wealth. (Or—Do not covet, for whose is wealth?)[21]

> The whole world is to be dwelt in by the Lord,
> whatever living being there is in the world.
> So you should eat whatever has been abandoned;
> and do not covet anyone's wealth.[22]

As one can see there are a variety of ways of translating this *mantra*. "Veiled," "inhabited," "enveloped," "covered," "dwelt in," all these are used just to translate the word *āvāsya*. All are correct, or, at least possible, but which of them is the best? It is often very hard to tell. This is another reason we have translated this Upaniṣad in the way we have. The translations above and the ones we have provided in the body of this work are best regarded as provisional translations. Readers are given the tools in this book to improve on our translations. The major meanings of each of the words in the text, their grammatical identifications, information about unusual word usages and phrases, and at least two commentaries with radically different interpretations of the text are provided for each *mantra* of the Upaniṣad. For instance, there are three main meanings for the three verbal roots in Sanskrit that have the form *vas*, any of which could be the basis of the word *āvāsya* in this *mantra*. They are "to dwell," "to clothe," and "to perfume." The translations above reflect only the first two meanings, dwell and clothe. "The world is perfumed by the Lord" may seem a bit farfetched, but taken as a metaphor it has a certain poetic or aesthetic beauty to it. Keeping this in view, we have used the word "infused," some of the meanings of which are "to inspirit or animate" or "to

[17] Hiriyanna, M., trans. *Īshāvāsyopanishad*, 4. (Srirangam: Sri Vani Vilas Press, 1911)

[18] Śrī Aurobindo, *The Complete Works of Aurobindo*, Volume 17, *Isha Upanishad*, 5. Originally published in 1914.

[19] Robert Ernest Hume, trans., *The Thirteen Principal Upanishads*, 362. (London, Oxford, New York: Oxford University Press, repr. 1977 [1st ed. 1921])

[20] Radhakrishnan, S., trans., *The Principal Upaniṣads*, 567. (New Delhi: Indux [an imprint of HarperCollins Publishers India], repr. 1994 [1953])

[21] Swami Gambhirananda, trans., *Eight Upaniṣads*, 1, 4. (Calcutta: Advaita Ashrama, 4th impression 1977 [1st 1957])

[22] Olivelle, Patrick, trans., *Upaniṣads*, 249. (Oxford, New York: Oxford University Press, 1996)

fill." That seems to us to be closest to what the author of the *mantra* wishes to say: that the Lord "inspirits" or "animates" all the moving or living beings in the world. Thus, they are the Lord and the Lord is they. One could not arrive at such a refinement, if indeed a refinement it is, without weighing all the various possibilities.[23]

The Īśopaniṣad

There are too many translations of the *Īśā* to mention. Like the *Bhagavad-gītā* ("The Lord's Song") it seems as if almost everyone has tried his or her hand at translating it, whether or not s/he has studied the Sanskrit language in which the text is written.[24] Aurobindo before publishing his final translation of the Upaniṣad wrote ten commentaries in varying states of completion on the text.[25]

As far as Sanskrit commentaries go, a recent two-volume work has collected fifty-one Sanskrit commentaries on the text and there are still more besides.[26] One might reasonably argue that the *Īśā Upaniṣad* is one of the most influential texts of the Hindu tradition after the *Bhagavad-gītā*. For those who know both texts, it is clear that the *Īśā* itself has influenced the *Gītā*.

What is it about the *Īśā Upaniṣad* that has attracted so much attention and interest? In the first place it is short. Other than the *Māṇḍūkya Upaniṣad*, it is the shortest of the Upaniṣads. Moreover, unlike the *Māṇḍūkya*, the *Īśā* is entirely in verse, making it easier to memorize. It consists of only eighteen *mantras*.[27] In addition to this, the *Īśā* bears a close connection to one of the earliest and longest of the Upaniṣads, the *Bṛhad-āraṇyaka Upaniṣad* (BU). Five and most of a sixth of the *Īśā*'s eighteen verses are drawn from the *Bṛhad-āraṇyaka*.[28] That is about a third of the verses in the text. The sixth verse, ĪU verse 3, is only partially the same as its source, BU 4.4.11.[29] Moreover, the invocation at the beginning of the ĪU is also a verse from the BU.[30] This suggests that the *Īśā* may have been created as a brief, versified summary of the main teachings of the *Bṛhad-āraṇyaka*, once again, all the more useful because it is easy to memorize.

Most scholars think the BU is the oldest of the Upaniṣads. Olivelle, for instance says:

> On linguistic and other grounds, there is general agreement that the Bṛhadāraṇyaka, as a whole, is the oldest of the Upaniṣads, even though individual passages in it may be younger than those of others, especially those of the Chāndogya. Together with the latter, the Bṛhadāraṇyaka not only constitutes about two-thirds of the corpus of ancient Upaniṣadic documents but also represents the oldest and the most important part of this literature.[31]

It appears that the BU was added on to the end of the *Śatapatha Brāhmaṇa* which is the explanation or commentary on the *Vājasaneyī Saṃhitā*. However, since there was no chapter of the VS that the BU could be considered a commentary or explanation of, the ĪU was composed as a summary of the BU and added on as the fortieth chapter of the VS sometime after the BU was added to the *Śatapatha Brāhmaṇa*. Thus, the *Vājasaneyī Saṃhitā* and the *Śatapatha Brāhmaṇa* were synchronized.

Structurally, however, we are meant to believe that the opposite is the case, that the BU is the commentary or explanatory expansion (*brāhmaṇa*) of the *Īśā Upaniṣad*. As mentioned before, the Īśā is the final (fortieth) chapter of the *Vājasaneyī Saṃhitā* or the *White Yajur Veda*. The BU, in turn, is the final portion of the *Śatapatha Brāhmaṇa*, the explanatory text of the *Vājasaneyi Saṃhitā*. Just as the earlier portions of the *Śatapatha Brāhmaṇa* comment on the earlier chapters of the *Vājasaneyī Saṃhitā*, the BU is meant to be understood as

[23] There is a fourth possible root having the form *vas*, a Vedic verbal root related to *uṣ* (related to *uṣas*, "morning light," "dawn"). It means "to shine" or "grow bright." If this meaning is accepted we might take the first half of the *mantra* to mean, "the whole world is illumined or brightened by the Lord."

[24] Take for instance poet Stephen Mitchell's translation of the *Bhagavad-gītā*. Mitchell knows no Sanskrit at all, but he is a poet.

[25] See Volume 17 of his collected works which is available for free online.

[26] Shastri, Dr. Yajneshwar S. and Sunanda Y. Shastri, eds., *Īśāvāsyopaniṣad with 51 Sanskrit Commentaries*, 2 vols. (Ahmedabad: Sriyogi Publications, 2013)

[27] In one of its two versions it has only seventeen *mantras*.

[28] ĪUK 10 = BUK 4.4.10, ĪU 15-18 = BUK 5.15.1-4.

[29] Īśā verse 3 begins with *asuryāḥ*, "infernal, demonic," or, *asūryāḥ*, "sunless," while the BUK verse begins with *anandāḥ*, "joyless." In addition, the last quarter of the verse is different in the BUK version, reading *avidvāṃso 'budho janāḥ*, "people who are ignorant, unawakened," instead of *ye ke cātmahano janāḥ*, "those people who are killers of the Self." The BUM (Mādhyandina) version of the verse, however, has the same as the ĪU reading.

[30] BU 5.1.1

[31] Patrick Olivelle, *Upaniṣads*, 3-4. (Oxford, New York: Oxford University Press, 1996)

commentary on the ĪU.[32]

I don't know if the ĪU has ever been read in this way, however. Can one connect the various verses or groups of verses of the ĪU to specific sections of the BU? It may be possible. The first verse of the ĪU, for instance, is about the Lord inhabiting or infusing the whole moving world. The first chapter of the BU starts with a description of the ritual dismemberment of a horse in the horse sacrifice (*aśvamedha*) in which each of the parts of the horse becomes a part of the world: the horse's head becomes dawn, the horse's eye becomes the sun, and so on. In other words, Īś, the Lord, here represented as the sacrificial horse, comes to inhabit the world, comes to move the world. This echoes the famous creation hymn from the Ṛg Veda known as the *Puruṣa-sūkta* (10.90). In that hymn a divine being named Puruṣa is similarly sacrificed at the beginning of the world in order to create the world. His various parts became things in the world, his eye the sun, his mind the moon, his bones the mountains, his blood the rivers and seas. In this way sacrifice was praised as having the power to create the world, and the world itself is recognized as rooted in the divine because it is made of the parts of a primordial divine being.

Following the passage on the horse, several other creation accounts are given (creation from death, creation from the Self, creation from *brahman*). In this example, the BU does seem to expand on the teaching of the first verse of the ĪU. Does this hold throughout the text, however? That is harder to demonstrate. Take, for instance, the next verse which teaches that performing actions without attachment to their results keeps the consequences of action from sticking to one. It is hard to connect that to particular passages of the BU. Much is said about ritual action in the BU, but the point often is that without knowing the meaning of the rituals one is placing oneself in danger. This is expressed by the claim, met several times in the BU, that one's head will fall off if one does not know the correct meaning of the rites and yet performs them. Maybe this is the same point being made by the second verse of the ĪU. If one acts without knowing that everything in the world is infused or owned by the Lord, one will be plastered over by the results of one's actions and one will have to die and be reborn again and again. It is difficult to find one to one correspondences between the verses of the ĪU and specific passages or teachings of the BU. Nevertheless, there is no doubt that two are more closely related to each other than any other pair of Upaniṣads in the whole corpus.

There are other features of the *Īśā* that make it an ideal text for an introduction to the language and thought of the early Upaniṣads. Because of the fact that there are two versions of it and because of the text-critical work of great scholars like Paul Thieme and Mislav Ježić we know a good deal about the history of the text, how it changed over time, and in some cases why. Moreover, the text combines two important strains of later Vedāntic thinking: theism and non-dualism. The theism of the *Īśā* is an ancient form, much too early to be identified with the sectarian forms of theism that developed later. The non-dualism is similarly primitive and the authors of the text or its redactors saw no problem in combining the two, or in allowing them to co-exist, or even in treating them as the same thing. In the later tradition theism and non-dualism will compete against each other for the highest honors, some placing non-dual Brahman at the top of the hierarchy and others placing Bhagavān or Bhagavatī, the supreme personal god or goddess, above Brahman. There is also in this text perhaps the earliest expression of unselfish or selfless action (*naiṣkāmya-karma*) and non-violence (*ahiṃsā*) which later became some of the foundations of Indian ethical thinking. Thus, in the *Īśā* we find a garden filled with young plants that will grow, mature, gain strength, and finally bear fruit many times over in the classic philosophies and literatures of the later Hindu tradition.

In providing the most common meanings of the Sanskrit words of the ĪU, we have made use of the ample lexical resources available on the internet these days. The set of Sanskrit-English (and English-Sanskrit) Dictionaries maintained online by the Institute of Indology and Tamil Studies at the University of Cologne (http://www.sanskrit-lexicon.uni-koeln.de/) is an extraordinary help to scholars and translators of Sanskrit texts. We drew the primary meanings of the Sanskrit words from either the *Monier-Williams Sanskrit-English Dictionary* or the *Apte Practical Sanskrit-English Dictionary* or the *Sanskrit and Tamil Dictionaries* resources available there. For the grammatical analyses of the words we used Kale's text *A Higher Sanskrit Grammar* (1894), a scanned version of which is also available at the University of Cologne site. Occasionally, we referred to Mac-

[32]The *Vājasaneyī Saṃhitā* or *White Yajur Veda* represents a reorganization and revision of the somewhat disorganized and mixed *Black Yajur Veda*. It is thus later than the *Black Yajur Veda* and later than even the *Atharva Veda* from which it also borrows. In the *Black Yajur Veda* the *mantra* or verse sections are interspersed with *brāhmaṇa*, or commentarial, sections. In the *White Yajur Veda*, the *brāhmaṇa* portions are removed and a separate *brāhmaṇa*, the *Śatapatha Brāhmaṇa* was composed to accompany the restructured *White Yajur Veda*. See Staal's discussion of the four Vedas in *Discovering the Vedas*, 69-86.

[33]Arthur A. MacDonell, *A Sanskrit Grammar for Students*. (Oxford: Oxford University Press, [3rd ed.] 1927 [repr.] 1962)

[34]William Dwight Whitney, *Sanskrit Grammar*. (Cambridge, Mass and London, England: Harvard University Press, [2nd ed.] 1889, [repr.]

Donell's *A Sanskrit Grammar for Students*[33] and Whitney's *Sanskrit Grammar*.[34] On rare occasions we referred to MacDonell's *A Vedic Grammar for Students*.[35]

I wish to express my deep gratitude to J. Prabhakara Sastri who through his affection, encouragement, and excellent teaching skills in the subjects of Sanskrit grammar and literary criticism helped me overcome many of the hurdles faced by students of Sanskrit. Some of his inexhaustible enthusiasm for the great language has rubbed off on me; may it also spread to and enliven the readers of this book.

Welcome, then, to the world of the ancient sages and seers of India who studied and contemplated the world around them with all the means at their disposal and who recorded their discoveries, intuitions, hypotheses, and creative imaginings in the richly poetic and insightful texts of the Vedic corpus, the final or concluding portions of which are the Upaniṣads.

1975)

[35] Arthur A. MacDonell, *A Vedic Grammar for Students*. (New Delhi: D. K. Printworld Ltd., 1999 [based on the 1916 ed.])

Abbeviations

Texts Cited

AS *Atharva-saṃhitā*
BG *Bhagavad-gītā*
BU *Bṛhad-āraṇyaka Upaniṣad*
BUK *Bṛhad-āraṇyaka Upaniṣad* of the Kāṇva recension
BUM *Bṛhad-āraṇyaka Upaniṣad* of the Mādhyandina recension
CU *Chāndogya Upaniṣad*
ĪU *Īśā Upaniṣad*
ĪUK *Īśā Upaniṣad* of the Kāṇva recension
ĪUM *Īśā Upaniṣad* of the Mādhyandina recension
KaU *Kaṭha Upaniṣad*
KeU *Kena Upaniṣad*
MBhĪU *Mādhva-bhāṣya* on the ĪU
MāU *Māṇḍukya Upaniṣad*
MtU *Maitrāyaṇīya (Maitrī) Upaniṣad*
ṚS *Ṛg-saṃhitā*
ṚV *Ṛg Veda*
SK *Sāṃkhya-kārikā* by Īśvarakṛṣṇa
ŚU *Śvetāśvatara Upaniṣad*
ŚB *Śatapatha Brāhmaṇa*
ŚBhĪU *Śāṅkara-bhāṣya* on the ĪU
ŚBhBU *Śāṅkara-bhāṣya* on the BUK
US *Upadeśa-sāhasrī* by Śaṅkara
BS/VS *Brahma-sūtra* or *Vedānta-sūtra* by Bādarāyaṇa
VāS *Vājasaneyī Saṃhitā (White Yajur Veda)*
YS *Yoga-sūtra* by Patañjali

Abbreviations

[These abbreviations are a subset of those used in the *Monier-Monier Williams Sanskrit-English Dictionary* with a few of our own additions.]

Ā. the *ātmanepada* ("word for itself," or intransitive) form of a verb. Verbs are Ātmanepada or Parasmaipada or Ubhayapada. See below.
abl. the ablative or fifth (*pañcamī*) case.
acc. the accusative or second (*dvitīyā*) case.
adj. adjective (cf. mfn.)
adv. adverb
anom. anomalous
aor. aorist—a kind of past tense that expresses past action indefinitely. It refers to a recent action or one done during the course of the present day. (See Kale, 523.) It corresponds to the present perfect in English: "I have eaten already." (See Macdonell, 206.)
c. case
caus. causal, causative
cf. confer, compare
cl. one of the ten classes of verbal roots in the present system (i.e., the present, the imperative, the optative, and the imperfect).
class. classical
comm. commentator or commentary
comp. compound
compar. comparative degree
cond. conditional mood of verb.
conj. conjunctive
dat. dative or fourth (*caturthā*) case
dem. demonstrative
desid. desiderative
dimin. diminutive
du. dual number
ed. edition
e.g. *exempli gratia*, 'for example'
Eng. English
esp. especially
etym. etymology
f. feminine
fig. figuratively

fut. future
fut.p.p. future passive participle
gen. genitive case or sixth (*ṣaṣṭhī*)
gend. gender
ger. the gerund form of the verb.
Germ. German
Gk. Greek
gr. grammar
ibid. *ibidem* or 'in the same place or book or text' as the preceding
ibc. in the beginning of a compound
i.e. *id est*, "that is"
ifc. *in fine compositi* or 'at the end of a compound'
impers. impersonal or used impersonally
impf. imperfect tense
impv. imperative
ind. indeclinable particle.
inf. infinitive mood
instr. the instrumental or third (*tṛtīyā*) case.
intens. intensive
interj. interjection
interr. interrogative
irr. irregular
Lat. Latin
lit. literally
loc. the locative or seventh (*saptamī*) case.
log. logic
m. the masculine grammatical gender.
mfn. masculine, feminine, and neuter; or adjective
no. noun
n. neuter gender
nom. the nominative or first (*prathamā*) case.
opt. optative or benedictive mood of the verb.
P. the *parasmaipada* ("word for another," or transitive) form of a verb.
p. page
part. participle
partic. particle
pass. passive voice
patr. patronymic
pers. person
pf. perfect tense
phil. philosophy
pl. plural
pot. potential
p.p. past participle
Prāk. Prakrit
prep. preposition
pres. present tense
priv. privative
prob. probably
pron. pronoun
pronom. pronominal
redupl. reduplicated
reflex. reflexive or used reflexively
Russ. Russian
sing. the singular number of either nouns or verbs.
subj. subjunctive
superl. superlative degree
U. the *ubhayapada* ("word for both,") identification of a verb. This means that a given verb can be either *ātmanepada* or *parasmaipada*. See above.
v. verb
Ved. Vedic or Veda
voc. vocative case or the eighth case (*aṣṭamī*)
$\sqrt{xxx}$ sign for the root of a verb as in $\sqrt{bh\bar{u}}$, "to be."

Part I

Mādhyandina Īśopaniṣad

Mādhyandina Version

The following presentation of the Mādhyandina version of the *Īśopaniṣad* is based on the extraordinary work of Mislav Ježić.[1] The Mādhyandina version is, according to Ježić, the earliest version of the *Īśā Upaniṣad*. The later and most commonly commented on version of the Upaniṣad is the Kāṇva version. Kāṇva and Mādhyandina refer to two separate branches of the *White Yajur Veda* (the *Vājasaneyī Saṃhitā*), the latest of the Vedas to be composed,[2] through which the *White Yajur Veda* was preserved, memorized, and passed down in India. In the case of the *Īśā* and the *Bṛhad-āraṇyaka Upaniṣads* of each of the branches, there are numerous differences that give us insight into the historical development of the *Īśopaniṣad*. On the basis of these comparisons, Ježić has attempted to reconstruct the earliest version of the text and call attention to ways in which the text was added to and reorganized at later periods. In doing this, he also has suggested ways of altering the text to recover its original, metrically correct form. As mentioned above, however, the Kāṇva version is the version that been commented on the most in the long history of the interpretation of this text. There are only a few commentaries that take the Mādhyandina version as their root text.[3] Later in this book, when we present our full grammatical analysis of the Upaniṣad with a translation of both the text and Śaṅkara's (7th cent. CE) commentary on the text, we present the standard Kāṇva version (without Ježić's emendations) since that is the version on which Śaṅkara commented. Here, though, we present the earlier Mādhyandina version with Ježić's suggested emendations and annotations since it represents the best current reconstruction of the original text.

We have included the invocation with the text here. Strictly speaking the invocation associated with the Īśā is not part of the Upaniṣad. None of the commentators comment on it as part of the Upaniṣad. When it was attached to the Upaniṣad is not clear. At some point, probably after the principal Upaniṣads were separated from their *brāhmaṇa*, *āraṇyaka*, or *saṃhitā* contexts and treated as a distinct group within Vedic literature, they were each given invocations. As it happens, the invocation of the Īśā is a verse from its sister Upaniṣad, the *Bṛhad-āraṇyaka Upaniṣad* (BU). That verse opens one of the appendices of the BU, the Fifth Chapter (5.1.1), where several other verses of the Īśā are also found (5.15.1-3).

[1] The text and notes are taken from his paper, "Īśā-Upaniṣad: History of the Text in the Light of the Upaniṣadic Parallels," 19-21. The entire paper is published here in this volume as Appendix A.

[2] The *White Yajur Veda* represents a reorganization and revision of the somewhat disorganized and mixed *Black Yajur Veda*. It is thus later than the *Black Yajur* and later than even the Atharva Veda from which it also borrows. In the *Black Yajur Veda* the *mantra* or verse sections are interspersed with *brāhmaṇa*, or commentarial, sections. In the *White Yajur Veda*, the *brāhmaṇa* portions are removed and a separate *brāhmaṇa*, the *Śatapatha Brāhmaṇa* was composed to accompany the restructured *White Yajur Veda*. See Staal's discussion of the four Vedas in *Discovering the Vedas*, 69-86.

[3] In a recent publication of fifty-one Sanskrit commentaries on the Īśā only ten of them were written on the basis of the Mādhyandina version of the text. These are the *Īśāvāsya-bhāṣya* by Uvaṭācārya (1050 CE), *Īśāvāsya-dīpa* by Mahīdhara (16th cent. CE), *Īśāvāsya-rahasya* by Brahmānanda Sarasvatī (n.d.), *Īśāvāsya-rahasya-vivṛti* by Rāmacandra Paṇḍita (1769-1830 CE), *Īśāvāsya-artha-prakāśa* by Digambarānucara (n.d.), *Īśāvāsya-dinakara-vyākhyā* by Vellamkoṇḍa Rāmarāyakavi (1875-1914 CE), *Yogapakṣīya-prakāśa-bhāṣya* by an unknown author, *Īśāvāsya-ṭīkā* by Śrī Mohana (20th cent. CE), *Īśāvāsyopaniṣad-bhāṣya* Swāmī Dayānanda Sarasvatī (1824-1883 CE), *Īśāvāsyopaniṣad-saṃskāra-bhāṣya* by Bhagavadācārya (20th cent. CE). See *Īśāvāsyopaniṣad with 51 commentaries*, part I, edited by Acarya Prof. Dr. Yajneshwar S. Shastri and Dr. Sunanda Y. Shastri, lviii-lxiii.

Invocation

oṁ pūrṇamadaḥ pūrṇamidaṃ
pūrṇātpūrṇamudacyate |
pūrṇasya pūrṇamādāya
pūrṇamevāvaśiṣyate ||[4]
|| *oṁ śāntiḥ śāntiḥ śāntiḥ oṁ* ||

Oṁ, That is full; this is full;
From Fullness arises Fullness;
Subtract Fullness from Fullness,
What remains is still Fullness.
Oṁ Peace, peace, peace! Oṁ

First triplet

īśā́vāsyàm idaṁ sárvaṃ
yát kiṃca jágatyāṃ jágat|
téna tyakténa bhuñjīthā
mā́ gṛdhaḥ kásya svid dhánam|| *1*||

1. Oṁ. By the Owner infused is all this,
Whatever moves in the world of motion.
Enjoy that which is let go of;
Don't hold on; whose property is it?

kurvánn evéhá kármāṇi
jijīviṣéc[5] *chatáṁ sámāḥ*|
evámṃvídi[6] *nā́nyátheti*[7]
ná kárma lipyate náre|| *2*||

2. In this way by performing actions here,
One should live a hundred years.
So there is no other way for you,
No *karma* thus adheres to one.

asūryā́[8] *nā́ma te lokā́*
andhéna tamasā́vṛtāḥ|
tā́ṁs te prétyā́pi gacchanti[9]
yé ké cātmaháno jánāḥ|| *3*||

3. Veiled indeed are those worlds,
Infused with blind darkness,
To which they go after death,
Those people who smother the Self.

Triṣṭubh 1

ánejad ékaṃ mánaso jávīyo
naínad devā́ āpnuvan pū́rvam árṣat|
tád dhā́vato'nyā́n átyeti tíṣṭhat
tásminn apó mātaríśvā dadhāti|| *4*||

4. One, unmoving, faster than the mind,
It rushes ahead of the gods, [who are] unable to overtake it.
Though unmoving, it passes up the other runners.
In it, Life-energy generates all activity.

Second triplet

tád ejati tán naijati
tád dūré tád u antiké|
tád antár asya sárvasya
tád u sárvasya bāhyatáḥ[10]|| *5*||

5. It vibrates; it is still.
It is far away, but it is near.
It is within everything,
But outside all of this too.

---

[4]BUM 5.1.1.

[5]*jijīviṣa it* (Thieme) = impv. If we accept Ježić's emendation of the third line to *evámṃvídi*, Thieme's suggestion is unnecessary since the verse is not a construction in the second person.

[6]In place of *evaṃ tvayi*. Goes better with *nare* later in the verse.

[7]In place of *nānyatheto'sti* which makes the verse hypermetrical.

[8]Alt. reading: *asuryā́ nā́ma*: demonic.

[9]ĪUM 3abc = BUM 4.4.1.

[10]The verse as it stands is hypermetrical. Therefore, the second *asya* has been removed, as per Thieme and Ježić.

yás tú sárvāṇi bhūtā́ni
ātmánn evā́nu paśyati|
sarvabhūtéṣu cātmā́nam
táto ná vi cikitsati|| 6||[11]

6. But one who sees
All beings in this very Self
And this Self in all beings
Because of this does not doubt.[4]

yásmint sárvāṇi bhūtā́ny
ātmaivā́bhūd vijānatáḥ|
tátra kó móhaḥ káḥ śóka
ekatvám anupáśyataḥ|| 7||

7. When one realizes "the Self
Has become all beings,"
Then for the seer of oneness
What delusion and sorrow can there be?

Triṣṭubh 2

sá páryagāc chukrám akāyám avraṇám
asnāvirám̐ śuddhám ápāpaviddham|
kavir manīṣī́ paribhū́ḥ svayaṃbhū́r
árthān vyàdadhāc chā́śvatī́bhyaḥ sámābhyaḥ[12]*||*
8||

8. He permeates everything, luminous,
Incorporeal, flawless, without nerves,
Immaculate, impervious to evil,
Enlightening, sage, all-encompassing,
Self-sufficient; he allots all things
As needed for aeons eternal.

Third triplet

andhám̐ támaḥ prá viśanti
yé 'sàṃbhūtim upā́sate|
táto bhū́ya iva té támo
yá u sáṃbhūt(i)yām̐ ratā́ḥ|| 9||[13]

9. They enter into blind darkness
Who devote themselves to regression.
To greater gloom than that go they
Who desire progression.

anyád evā́húḥ saṃbhavā́d
(a)nyád āhur ásaṃbhavāt|
íti śuśruma dhī́rāṇām
yé nas tád vicacakṣiré|| 10||

10. They say one thing indeed
Results from progression.
Another from regression, they say.
Thus have we heard from the wise,
Those who have perceived it for us.

sáṃbhūtiṃ ca vināśáṃ ca
yás tád védobháyam̐ sahá|
vināśéna mṛtyúṃ tīrtvā́
sáṃbhūtyāmṛ́tam aśnute|| 11||

11. Progression and destruction,
One who knows both together
Crossing death by destruction
Gains immortality by progression.

[11]cf. ĪUK 6d, BUK 4.4.15d, BUM 4.4.18d, and KaU 4.5 (2.1.5). All have *tato na vi jupupsate.*

[12]8d is hypermetrical. Omitting *yāthātathyataḥ* fixes the *triṣṭubh* meter.

[13]ĪUM 9 = BUM 4.4.13.

[4]In the case of *vi jugupsate*: Because of this he does not recoil.

Here ends the original ĪU

First extension: Fourth Triplet

andhám̥ támaḥ prá viśanti
yé (á)vidyām upā́sate|
táto bhū́ya iva té támo
yá u vidyā́yām̐ ratā́ḥ|| 12||[14]

12. They enter into blind darkness
Who devote themselves to ignorance;
To greater gloom than that go they
Who desire knowledge.

anyád evā́húr vidyáyā
(a)nyád āhur ávidyayā|[15]
íti śuśruma dhī́rāṇām̥
yé nas tád vicacakṣiré|| 13||

13. They say one thing indeed
Results from knowledge.
Another from ignorance, they say.
Thus have we heard from the wise,
Those who have perceived it for us.

vidyā́m̥ cā́vidyām̥ ca
yás tád védobháyam̐ sahá|
ávidyayā mr̥tyúm̥ tīrtvā́
vidyáyāmŕ̥tam aśnute|| 14||

14. Knowledge and ignorance,
One who knows both together,
Crossing death by ignorance,
Gains immortality by knowledge.

Second extension: Fifth Triplet

vayúr ánilam amŕ̥tam
áthedám̥ bhásmāntam̐ śarīram|
óm̥ kráto smára klibé smara
kráto smára kr̥tám̐ smara|| 15||[16]

15. [May my] vital breath [repair] to immortal air,
And this body now to its end in ashes;
Om̥, remember, oh Mental Fire, remember for the sake of merited worlds,
Remember, oh Mental Fire, remember what has been done!

ágne náya supáthā rāyé asmā́n
víśvāni deva vayū́nāni vidvā́n|
yuyodhi àsmáj juhurāṇám éno
bhū́yiṣṭhām̥ te námauktim̥ vidhema|| 16||[17]

16. Oh Sacred Fire, lead us for glory on the path of light!
Oh God, knowing all [our] ways,
Overcome our crooked misdeeds.
We offer to you the greatest praise!

hiraṇmáyena pā́treṇa
satyásyā́pihitam̥ múkham|
yo 'sā́v ādityé púruṣaḥ
só 'sā́v ahám ó3m khám̥ bráhma|| 17||

17. By a golden disc
The door of truth is hid.
He who is that person in the sun,
That one indeed am I.
Om̥! Space is Brahman!

[14]ĪUM 12-14 = ĪUK 9-11; ĪUK 9 = BUK 4.4.10.

[15]The reading: *anyád evā́húr vidyā́yā anyád āhur ávidyāyāḥ* is preferred by Thieme, the ablative case being more suitable here. The verse using the instrumental, however, is short a syllable because of *sandhi*.

[16]ĪUM 15-16 = BUM 5.3; addition of ĪUM 17.

[17]This verse is from the *R̥g-sam̥hitā*, 1.189.1. And 16b is from *Atharva-sam̥hitā*, 4.39.10b.

Part II

Kāṇva Īśopaniṣad

Kāṇva Version

The Kāṇva version of the Īśā is presented here. The Kāṇva version is the one upon which the most commentators wrote. Among them is Śaṅkara (7th cent. CE) whose commentary is the earliest of the surviving commentaries and the most prestigious. The Kāṇva version tends to be more prominent in South India, the Mādhyandina more prominent in North India. We include the invocation here along with the Upaniṣad though it is not strictly speaking a part of the text. See our note before the Mādhyandina version of the text.

oṁ pūrṇamadaḥ pūrṇamidaṃ
pūrṇātpūrṇamudacyate |
pūrṇasya pūrṇamādāya
pūrṇamevāvaśiṣyate ||[1]
|| oṁ śāntiḥ śāntiḥ śāntiḥ oṁ ||

Oṁ, That is full; this is full;
From Fullness arises Fullness;
Subtract Fullness from Fullness,
What remains is still Fullness.
Oṁ Peace, peace, peace! Oṁ

Oṁ. īśā́vāsyàm idaṁ sárvaṃ
yát kiṃca jágatyāṃ jágat|
téna tyakténa bhuñjīthā
mā́ gṛdhaḥ kásya svid dhánam|| 1||

1. Oṁ. By the Owner infused is all this,
Whatever moves in the world of motion.
Enjoy that which is let go of;
Don't hold on; whose property is it?

kurvánn evéhá kármāṇi
jijīviṣéc chatáṁ sámāḥ|
eváṃ tvayi nā́nyátheto'sti
ná kárma lipyate náre|| 2||[2]

2. In this way by performing actions here,
One should live a hundred years.
So there is no other way for you,
No *karma* thus adheres to one.

asuryā́ nā́ma te lokā́[3]
andhéna tamasā́vṛtāḥ|
tā́ṁs te prétyā́bhigacchanti[4]
yé ké cātmaháno jánāḥ|| 3||[5]

3. Veiled indeed are those worlds,
Infused with blind darkness,
To which they go after death,
Those people who smother the Self.

ánejad ékaṃ mánaso jávīyo
naínad devā́ āpnuvan pū́rvam árṣat|[6]
tád dhā́vato'nyā́n átyeti tíṣṭhat
tásminn apó mātaríśvā dadhāti|| 4||

4. One, unmoving, faster than the mind,
It rushes ahead of the gods, [who are] unable to overtake it.
Though unmoving, it passes up the other runners.
In it, Life-energy generates all activity.

tád ejati tán naijati
tád dūré tád u antiké|
tád antár asya sárvasya
tád u sárvasyāsya bāhyatáḥ[7] *|| 5||*

5. It vibrates, it is still.
It is far away, but it is near.
It is within everything,
But outside all of this too.

yás tú sárvāṇi bhūtā́ni
ātmánn evā́nu paśyati|
sarvabhūtéṣu cātmā́nam
táto ná vi jugupsate|| 6||[8]

6. But one who sees
All beings in this very Self
And this Self in all beings
Because of this does not recoil.[1]

[1] BUK 5.1.1.
[2] cf. ĪUd and BUK 4.4.23, BUM 4.4.28, both may reference CU 4.14.3.
[3] *asūrya*, sunless, possible; BUK *anandā*, joyless
[4] M = *prétyā́pi gacchanti*
[5] BUK 4.4.14abc, BUM 4.4.11abc; cf. BG 13.28
[6] M = *árśat.*
[7] The verse as it stands is hypermetrical, that is, it has too many syllables for the *anuṣṭubh* meter it is written in. The fourth quarter has nine instead of eight. Therefore, Thieme and Ježić recommend removing the second *asya*.
[8] ĪUM = *vi cikitsati*; ĪUK 6d is similar to BUK 4.4.15d, BUM 4.4.18d, and KaU 4.5 (2.1.5). All have *tato na vi jupupsate.*

[1] In the case of *vi cikitsati*: Because of this he does not doubt.

yásmint sárvāṇi bhūtā́ny
ātmaivā́bhūd vijānatáḥ|
tátra kó móhaḥ káḥ śóka
ekatvám anupáśyataḥ|| 7||[9]

7. When one realizes "the Self
Has become all beings,"
Then for the seer of oneness
What delusion and sorrow can there be?

sá páryagāc chukrám akāyám avraṇám
asnāvirám̐ śuddhám ápāpaviddham|
kavir manīṣī́ paribhū́ḥ svayaṃbhū́r
yāthātathyató'rthān vyàdadhāc chā́śvatī́bhyaḥ
sámābhyaḥ[10]*|| 8||*[11]

8. He permeates everything, luminous,
Incorporeal, flawless, without nerves,
Immaculate, impervious to evil,
Enlightening, sage, all-encompassing,
Self-sufficient; he allots all things
As needed for aeons eternal.

andháṃ támaḥ prá viśanti
yé (á)vidyām upā́sate|
táto bhū́ya iva té támo
yá u vidyā́yām̐ ratā́ḥ|| 9||[12]

9. They enter into blind darkness
Who devote themselves to ignorance;
But into greater gloom than that go they
Who desire knowledge.

anyád evā́húr vidyáyā
(a)nyád āhur ávidyayā|[13]
íti śuśruma dhī́rāṇāṃ
yé nas tád vicacakṣiré|| 10||(cf. KeU 4 [1.4])[14]

10. They say one thing indeed
Results from knowledge.
Another from ignorance, they say.
Thus have we heard from the wise,
Those who have perceived it for us.

vidyā́ṃ cā́vidyāṃ ca
yás tád védobháyam̐ sahá|
ávidyayā mṛtyúṃ tīrtvā́
vidyáyāmṛ́tam aśnute|| 11||

11. Knowledge and ignorance,
One who knows both together,
Crossing death by ignorance,
Gains immortality by knowledge.

andháṃ támaḥ prá viśanti
yé 'sàṃbhūtim upā́sate|
táto bhū́ya iva té támo
yá u sáṃbhūt(i)yām̐ ratā́ḥ|| 12||

12. They enter into blind darkness
Who devote themselves to regression.
To greater gloom than that go they
Who desire progression.

anyád evā́húḥ saṃbhavā́d
(a)nyád āhur ásaṃbhavāt|
íti śuśruma dhī́rāṇāṃ
yé nas tád vicacakṣiré|| 13||

13. They say one thing indeed
Results from progression.
Another from regression, they say.
Thus have we heard from the wise,
Those who have perceived it for us.

---

[9] cf. BG 6.29-30.

[10] 8d is hypermetrical. Omitting *yāthātathyataḥ* fixes the *triṣṭubh* meter.

[11] cf. KaU 5.13 (2.2.13), ŚU 6.13

[12] BUK 4.4.10.

[13] The reading: *anyád evā́húr vidyā́yā anyád āhur ávidyāyāḥ* is preferred by Thieme, the ablative case being more suitable here. The verse using the instrumental, however, is short a syllable because of *sandhi*.

[14] *anyad eva tad-viditād atho aviditād adhi| iti śuśruma pūrveṣām ye nas tad vyācacakṣire||*

sáṃbhūtiṃ ca vināśáṃ ca
yás tád védobháyaṁ sahá|
vināśéna mṛtyúṃ tīrtvā́
sáṃbhūtyāmŕ̥tam aśnute|| 14||

14. Progression and destruction,
One who knows both together
Crossing death by destruction
Gains immortality by progression.

hiraṇmáyena pā́treṇa
satyásyā́pihitaṃ múkham|
tat tvaṃ pū́ṣann apā́vṛṇu
satyadharmāya dṛṣṭaye|| 15||[15]

15. By a golden disc
The door of truth is hid.
Do thou uncover it, Oh Nourishing Sun,
Reveal it for one firm in the Truth.

pū́ṣann ekarṣe yama sūrya prā́jāpatya
vyū̀ha raśmī́nt sámūha téjaḥ|
yát te rūpáṃ kályāṇatamaṃ tát te paśyāmi
yo 'sā́v asaú púruṣaḥ só 'hám asmi|| 16K||[16]

16. Oh Nourishing Sun, the One Seer, Psychopomp,
Solar Orb, Scion of the Lord of Progeny,
Disperse your rays, gather up your brilliance:
So that I take in that most auspicious form of yours—
That very Person, that am I!

vayúr ánilam amŕ̥tam
áthedáṃ bhásmāntaṁ śarīram|
óm kráto smára kṛtáṁ smara
kráto smára kṛtáṁ smara|| 17K||[17]

17. [May my] vital breath [repair] to immortal air,
And this body now to its end in ashes;
Oṃ remember, oh Mental Fire, remember what has been done,
Remember, oh Mental Fire, remember what has been done!

ágne náya supáthā rāyé asmā́n
víśvāni deva vayúnāni vidvā́n|
yuyodhi àsmáj juhurāṇám éno
bhū́yiṣṭhāṃ te námauktiṃ vidhema|| 18||[18]

18. Oh Sacred Fire, lead us for glory on the path of light!
Oh God, knowing all our ways,
Overcome our crooked misdeeds.
We offer to you the greatest praise!

[15]BUK 5.15.1.
[16]BUK 5.15.2.
[17]BUK 5.15.3; 15M with variation.
[18]This verse is from the *Ṛg-saṃhitā*, 1.189.1. And 16b is from *Atharva-saṃhitā*, 4.39.10b.

Part III

Mādhyandina and Kāṇva Versions Compared

Mādhyandina & Kāṇva Versions (Side by Side)

The following presentation of the Kāṇva and the Mādhyandina versions of the *Īśopaniṣad* shows the differences between the texts of the two recensions. Though the texts are largely the same, there are some substantial differences between them, differences of verse order, differences in number of verses, and differences within the verses themselves. The best way to make the differences easily apparent is to place the two versions side-by-side so that they can be compared on a verse-by-verse, triplet-by-triplet basis. It bears remembering that of the two, the Mādhyandina version is considered older, but the Kāṇva version is the one upon which most commentators have commented. Both versions have been altered from the received or "vulgate" versions on the basis of Thieme's and Ježić's suggestions.

The Mādhyandina version is presented in the left column. If there is nothing in the right column, it is because the two versions, Mādhyandina and Kānva, are the same for those verses. When both columns are occupied, it is because the Mādhyandina and the Kāṇva versions differ from each other. To make things clearer, each verse is labeled with either an M, for Mādhyandina version, or with K, for Kāṇva version, or with both when the verse is the same in both.

Invocation

oṁ pūrṇamadaḥ pūrṇamidaṃ
pūrṇātpūrṇamudacyate |
pūrṇasya pūrṇamādāya
pūrṇamevāvaśiṣyate ||[1]

|| *oṁ śāntiḥ śāntiḥ śāntiḥ oṁ* ||

Oṁ, That is full; this is full;
From Fullness arises Fullness;
Subtract Fullness from Fullness,
What remains is still Fullness.

Oṁ Peace, peace, peace! Oṁ

[1] BUK 5.1.1.

Mādhyandina

Kānva

Oṁ. īśā́vāsyàm idaṁ sárvaṃ
yát kiṃca jágatyāṃ jágat|
téna tyakténa bhuñjīthā
mā́ gṛdhaḥ kásya svid dhánam|| 1KM||

MK1. Oṁ. By the Owner infused is all this,
Whatever moves in the world of motion.
Enjoy that which is let go of;
Don't hold on; whose property is it?

kurvánn evéhá kármāṇi
jijīviṣéc chatáṁ sámāḥ|
eváṃ tvayi nā́nyátheto'sti
ná kárma lipyate nárе|| 2KM||[2]

MK2. In this way by performing actions here,
One should live a hundred years.
So there is no other way for you.
No *karma* thus adheres to one.

asuryā́ nā́ma te lokā́[3]
andhéna tamasā́vṛtāḥ|
tā́ṁs te prétyā́bhigacchanti[4]
yé ké cātmaháno jánāḥ|| 3KM||[5]

MK3. Veiled indeed are those worlds,
Infused with blind darkness,
To which they go after death,
Those people who smother the Self.

ánejad ékaṃ mánaso jávīyo
naínad devā́ āpnuvan pū́rvam árṣat|[6]
tád dhā́vato'nyā́n átyeti tíṣṭhat
tásminn apó mātaríśvā dadhāti|| 4KM||

MK4. One, unmoving, faster than the mind,
It rushes ahead of the gods, [who are] unable to overtake it.
Though unmoving, it passes up the other runners.
In it, Life-energy generates all activity.

tád ejati tán naijati
tád dūré tád u antiké|
tád antár asya sárvasya
tád u sárvasyāsya bāhyatáḥ[7]*|| 5KM||*

MK5. It vibrates, it is still.
It is far away, but it is near.

[2]cf. ĪUd and BUK 4.4.23, BUM 4.4.28; both may reference CU 4.14.3.

[3]*asūrya*, sunless, possible; BUK *anandā*, joyless

[4]M = prétyā́pi gacchanti

[5]BUK 4.4.14abc, BUM 4.4.11abc; cf. BG 13.28

[6]M = árśat.

[7]The verse as it stands is hypermetrical. Therefore, Thieme and Ježić recommend removing the second *asya*.

It is within everything,
But outside all of this too.

yás tú sárvāṇi bhūtā́ni
ātmánn evā́nu paśyati|
sarvabhūtéṣu cātmā́nam
táto ná vi jugupsate|| 6KM||[8]

MK6. But one who sees
All beings in this very Self
And this Self in all beings
Because of this does not recoil.[9]

yásmint sárvāṇi bhūtā́ny
ātmaivā́bhūd vijānatáḥ|
tátra kó móhaḥ káḥ śóka
ekatvám anupáśyataḥ|| 7KM||[10]

MK7. When one realizes "the Self
Has become all beings,"
Then for the seer of oneness
What delusion and sorrow can there be?

sá páryagā́c chukrám akāyám avraṇám
asnāvirám̐ śuddhám ápāpaviddham|
kavir manīṣī́ paribhū́ḥ svayaṃbhū́r
yāthātathyató'rthān vyàdadhāc chā́śvatī́bhyaḥ
sámābhyaḥ[11] *|| 8KM||*[12]

MK8. He permeates everything, luminous,
Incorporeal, flawless, without nerves,
Immaculate, impervious to evil,
Enlightening, sage, all-encompassing,
Self-sufficient; he allots all things
As needed for aeons eternal.

andhám̐ támaḥ prá viśanti
yé 'sàṃbhūtim upā́sate|
táto bhū́ya iva té támo
yá u sáṃbhūt(i)yām̐ ratā́ḥ|| 9M (12K)||[13]

M9. They enter into blind darkness
Who devote themselves to regression.
To greater gloom than that go they
Who desire progression.

anyád evā́húḥ saṃbhavā́d
(a)nyád āhur ásaṃbhavāt|
íti śuśruma dhī́rāṇāṃ
yé nas tád vicacakṣiré|| 10M (13K)||

M10. They say one thing indeed

[8]ĪUM = vi cikitsati; ĪUK 6d, BUK 4.4.15d, BUM 4.4.18d, and KaU 4.5 (2.1.5) all have *tato na vi jupupsate.*

[9]In the case of *vi cikitsati*: Because of this he does not doubt.

[10]cf. BG 6.29-30.

[11]8d is hypermetrical. Omitting *yāthātathyataḥ* fixes the *triṣṭubh* meter.

[12]cf. KaU 5.13 (2.2.13), ŚU 6.13

[13]9M = BUM 4.4.13.

andhám̐ támaḥ prá viśanti
yé (á)vidyām upā́sate|
táto bhū́ya iva té támo
yá u vidyā́yām̐ ratā́ḥ|| 9K (12M)||[1]

K9. They enter into blind darkness
Who devote themselves to ignorance;
But into greater gloom than *that* go they
Who desire knowledge.

anyád evā́húr vidyáyā
(a)nyád āhur ávidyayā|[2]
íti śuśruma dhī́rāṇāṃ
yé nas tád vicacakṣiré|| 10K (13M)||[3]

K10. They say one thing indeed
Results from knowledge.

[1]9K = BUK 4.4.10.

[2]The reading: *anyád evā́húr vidyā́yā anyád āhur ávidyāyāḥ* is preferred by Thieme, the ablative case being more suitable here. The verse using the instrumental, however, is short a syllable because of *sandhi.*

[3]cf. KeU 4 [1.4]: *anyad eva tad-viditād atho aviditād adhi| iti śuśruma pūrveṣām ye nas tad vyācacakṣire||*

Results from progression,
Another from regression they say.
Thus have we heard from the wise,
Those who have perceived it for us.

sáṃbhūtiṃ ca vināśáṃ ca
yás tád védobháyaṁ sahá|
vināśéna mṛtyúṃ tīrtvā́
sáṃbhūtyāmṛ́tam aśnute|| 11M (14K)||

M11. Progression and destruction,
One who knows both together
Crossing death by destruction
Gains immortality by progression.

andháṃ támaḥ prá viśanti
yé (á)vidyām upā́sate|
táto bhū́ya iva té támo
yá u vidyā́yāṁ ratā́ḥ|| 12M (9K)||

M12. They enter into deeper darkness
Who devote themselves to ignorance;
To greater gloom than that go they
Who desire knowledge.

anyád evā́húr vidyáyā
(a)nyád āhur ávidyayā|
íti śuśruma dhī́rāṇāṃ
yé nas tád vicacakṣiré|| 13M (10K)||

M13. They say one thing indeed
Results from knowledge.
Another from ignorance they say.
Thus have we heard from the wise,
Those who have perceived it for us.

vidyā́ṃ cā́vidyāṃ ca
yás tád védobháyaṁ sahá|
ávidyayā mṛtyúṃ tīrtvā́
vidyáyāmṛ́tam aśnute|| 14M (11K)||

M14. Knowledge and ignorance,
One who knows both together
Crossing death by ignorance,
Gains immortality by knowledge.

Another from ignorance they say.
Thus have we heard from the wise,
Those who have perceived it for us.

vidyā́ṃ cā́vidyāṃ ca
yás tád védobháyaṁ sahá|
ávidyayā mṛtyúṃ tīrtvā́
vidyáyāmṛ́tam aśnute|| 11K (14M)||

K11. Knowledge and ignorance,
One who knows both together
Crossing death by ignorance,
Gains immortality by knowledge.

andháṃ támaḥ prá viśanti
yé 'sàṃbhūtim upā́sate|
táto bhū́ya iva té támo
yá u sáṃbhūt(i)yāṁ ratā́ḥ|| 12K (9M)||

K12. They enter into blind darkness
Who devote themselves to regression.
To greater gloom than that go they
Who desire progression.

anyád evā́húḥ saṃbhavā́d
(a)nyád āhur ásaṃbhavāt|
íti śuśruma dhī́rāṇāṃ
yé nas tád vicacakṣiré|| 13K (10M)||

K13. They say one thing indeed
Results from progression.
Another from regression, they say.
Thus have we heard from the wise,
Those who have perceived it for us.

sáṃbhūtiṃ ca vināśáṃ ca
yás tád védobháyaṁ sahá|
vināśéna mṛtyúṃ tīrtvā́
sáṃbhūtyāmṛ́tam aśnute|| 14K (11M)||

K14. Progression and destruction,
One who knows both together
Crossing death by destruction[4]
Gains immortality by progression.

[4]Here, instead of using *sambhūti* or *sambhava*, the word used is *vināśa*. This suggests that *vināśa*, destruction, is a synonym of *asambhūti* which we have been translating as "regression."

vayúr ánilam amṛ́tam
áthedáṃ bhásmāntaṁ śarīram|
ó3m kráto smára klibé[14] *smara*
kráto[15] *smára kṛtáṁ smara|| 15M||*[16]

M15. [May my] vital breath [repair] to immortal air,
And this body now to its end in ashes;
Oṃ, remember, oh Mental Fire, remember for the sake of merited worlds,
Remember, oh Mental Fire, remember what has been done!

ágne náya supáthā rāyé asmā́n
víśvāni deva vayúnāni vidvā́n|
yuyodhi àsmáj juhurāṇám éno
bhū́yiṣṭhāṃ te náma uktiṃ vidhema[17] *|| 16M||*

M16. Oh Sacred Fire, lead us for glory on the path of light!
Oh God, knowing all [our] ways,
Overcome our crooked misdeeds.
We offer to you the greatest praise!

hiraṇmáyena pā́treṇa
satyásyā́pihitaṃ múkham|
yo 'sā́v ādityé púruṣaḥ
só 'sā́v ahám óm kháṃ bráhma|| 17M||[18]

M17. By a golden disc
The door of truth is hid.
He who is that person in the sun,
That one indeed am I.
Oṃ! Space is Brahman!

[14]*Klib* (*kḷb*), (f.) created world, accomplishment, "remember for the sake of the world (heaven) created by (meritorious) karma."

[15]*Kratu* probably means sacrifice, personalized as Agni, the sacrificing priest for all fire (*agni*) worship, indwelling in humans also as inner light of intelligence as well as light of the sun (*āditya*) and lightning.

[16]BUM 5.15.3; 17K with variation.

[17]This verse is from the *Ṛg-saṃhitā*, 1.189.1. And 16b is from *Atharva-saṃhitā*, 4.39.10b.

[18]First half the same as 15K.

hiraṇmáyena pā́treṇa
satyásyā́pihitaṃ múkham|
tat tvaṃ pū́ṣann apā́vṛṇu
satyadharmāya dṛṣṭaye|| 15K||[5]

K15. By a golden disc
The door of truth is hid.
Do thou uncover it, Oh Nourishing Sun,
Reveal it for one firm in the Truth.

pū́ṣann ekarṣe yama sūrya prā́jāpatya
vyū̀ha raśmī́nt sámūha téjaḥ|
yát te rūpáṃ kályāṇatamaṃ tát te paśyāmi
yo 'sā́v asaú púruṣaḥ só 'hám asmi|| 16K||[6]

K16. Oh Nourishing Sun, the One Seer, Psychopomp,
Solar Orb, Scion of the Lord of Progeny,
Disperse your rays, gather up your brilliance:
So that I take in that most auspicious form of yours—
That very Person, that am I!

vayúr ánilam amṛ́tam
áthedáṃ bhásmāntaṁ śarīram|
óm kráto smára kṛtáṁ smara
kráto smára kṛtáṁ smara|| 17K||[7]

K17. [May my] vital breath [repair] to immortal air,
And this body now to its end in ashes;
Oṃ remember, oh Mental Fire, remember what has been done,
Remember, oh Mental, remember what has been done!

ágne náya supáthā rāyé asmā́n
víśvāni deva vayúnāni vidvā́n|
yuyodhi àsmáj juhurāṇám éno
bhū́yiṣṭhāṃ te náma uktiṃ vidhema|| 18K||

K18. Oh Sacred Fire, lead us for glory on the path of light!
Oh God, knowing all our ways,
Overcome our crooked misdeeds.
We offer to you the greatest praise!

[5]BUK 5.15.1.

[6]BUK 5.15.2.

[7]BUK 5.15.3; 15M with variation.

26542

Part IV

Kāṇva Īśopaniṣad with Śaṅkara's Commentary

Invocation

ॐ। पूर्णमदः पूर्णमिदं
पूर्णात्पूर्णमुदच्यते।
पूर्णस्य पूर्णमादाय
पूर्णमेवावशिष्यते॥

॥ॐ शान्तिः शान्तिः शान्तिः ॐ॥

Oṁ. That is Full; this is Full;
From Fullness arises Fullness;
Subtract Fullness from Fullness,
What remains is still Fullness.
Oṁ! Peace, peace, peace! Oṁ!

oṁ pūrṇamadaḥ pūrṇamidaṃ
pūrṇātpūrṇamudacyate|
pūrṇasya pūrṇamādāya
pūrṇamevāvaśiṣyate||

|| oṁ śāntiḥ śāntiḥ śāntiḥ oṁ ||

ॐ। पूर्णमदः पूर्णमिदं
पूर्णात्पूर्णमुदच्यते।
पूर्णस्य पूर्णमादाय
पूर्णमेवावशिष्यते॥

॥ॐ शान्तिः शान्तिः शान्तिः ॐ॥

ॐ। पूर्णमदः पूर्णमिदं
oṁ pūrṇam adaḥ pūrṇam idaṃ
Oṁ. Full is that; full is this;

पूर्णात्पूर्णमुदच्यते।
pūrṇāt pūrṇam udacyate|
From fullness fullness arises;

पूर्णस्य पूर्णमादाय
pūrṇasya pūrṇam ādāya
From fullness fullness subtracting,

पूर्णमेवावशिष्यते॥
pūrṇam eva avaśiṣyate||
Fullness itself remains.

॥ॐ शान्तिः शान्तिः शान्तिः ॐ॥
oṁ śāntiḥ śāntiḥ śāntiḥ oṁ
Oṁ. Peace, peace, peace! Oṁ.

oṁ ind.: "a word of solemn affirmation and respectful assent, sometimes translated by 'yes, verily, so be it.'" —Monier Williams
pūrṇam (n. nom. sing.) *pūrṇa*: "full, complete."
adaḥ (pers. pron., n. nom. sing.) *adas*:[1] "that." This is a demonstrative pronoun used for persons or things that are some distance away.
pūrṇam See above.
idam (demon. pron., n. nom. sing.) *idam*: "this."
pūrṇāt (n. abl. sing.) "from the full."
pūrṇam (n. acc. sing.) "the full."
udacyate (3rd. pers. pass. sing.) *ud*[2] + $\sqrt{\text{añc}}$ (cl. 1, P.): "to be thrown out, to come forth, to proceed [from]." Here: "comes forth [from]."
pūrṇasya (n. gen. sing.) "of the the full."
pūrṇam (n. acc. sing.) "the full."
ādāya ger. of *ā* + $\sqrt{\text{dā}}$ (cl. 3, U.): "take, accept, receive from; to seize, take away, carry off, rob, take back, reclaim."
pūrṇam (n. nom. sing.) "the full."
eva ind.: "so, just so, exactly so."
avaśiṣyate (3rd. pers. pass. sing.) *ava* + $\sqrt{\text{śiṣ}}$: "to be left as a remnant, to remain."
oṁ ind.: see above
śāntiḥ (f. nom. sing.) *śānti*: "tranquillity, peace, quiet, peace or calmness of mind, absence of passion, averting of pain."

[1]By *sandhi* rules, or rules of euphonic combination, a final "s" changes to *visarga* (ḥ).
[2]See the appendix for verbal prefixes.

Oṁ. That is Full; this is Full;
From Fullness arises Fullness;
Subtract Fullness from Fullness,
What remains is still Fullness.
Oṁ! Peace, peace, peace! Oṁ!

Śaṅkara's commentary on *Bṛhad-āraṇyaka Upaniṣad* 5.1 (Invocation)

pūrṇam ada *ityādi khilakāṇḍam ārabhyate| adhyāyacatuṣṭayena yad eva sākṣād aparokṣād brahma ya ātmā sarvāntaro nirupādhiko'śanāyādyatīto neti netīti vyapadeśyo nirdhārito yad vijñānaṃ kevalam amṛtatvasādhanam adhunā tasyaivātmanaḥ sopādhikasya śabdārthādivyavahāraviṣayāpannasya purastād anuktāny upāsanāni karmabhir aviruddhāni prakṛṣṭābhyudayasādhanāni kramamuktibhāñji ca tāni vaktavyānīti paraḥ sandarbhaḥ sarvopāsanaśeṣatvenoṅkāro damaṃ dānaṃ dayām ity etāni ca vidhitsitāni|*

This appendix [of the BU] begins with the words: **That is full**. With the first four chapters [of the BU], Brahman which is the Self within all was revealed immediately and directly as free of limiting qualifications, beyond hunger, thirst, and so forth, and indicated by "not this, not this." Knowledge of that Brahman was revealed as the only means to immortality. Now, meditations, not mentioned before [in the BU], on that very Self, which is now qualified and verbally discussed—that is, meditations which are not incompatible with ritual actions, are the preeminent means for personal growth. They lead to gradual liberation and will be described in the following treatise. The *mantra* "*oṁ*" along with self-control (*dama*), charity (*dāna*), and compassion (*dayā*) are to be the complements of all meditations.

pūrṇam adaḥ *pūrṇaṃ na kutaścid vyāvṛttaṃ vyāpīty etat| niṣṭhā ca kartari draṣṭavyā|* **ada** *iti parokṣābhidhāyi sarvanāma tatparaṃ brahmety arthaḥ| tatsaṃpūrṇam ākāśavad vyāpi nirantaraṃ nirupādhikaṃ ca| tad eva* **idaṃ** *sopādhikaṃ nāmarūpasthaṃ vyavahārāpannaṃ pūrṇaṃ svena rūpeṇa paramātmanā vyāpyeva nopādhiparicchinnena viśeṣātmanā| tad* **idaṃ** *viśeṣāpannaṃ kāryātmakaṃ brahma pūrṇāt kāraṇātmana* **udacyata** *udricyata udgacchatītyetat| yadyapi kāryātmanodricyate tathāpi yat svarūpaṃ pūrṇatvaṃ paramātmabhāvaṃ tan na jahāti pūrṇam evodricyate| pūrṇasya kāryātmano brahmaṇaḥ pūrṇaṃ pūrṇatvam* **ādāya** *gṛhītvātmasvarūpaikarasatvam āpadya vidyayā 'vidyākṛtaṃ bhūtamātropādhisaṃsargajam anyatvāvabhāsaṃ tiraskṛtya pūrṇam evānantaram abāhyaṃ prajñānaghanaikarasasvabhāvaṃ kevalaṃ brahma* **avaśiṣyate**|

That is full; *full* means not absent from anywhere, in other words, this is "all-pervasive." It [full or the full, *pūrṇam*] is to be regarded as the subject of the sentence. **That** is a pronoun meaning "imperceptible," referring to Brahman which has the same meaning. It is complete, all-pervasive like space, unbroken, and free of limitations. **This** fullness, which is limited, characterized by name and form, and expressed in relative terms (*vyavahāra*), is all-pervasive through its essential nature, the highest Self (*paramātman*), but not through its appearance as truncated by limitations and distinctions. **This** Brahman which has become distinct and is an effect **arises**, (that is, swells up, issues) out of the full which is the cause. Even though this effect-Brahman arises [from the cause-Brahman] it does not give up its true nature, fullness, and its being as the highest Self; the full itself arises. The fullness which is effect-Brahman **reclaims**[3] the fullness of identity with the true nature of the Self. Through knowledge it removes the appearance of being different, which is caused by ignorance linked with the limiting adjuncts of the material elements. The fullness [so reclaimed] is Brahman alone, without interior or exterior, unmixed by nature, sheer homogeneous consciousness; it **alone remains**.

yad uktaṃ brahma vā idamagra āsīt tadātmānam evāvet tasmāt tat sarvam abhavad ity eṣo 'sya mantrasyārthaḥ| tatra brahmety asyārthaḥ **pūrṇam ada** *iti|* **idaṃ pūrṇam** *iti brahma vā idam agra āsīd ity asyārthaḥ| tathā ca śrutyantaram "yad eveha tad amutra yad amutra tad anviha" iti| ato adaḥśabdavācyaṃ pūrṇaṃ brahma tad evedaṃ pūrṇaṃ kāryasthaṃ nāmarūpopādhisaṃyuktam avidyayodriktam| tasmād eva paramārthasvarūpād anyad iva pratyavabhāsamānam| tadyad ātmānam eva paraṃ pūrṇaṃ brahma viditvā 'ham adaḥ pūrṇaṃ brahmāsmīty evaṃ pūrṇam ādāya tiraskṛtyāpūrṇasvarūpatām avidyākṛtāṃ nāmarūpo-*

When it was said before (BU 1.4.10): "In the beginning Brahman indeed became this: it knew only itself and therefore it became all," this is the meaning of this *mantra*. There [in that passage], by **that is full** *Brahman* is meant, and by **this is full**, "in the beginning Brahman indeed was *this*" is meant. It is also said in another *śruti* (KaU 4.10 or 2.1.10): "whatever is here is there;

[3]Our translation of the invocation, which is the more usual translation, renders *ādāya* as **subtract**: (**subtract [relative] fullness from [absolute] fullness**). Śaṅkara on the other hand uses an alternative meaning **reclaim fullness from fullness** for his own purposes.

pādhisaṃparkajām etayā brahmavidyayā **pūrṇam eva kevalam avaśiṣyate**| *tathā coktam "tasmāt tatsarvam abhavat"iti*| *yaḥ sarvopaniṣadartho brahma sa eṣo 'nena mantreṇānūdyata uttarasaṃbandhārtham*| *brahmavidyāsādhanatvena hi vakṣyamāṇāni sādhanāny oṃkāradamadānadayākhyāni vidhitsitāni khilaprakaraṇasaṃbandhāt sarvopāsanāṅgabhūtāni ca*|

whatever is there is here." Therefore, the full Brahman conveyed by the word "that" *is* [actually the same as] "this" full [relative Brahman] which is an effect linked with the limiting factors of name and form, emerging from ignorance. Therefore, it appears as different from its ultimate, true nature. Knowing itself to be that highest fullness, Brahman, thinking "I am that full Brahman," it reclaims that fullness and, through knowledge of Brahman, dissolves its incomplete nature created by ignorance and linked with the limiting factors of name and form: and **what remains is only fullness**. And that is stated in the earlier passage (BU 1.4.10): "therefore, it became all." This Brahman, which is the meaning of all the Upaniṣads, is reintroduced by this *mantra* to connect it with what follows, because the methods that are going to be described as ways of attaining knowledge of Brahman, namely, the saced syllable *Oṁ*, self-restraint, charity, and compassion, are to be parts of all forms of meditation (*upāsanā*) because of their connection with the appendix of this Upaniṣad.[4]

[4]Śaṅkara's commentary on the invocation of the ĪU, which is first found at BU 5.1, continues on but his analysis of the meaning of the invocation is complete here. So we discontinue our translation.

Discussion

This famous verse is first seen in the BU 5.1. It is not known when it was first attached as an invocation to the ĪU. Śaṅkara, for example, does not comment on it here, as an invocation, though he comments on the verse in its original context in the BU. It is possible that this verse is used as an invocation because later editors found that it offered a concise summary of the meaning of the Upaniṣad and was in close proximity to four of the other verses of the BU (5.15.1-4) that recur in the ĪU. This pregnant invocation in the BU is followed immediately by the following passage:

> *oṁ khaṃ brahma*| *khaṃ purāṇaṃ vāyuraṃ kham iti ha smāha kauravyāyanī-putro vedo'yaṃ brāhmaṇā vidur vedainena yad veditavyam*|| *1*||
>
> "Oṁ! Space is Brahman. The son of Kauravyāyanī used to say: "Space is ancient [eternal]. Space holds the wind [breath]. The knowers of Brahman (*brāhmaṇas*) knew that this [*oṁ*] is the Veda, since by it one knows what is to be known."

In Vedic literature the all-inclusive *mantra oṁ* is often identified with the ultimate, whether as personal lord or impersonal absolute. For example, see the unpacking of the *oṁ* in the *Māṇḍūkya Upaniṣad*, and as the *udgītha* (high chant) in the *Chāndogya Upaniṣad*.

Study Questions

1. In what way would you say this invocation, quoting the famous first half of BU 5.1.1 encapsulates the wisdom of the Upaniṣads?
2. Why is the binary of "*That*" versus "*This*" significant? What other binary oppositions are important in Upaniṣadic thinking?
3. If you think of *This* as waves and *That* as ocean, how might one use the analogy of an ocean and its waves to understand that "fullness" remains?
4. Restate the *mantra* in your own words and be prepared to explain your choices.

Mantra One

Śaṅkara's Introduction to the Īśā Upaniṣad

śrīgaṇeśāya namaḥ

I bow to Śrī Gaṇeśa!

īśitā sarvabhūtānāṃ
sarvabhūtamayaś ca yaḥ |
īśā āvāsyena sambodhyam
īśvaraṃ taṃ namāmy aham ||

To that Ruler of all beings,
Who also pervades all beings
Enlightening us with the Īśā Upaniṣad[5]
To that Lord I bow down.

īśā āvāsyam ity ādayo mantrāḥ karmasv aviniyuktāḥ| teṣām akarmaśeṣasya ātmano āyatimātraprakāśakatvāt| āyatimātraṃ ca ātmanaḥ śuddhatva-apāpaviddhatva-ekatva-nityatva-aśarīratva-sarvagatatvādi vakṣyamāṇam| tacca karmaṇā virudhyeta iti yukta eva eṣāṃ karmasv aviniyogaḥ|

The *mantras*, beginning with *īśāvāsyam*, are not used in rituals, because they reveal the pure majesty[6] of the Self which is not involved in action. And that pure majesty of the Self will be described as purity, freedom from harm, oneness, eternity, non-physicality, all-pervasiveness, and so forth. And that would be incompatible with action. Thus, it is fitting that these hymns are not used in rites.

na hy evaṃ lakṣaṇam ātmano āyatimātram utpādyaṃ vikāryam āpyaṃ saṃskāryaṃ kartṛ-bhoktṛ-rūpaṃ vā yena karmaśeṣatā syāt| sarvāsām upaniṣadām ātmāyatimātranirūpaṇena eva upakṣayāt| gītānāṃ mokṣadharmāṇāṃ ca evaṃparatvāt| tasmād ātmano 'nekatvakartṛtvabhoktṛtvādi ca aśuddhatvapāpaviddhatvādi ca upādāya lokabuddhisiddhaṃ karmāṇi vihitāni|

Nor could the pure majesty of the Self as defined above be subject to creation, alteration, attainment, improvement, agency or enjoyment or [in any way] involved in action. And that, too, is so because all the Upaniṣads have exhausted themselves on the investigation of nothing other than the pure majesty of the Self and also because the *Gītā* and the *Mokṣa-dharma*[7] are similarly devoted to that. And therefore, assuming [mistaken] ideas like the Self's plurality, its agency, its enjoyership, its impurity, its vulnerability to harm, and so forth, the ordinary intellect is formed and rites are prescribed.

yo hi karmaphalena arthī dṛṣṭena brahma-varcasādinā adṛṣṭena svargādinā ca dvijātirahaṃ na kāṇakubjatvādyanadhikāraprayojakadharmavānityātmānaṃ manyate so 'dhikriyate karmasv iti hy adhikāravido vadanti|

One, indeed, who wants the results of Vedic rituals, both visible, such as charismatic power, and invisible, like the celestial worlds and such, and who thinks to himself: "I am twice-born and do not have any of the

[5]Or, "Who is revealed through the Īśā Upaniṣad."

[6]*Āyatimātra.* Another version has *yāthātmya* (याथात्म्य) instead of *āyatimātra* (आयतिमात्र). That would mean true nature of the self.

[7]That is, the *Bhagavad-gītā* and the *Mokṣa-dharma* sections of the *Mahābhārata.*

disqualifying flaws like being blind in one eye, being humpbacked and the rest"—such a person is qualified for Vedic rituals. So say the experts on ritual qualification.

tasmād ete mantrā ātmano āyatimātraprakāśanena ātmaviṣayaṃ svābhāvikam ajñānaṃ nivartayantaḥ śokamohādisaṃsāradharmavicchittisādhanam ātmaikatvādivijñānam utpādayanti| ityevam uktādhikāryabhidheyasambandhaprayojanān mantrān saṃkṣepato vyākhyāsyāmaḥ ||

Therefore, these *mantras*, while negating inherent ignorance of the Self by revealing the Self's pure majesty, produce knowledge of the essential oneness, etc. of the Self, and that brings about a severing of the features of the cycle of birth and death such as sorrow, delusion, and the rest. Having described the one qualified [to study this text], the meaning to be conveyed, the relationship between this text and that meaning, and the goal of this discourse, I will briefly explain the *mantras*.[8]

[8] Śaṅkara here refers to the four connecting links (*anubandha*) for undertaking the study of this text— (1) the qualifications expected of the student or the intended audience; (2) the subject matter to be conveyed by the text; (3) the relationship between the text and its subject; and (4) the purpose or result arising from studying the text. It was believed that if these are not mentioned at the beginning of a book a qualified reader will not be inclined to take up the study.

ॐ ईशावास्यमिदꣳ सर्वं
यत्किंच जगत्यां जगत् ।
तेन त्यक्तेन भुञ्जीथा
मा गृधः कस्य स्विद्धनम् ॥१॥

Oṁ. By the Owner infused is all this,
Whatever moves in the world of motion.
Enjoy that which is let go of;
Don't hold on; whose property is it?

oṁ īśāvāsyamidaṁ sarvaṃ
yatkiṃca jagatyāṃ jagat|
tena tyaktena bhuñjīthā
mā gṛdhaḥ kasya sviddhanam|| 1||

ॐ ईशावास्यमिदꣳ सर्वं
यत्किंच जगत्यां जगत्।
तेन त्यक्तेन भुञ्जीथा
मा गृधः कस्य स्विद्धनम्॥ १॥

ॐ ईशा आवास्यम् इदꣳ सर्वं
oṁ īśā āvāsyam idaṁ sarvaṃ
Oṁ. By the Owner infused is this all

यत् किंच जगत्यां जगत्।
yat kiṃca jagatyāṃ jagat|
Whatever in the world moves.

तेन त्यक्तेन भुञ्जीथा
tena tyaktena bhuñjīthā
Therefore, with that which left enjoy;

मा गृधः कस्य स्विद् धनम्॥
mā gṛdhaḥ kasya svid dhanam||
Don't hold on; whose is it property?

oṁ ind.: a mystic monosyllable set forth as an object of profound religious meditation. The highest spiritual efficacy is attributed not only to the whole word but also to the three sounds *a*, *u*, *ṁ*, of which it consists.

īśā (m. inst. sing.) *īś* (from the root √*īś* (or √*īṭ*) (cl. 2, Ā. *iṣṭe*): "to own, possess, be master of." Here: "by the master, by the possessor."

āvāsyam (n. nom. sing.) *āvāsya* from the root *ā* + √*vas* (cl. 5, P.): "to abide, dwell; to spend (time); to enter, inhabit; to take possession of," or as caus. "to perfume."

idam (n. nom. sing.) the dem. pron. *idam*: "this." Used with reference to a person or thing near at hand.

sarvam (n. nom. sing.) mfn. pron. *sarva*: "whole, entire, all, every."

yat (rel. pron.) *yad*: "who, which, what. whichever."[9]

kiṃca a combination of the pron. of interrogation *kim* ("what") and the copulative particle *ca* ("and"). Together they mean "moreover, further" or as in this case "to a certain degree, a little."

jagatyām (f. loc. sing.) *jagatī*, the f. form of *jagat*: "the earth, people, the world, the universe."

jagat (n. nom. sing.) from the redupl. rt. √*gam*, (cl. 1, P., irr. *gamati, gacchati*): "to go." Here: "that which moves or is alive."

tena (m./n. instr. sing.) dem. pron. *tad*: "he, she, it." Here, "by him or it."

tyaktena (m. instr. sing.) *tyakta*, p.p. of √*tyaj* (cl. 1, P., *tyajati*): "to leave, abandon, quit." Here: "with that which is left."

bhuñjīthās (2nd pers. opt. sing.) √*bhuj* (cl. 7, U. *bhunakti* or *bhuṅkte*): "to enjoy." Here, "you may enjoy."

mā ind. partic. of prohibition or negation: "do not." Usually joined with the subj. mood of a verb.

gṛdhas (2nd pers. subj. sing.) √*gṛdh* (cl. 4, P. *gṛdhyati*): "to covet, desire, strive after greedily, be desirous of or eager for." Here, "do not hold on."

kasya (m. gen. sing.) the interrogative pron. *kim*: "what, who, which." Here: "whose."

svid an ind. of interrogation or inquiry or doubt translatable as: "do you think?, perhaps, indeed, any." Combined with an interrogative pron. like *kasya* it turns the interrogative into an indefinite: "whose" to "anyone's."

dhanam (n. acc. sing.) *dhana*: "wealth, riches, (movable) property, money, treasure."

[9]The final "d" is by *sandhi* changed to "t" before unvoiced consonants and when nothing follows.

Oṁ. By the Owner infused is all this,
Whatever moves in the world of motion
Enjoy that which is let go of
Don't hold on;
Whose property is it?[1]

[1]Alternative translation of the last two lines: "Enjoy that which is left aside by him. / Do not endeavor to take anyone's property."

Śaṅkara's Commentary on Mantra One

īśā *iṣṭa iti iṭ tena īśā|* **īśitā** *parama-īśvaraḥ parama-ātmā sarvasya| sa hi sarvam iṣṭe sarva-jantūnām ātmā san pratyag-ātmatayā tena svena rūpeṇa ātmanā* **īśā vāsyam** *ācchādanīyam|*

By the Owner (*īśā*), "he owns," from the root $\sqrt{\textit{īś}}$ (to own, to possess, to be master of), by him, by the Owner. **The owner** is the supreme Lord, the supreme Self of all. He indeed owns everything; by him, by being the Self of all that are born, as their inner Self, [i.e.] by his own form which is the Self. **By [that] Owner is all this infused**, that is to say, all this is enveloped.

kim? **idaṃ sarvaṃ yatkiṃca** *yatkiñcij* **jagatyāṃ** *pṛthivyāṃ* **jagat** *tatsarvaṃ svena ātmanā īśena pratyagātmatayā 'ham eva idaṃ sarvam iti parama-arthasatyarūpeṇa anṛtam idaṃ sarvaṃ carācaram ācchādanīyaṃ svena paramātmanā|*

What is? **All this, whatever moves in this world of motion**, that is, on this the earth. All of that is by his own Self, by the Owner as the inner Self, indeed, enveloped by supreme reality (*satya*): "I indeed am all this;" the fiction (*anṛta*), which is all this composed of the moving and unmoving, is enveloped by one's own supreme Self.

yathā candanāgarvāder udakādisambandhajakledādijam aupādhikaṃ daurgandhyaṃ tatsvarūpanigharṣaṇenācchādyate svena pāramārthikena gandhena| tadvad eva hi svātmany adhyastaṃ svābhāvikaṃ kartṛtvabhoktṛtvādilakṣaṇam **jagad** *dvaitarūpaṃ* **jagatyāṃ** *pṛthivyām,* **jagatyām** *iti upalakṣaṇa-arthatvāt sarvam eva nāmarūpakarmākhyaṃ vikārajātaṃ paramārthasatyātmabhāvanayā tyaktaṃ syāt|*

For example, a deceptive foul smell born of exposure to moisture in sandalwood, agarwood, and other fragrant substances is [eventually] enveloped by their own sublime fragrances through vigorous rubbing down to their inner essences. Just like that **whatever moves** (*jagat*) in the form of duality, defined as ordinary agency, enjoyership, etc., is imposed on one's own Self **in the world of motion**, that is, on the earth. Out of the implied sense of "**in the world**," we get everything born of change, known as name, form, and action, and that may be let go of by apprehension of the Self as the supreme Reality.

evam īśvarātmabhāvanayā yuktasya putrādyeṣaṇātrayasaṃnyāsa eva adhikāro na karmasu| **tena tyaktena** *tyāgena ity arthaḥ| na hi tyakto mṛtaḥ putro vā bhṛtyo vā ātmasambandhitāyā abhāvād ātmānaṃ pālayaty atas tyāgena ity ayam eva vedārthaḥ|* **bhuñjīthāḥ** *pālayethāḥ|*

Thus, one who has this apprehension of the Self of the Lord is qualified for the renunciation of the three obsessions, the obsession for sons, and so forth,[2] but not for Vedic ritual. "**That which is left**" means by renunciation. The rejected, dead son or servant, do not protect the Self because there is no relationship between them and the Self. Therefore, "by renunciation" is the meaning of the Veda. **You may enjoy** means "you may protect."

evaṃ tyakta-eṣanas tvaṃ **mā gṛdhaḥ**, *gṛdhim ākāṅksāṃ mā kārṣīr dhana-viṣayām|* **kasya-svid dhanaṃ** *kasya-cit parasya svasya vā dhanaṃ mā kāṅkṣīr ity arthaḥ| svid ity anarthako nipātaḥ|*

Thus, you who have rejected the three impulses don't hold on, do not have desires aimed at wealth. **Whose property is it** means do not desire anyone's, not someone else's nor your own, wealth. *Svid* is a meaningless particle.

athavā **mā gṛdhaḥ** *| kasmāt? kasya-svid dhanam ity ākṣepaartho na kasya-cid dhanam asti yad gṛdhyeta| ātmā eva idaṃ sarvam iti īśvara-bhāvanayā sarvaṃ tyaktam ata ātmana eva idaṃ sarvam ātmā eva ca sarvam ato mithyāviṣayāṃ gṛdhiṃ mā kārṣīr ity arthaḥ|| 1||*

Or, **don't hold on**. Why? An implied sense of **whose property is it** is [that] no one has any wealth for you to cling to. The Self alone is all this. Through this contemplation of the Lord everything is renounced. Therefore, all this belongs to the Self; the Self indeed is all. Therefore, don't hold on to something that is false. This is the meaning. (1)

---

[2]BUK 4.4.22. The other two are wealth (*vitta*) and worlds (*loka*).

Discussion

Points for Consideration

The first word brings attention to the possibility that this particular Upaniṣad is one that takes up the idea of the existence and nature of *Īś* (or *Īśa*). But wait, let's not go too fast; the phrase *īśāvāsyam*, like so many phrases in Sanskrit, could be interpreted in many ways. Because of the euphonic rules for combination of words and parts of words, the first word can be construed in at least these four ways:

1. *Īś*: master, lord, owner, supreme spirit, and much later a name of god Śiva.
2. *Īśa*: ruler, master, lord, a Rudra, a name of Śiva or Kuvera, a husband, the number 11.
3. *Īśā*: f. faculty , power, or dominion (and possibly a feminine form, for 1 and 2 above—mistress?, lady?, goddess?).
4. *Īśā*: The instrumental form of Īś: *Īśā*, by the master, the lord, the owner.

All of the above possible noun meanings are from the basic or root form of the verb √*īś*: to own, to belong to, dispose of, be valid or powerful, to be master of, to command, to rule, reign, to behave like a master, [cf. Goth. aigan, "to have;" Old Germ. eigan, "own;" Mod. Germ. eigen.]

This first word is combined with the second word in the verse, which may be one of the following:

1. *āvāsyam*
2. *vāsyam*
3. *a-vāsyam*
4. *ava-āsya*

This is a future passive participle which adds to the meaning of the verbal root "to be ... , fit for ... , fit to be ... , ought to be ... ," and is formed from one of the following verbs:

1. √*vas*: (cl. 1, P.) dwell, abide, stop at or stay at; (caus.) to cause to exist, to preserve, to cause to be inhabited.
2. √*āvas*: (cl. 1 + ā) dwell, abide, enter, take possession of, inhabit, settle, sleep with, receive hospitably.
3. √*vas*: (cl. 2, A.) to put on, invest, wear.
4. √*vas*: (cl. 6, P.) to shine, grow bright; (caus.) to cause to shine.
5. √*vās*: (cl. 10, P.) perfume, make fragrant, fumigate, scent, incense, steep.
6. √*āvās*: (cl. 10 + ā) to perfume.
7. √*vas* (cl. 10., P.) to love, to cut off; to accept, take; to offer; to kill.
8. √*avās* (cl. 2., P. + ava) to decline, to deteriorate, to decay; to put down (RV i, 140, 10); to be dropped/cast off (See Smith, 1968).

When the first two words are put together we have the following options:

1. *Īśā āvāsyam*: by the owner (master, Lord, Spirit, Power, God, Goddess, Śiva), to be indwelt, inhabited, possessed, infused, perfumed, invested. (Most likely)
2. *Īśā āvāsyam*: By the Lord to be illumined or brightened. (Possible reference here to the sun as the illuminating power of the world and symbol of or doorway to the highest Self.)
3. *Īśā āvāsyam*: By the Lord to be caused to be. (An ontological meaning depicting the Lord as creator of the world or as being itself.)
4. *Īśa-āvāsyam*: virtually the same as 1 except less probable since it takes *īśāvāsya* as a compound word. Compound words were not as common in Vedic and Upaniṣadic language as they were in the later language.
5. *Īśā-vāsyam*: by the goddess (power, dominion) to be indwelt (highly unlikely because of the nearly complete absence of goddesses in Vedic texts).
6. *Īśā-āvāsyam*: by the goddess (power, dominion) to be infused (perfumed) (even less likely than the previous option because infused and perfumed are less likely than indwelt or inhabited).
7. *Īśā avāsyam*: by the Lord to be uninhabited. (Another possibility with low probability, but one which oddly enough would fit with some later interpretations of the nature of the world: that the world is empty of the Lord, that the Lord is absent from this world, lives in another world or higher reality.)

8. *Īśā avāsyam*: by the Lord to be cast off, abandoned, destroyed. The use of the word *avāsya* in this sense is found in the Ṛg Veda (1.140.10). This is based on the suggestion of Morton Smith that the first verse or mantra might be about the death of the head of the family, owner of the family estate. So the meaning would be: "By the Lord is all this to be left behind, whatever moves on this property. What is left behind by him you (his heirs) may enjoy. Do not take anyone else's property (but for what you receive from him)." The basic meaning seems to be the same. Nothing belongs to you. It is his now, but it soon will be yours. After you your descendents will have it. Don't try to cling to it or steal anyone else's property.

However, the basic meaning seems to be the abstract concept of owning or possessing by way of indwelling or pervasion. All this, this whole world or reality, it is asserted, is owned and pervaded. This is further strengthened by the question at the end: whose property is [anything you may believe yourself to own or dispose of] anyway? We are faced immediately with being dispossessed of the world we have believed ourselves to own, master, or control. Instead, there is something or someone else who owns and controls everything (including our own bodies). We are not who we think we are—the concept of possession and property is directly related to identity in general; possibly the most important question in Indian philosophy—"What do I have?"—is but another way of asking the chief Upaniṣadic question,"Who am I?" The answer from the beginning is humbling: you are not the owner or the boss. The direct consequence is a lesson on how to live: "Let go!" Don't hold on to anything –(1) since you are not the real owner, and (2) since everything is also in motion—*anitya*, all is transient. The unstated condition is: "If you want to be happy." It is implied by the injunction to "enjoy" paradoxically, not by possessing (since someone else is the owner) or controlling, but by letting go, surrendering false ownership, false identity, and dropping attachment. This can be read as the earliest injunction for "*karma yoga*" (the discipline of action) and the "*niṣkāma-karma*" (acting without desire for results) of the later *Bhagavad-gītā*, eventually considered an honorary Upaniṣad. The implication is that property can be enjoyed—with the correct perspective. Enjoy not as the ego bound owner, but as the true owner, the egoless true Self. Though this can easily be interpreted as a call for total renunciation, the enjoinder to enjoy, may also be taken literally—true enjoyment is possible only with a wider perspective based on true identity.

Yat kiṃca jagatyāṃ jagat, "whatever moves," is probably a reference to all forms of animal life as contrasted with all forms of vegetation "*sthāvara*" (things that stand only), but as Thieme (1965) points out, it can also be taken broadly to include all living things. In modern terms, which seem consonant with Hindu thinking, everything in the relative world, since it is made of ever dynamic matter, *prakṛti*, is in constant motion and is thus infused by the Lord.

On the surface this enjoinder leaves the wandering ascetic to nourish himself with what his virtuous benefactors explicitly *give him as alms*. That is probably the most literal sense here. However, the Upaniṣad is not mostly about literal, restricted meanings, but as Upaniṣad seeks to take things to their ultimate extent by putting them in the widest context. So what is abandoned by the Owner? Nothing and everything! "Holding" or ownership is a mental act reflecting small selfhood. So who abandons, "lets go," of that which gives nourishment, provides enjoyment? Thieme asserts it is the religious benefactor and not the Lord referred to (p. 89). However, he may be missing the larger picture here: since the Lord, the spiritual Self as ultimate Owner, begins the Upaniṣad, and the verse, and dominates the whole, it seems more natural to understand that part of owning everything, infusing everything, is also sacrificing, donating, letting go of everything. Are we to see the Owner, the Lord, as the ultimate possessive tyrant—appropriating and jealously keeping everything from all lower creatures? Seems very doubtful. The Self is described as creating through self-sacrifice, self-offering (ex. Ṛg Veda, 10.90) and other creation accounts of the One becoming many, (see also *Bṛhadāraṇyaka Upaniṣad* (BU), 4.5). Humans are asked to only enjoy here in the moving world, with the same detachment, the same wide perspective, and the same compassion. (See also the *Bhagavad-gītā* 3.19 *et. al.* on detachment). The Owner paradoxically infuses all but does not stick to it. BU 4.5.15 for example characterizes the Self as *sa eṣa neti neti ātmā; agṛhyaḥ na hi gryate, aśīya, na hi śīryate, asaṅga na hi sajyate*: "This Self is not this, not that; it is not graspable and is not grasped, indestructible, not destroyed, not sticky, does not adhere to anything."

Thieme argues against Śaṅkara that "not coveting" (his translation of *mā gṛdhaḥ*) is not "a theoretical attitude," but "a prescription" for "religiously founded practical behavior." However, the issue seems to be wider here than an ascetic prohibition against taking, eating, enjoying no more than the food which is explicitly offered to ascetics, or what they glean on their wanderings. This is probably not a manual for ascetic behavior but indeed a wider philosophical/religious stance with respect to "ownership."

The question at the end asks, "Whose property is it [really]?" The answer is of course only the ultimate "Owner" who infuses all things, the Self. Gandhi's famous comment that this first verse encapsulates the main thrust of Hindu Dharma in general underscores the importance of this as a philosophical and ethical statement with broad ranging implications. Certainly, it is the most memorable verse of the whole Upaniṣad. Since everything is pervaded by a spiritual Self, the real Owner of all, how ought we to think and act? The answer is simply without holding on, mentally or physically to that which is "in motion" (and can't really be held) and which belongs to "another" who already "owns" the whole. Perhaps the point is one of perspective. The verse seems to be advising those seeking ultimate wisdom and happiness, which in the Indian tradition means freedom from suffering (*duḥkha*), not to live with a narrow perspective on enjoyment and ownership. We can see in this with Gandhi a basis for the ethic of *ahiṃsā*, non-violence, non-harming of anything that moves. This is not, however, a legal prohibition, but *pace* Thieme, a deeply philosophical change in perspective. It is not just about "taking what is not given" or against killing or stealing. It goes to the heart of "holding." Moving things are not to be "owned" or "held" separate by the small self, or suffering ensues. Can it be that everything else to come in the Upaniṣad is an unfolding of this wider view, from an analysis of the nature of the self, to a wider understanding of knowledge and the knower, to the proper exit from this moving universe at death? The Upaniṣad presents a grappling with the basic binary code of life: Owner and owned and their opposing natures and the consequences. If we stumble across an abandoned house, an unguarded treasure, or any object seen separate from the greater Whole, our first impulse is like children to exclaim, "finders, keepers." So Verse One clarifies: nothing is to be held onto! What can we enjoy? Only what has been abandoned (*tyaktena*, i.e., as an object of ownership).

Study Questions

1. What do you believe is the main point of this verse, and why? If this is the introductory verse it may have the highest signifigance. If so, what is the point of this Upaniṣad?
2. How is the invocation connected to Mantra One?
3. If *Īś* is translated as "Lord," what differences might obtain between a Judeo-Christian use of the word and that here? Why? Find the words used in other scriptural languages for "lord" (Hebrew, Greek, Arabic, Latin) and note differences in meaning. What is the etymology of the English word "Lord?" Is there an underlying meaning for the Lord word in Indo-European languages? In Semitic languages?
4. How important will it be to try to hold Western theological thinking in abeyance as you encounter this text, and why?
5. Why is the indwelling or pervasion by *Īś* central as a religious concept? Are there parallels in other religions? What is the difference?
6. What does it mean exactly to "own" something?
7. What does it mean to "let go" of ownership? What is the history of "renunciation" in Indian philosophy and religion? Is the intention here to promote "world negation?" Outside of Hindu thought, what other traditons encourage renunciation or monasticism?
8. What is implied by the pun "*jagatyāṃ jagat* "whatever moves in the world of motion?" How does this particular way of saying "everything" contribute to the main thrust of the second half of the *mantra*?
9. Compare Śaṅkara's commentary with that of Madhva (See Part V). Which do you find more helpful? Why?
10. Restate the *mantra* in your own words and be prepared to explain your choices.

Mantra Two

Śaṅkara's Introduction to Mantra Two

evam ātma-vidaḥ putra-ādyeṣaṇā-traya-saṃnyāsena ātma-jñāna-niṣṭha-tayā ātmā rakṣitavya ity eṣa veda-arthaḥ| atha itarasya anātma-jñatayā ātma-grahaṇāya aśaktasya idam upadiśati mantraḥ

For the knower of the Self the meaning of the Veda is [that] the Self is to be [as it were] maintained, with continuing renunciation of the three obsessions (with sons, etc.) by staying established in self-knowledge. Now then, this [next] mantra gives instruction for the opposite type of person, the one who has no capacity to grasp the Self because of ignorance of the Self:

कुर्वन्नेवेह कर्माणि
जिजीविषेच्छतं समाः।
एवं त्वयि नान्यथेतो ऽस्ति
न कर्म लिप्यते नरे॥

In this way by performing actions here,
One should live a hundred years.
So there is no other way for you,
No *karma* thus adheres to one. (2)

kurvanneveha karmāṇi
jijīviṣecchataṁ samāḥ|
evaṃ tvayi nānyatheto 'sti
na karma lipyate nare||

कुर्वन्नेवेह कर्माणि
जिजीविषेच्छतँ समाः।
एवं त्वयि नान्यथेतो ऽस्ति
न कर्म लिप्यते नरे॥

कुर्वन्नेवेह कर्माणि
kurvann eva iha karmāṇi
By performing, in this way, here, actions

जिजीविषेच्छतँ समाः।
jijīviṣec chataṁ samāḥ|
One may hope to live a hundred years

एवं त्वयि नान्यथेतो ऽस्ति
evaṃ tvayi na anyathā ito 'sti
So, for you, no other way, than this is there

न कर्म लिप्यते नरे॥
na karma lipyate nare||
No action is stuck to a person.

kurvan (m. pres. part.) $\sqrt{kṛ}$ (cl. 2, P.): "to do, make, perform, accomplish, cause, effect, prepare, undertake." Here: "doing, performing."
eva (ind. partic.) "so, just so, exactly so, indeed, truly, really."
iha (ind. partic.) "in this place, here."
karmāṇi (n. acc. pl.) *karman*: "act, action, performance, rite, business, the result of action (merit or demerit)."
jijīviṣet (3rd. pers. opt. sing.) Desid. form of $\sqrt{jīv}$ (cl. 1, P.), *jijīv*, "to wish to live, be or remain alive." Here: "one may wish or desire to live."
śatam (n. acc. sing.): "a hundred."[1]
samās (f. acc. pl.) *samā*: "year." *samās*: "years."
evam (ind. partic.): "thus, in this way, in such a manner."
tvayi (mfn. loc. sing.) pers. pron. *yuṣmad*: "you." Here: "in you," or "to you."
na (ind.): "not, no, nor, neither."
anyathā (ind.): "otherwise, in a different manner."
itas ind. from *i*, used like the abl. of the pronoun *idam*: "from this, than this."
asti (3rd. pers. sing.) $\sqrt{as}$ (cl. 2, P.): "to be, live, exist, be present, to take place, happen." Here, "there is."
na See above.
karma (n. nom. sing.) See *karman* above.
lipyate (3rd. pers. pass. sing.) $\sqrt{lip}$ (cl 6, U.): "to smear, besmear, anoint with (instr.), stain, soil, taint, pollute, defile." Here, "does [not] stick."
nare (m. loc. sing.) *nara*: "a man, a male, a person." Here: "to a man (person), to one."

[1] "With *śata* the counted object is added either in the gen., or in the same case as *śata*." In this verse *śata* is in the acc. sing. but the counted object, *samā*, year, is in the acc. pl.

In this way by performing actions here,
One should live a hundred years.
So there is no other way for you,
No *karma* thus adheres to one.

Śaṅkara's Commentary

kurvann eva iha *nirvartayann eva karmāṇy agnihotrādīni* **jijīviṣej** *jīvitum icchet|* **śataṃ** *śatasaṅkhyākāḥ* **samāḥ** *saṃvatsarān| tāvad dhi puruṣasya paramāyur nirūpitam| tathā ca prāptānuvādena yaj jijīviṣec chataṃ varṣāṇi tat kurvann eva karmāṇi ity etad vidhīyate|*

"**In this way by performing here,**" means carrying out Vedic rituals such as the Agnihotra. **One should live,** means may seek to live; **a hundred years**, that is, years (*sama*) numbering a hundred. That long is considered to be the longest life span of a person. Moreover, having reaffirmed that, the one hundred years that one may hope to live should be passed explicitly performing

evam *evaṃ-prakāreṇa* **tvayi** *jijīviṣati* **nare** *nara-mātra-abhimānini* **ita** *etasmād agni-hotra-ādīni karmāṇi kurvato vartamānāt prakārād* **anyathā** *prakāra-antaraṃ* **na asti** *yena prakāreṇa aśubhaṃ karma* **na lipyate** *karmaṇā na lipyata ity arthaḥ| ataḥ śāstra-vihitāni karmāṇy agni-hotra-ādīni kurvann eva jijīviṣet|*

Vedic rituals as it is ordained.

"**So**" (*evam*) means "in this way." When, **you**, a person (*nara*), **seek to live**. Person (*nara*) here means someone who regards himself as an ordinary person. **There is no other way**, that is, other than the received way of performing Vedic rituals such as the Agnihotra; there is no other way by which inauspicious action (*karma*) **does not adhere [to one]**. Therefore, an [ordinary] person may hope to live, performing ordained Vedic rituals such as the Agnihotra.

kathaṃ punar idam avagamyate pūrveṇa mantreṇa saṃnyāsino jñānaniṣṭhoktā dvitīyena tadaśaktasya karmaniṣṭhā ity ucyate|

[Objection:] How again are we to be sure that by the previous *mantra*, the renunciant's position of knowledge is indicated. And that by the second *mantra* the position of Vedic ritual of one incapable of that is indicated.

jñāna-karmaṇor virodhaṃ parvata-vad akampyaṃ yathā uktaṃ na smarasi kim? iha apy uktaṃ, yo hi jijīviṣet sa karma kurvan| īśā vāsyam idaṃ sarvaṃ tena tyaktena bhuñjīthāḥ mā gṛdhaḥ kasya svid dhanam iti ca| na jīvite maraṇe vā gṛdhiṃ kurvīta āraṇyam iyād iti ca padam| tato na punar iyād iti saṃnyāsa-śāsanāt| ubhayoḥ phala-bhedaṃ ca vakṣyati|

[Answer:] Our reply is that the incompatability between knowledge and Vedic ritual is unshakable like a mountain. Don't you remember? This is said here, too, "One who wants to live should perform Vedic ritual," and

> "By the Owner infused is all this
> Whatever moves in the world of motion.
> Enjoy [only] that which is let go of.
> Don't hold on: whose property is it?"[2]

And part of another verse, "Neither in life or death should you hold on to anything; you should go to the forest." "From that [the forest] you should not return," from the rule of renunciation. The different results of the two paths will be elucidated later.

imau dvāv eva panthānāv anuniṣkrāntatarau bhavataḥ kriyā-pathaś ca eva purastāt saṃnyāsaś ca uttareṇa nivṛtti-mārgeṇa eṣaṇā-trayasya tyāgaḥ| tayoḥ saṃnyāsa-patha eva atirecayati| nyāsa eva atyarecayad iti ca taittirīyake|

Indeed these two paths emerged (*anu*) in order—the first being the path of ritual action, and following that, the path of renunciation, that is, the path of cessation by way of the renunciation of the three obsessions. Indeed of the two, the path of renunciation is superior. As the *Taittirīya* [*Āraṇyaka*] says: "Renunciation is certainly superior."

> *dvāv imāv atha panthānau*
> *yatra vedāḥ pratiṣṭhitāḥ|*
> *pravṛtti-lakṣaṇo dharmo*
> *nivṛttaś ca vibhāvitaḥ|| [ma. bhā. 12.241.6] ityādi|*

> Now then there are these two paths on which
> The Vedas are established.
> One way (*dharma*) is characterized by activity
> And [the other] by cessation.[3]

putrāya vicārya niścitam uktaṃ vyāsena vedācāryeṇa bhagavatā| vibhāgaṃ cānayor darśayiṣyāmaḥ|| 2||

So said the blessed Vyāsa, the great teacher of the Vedas, definitively to his son, after deep reflection. And so we will now elucidate the difference between the two (paths). (2)

---

[2] Mantra One.

[3] *Mahābhārata*, 12.241.6.

Discussion

The question surfaces with Śaṅkara's commentary as to whether the Upaniṣad is mostly about delineating two paths, renunciation and ritual action/worship, showing the superiority of renunciation. I am not sold on this—I lean toward the idea that *karma* can have here just as easily the sense of general action and its fruit which can "smear" one. Certainly Śaṅkara has a horse to ride here and wishes to use the verses to make his point vociferously and in detail. The original sense of the verses may more likely be less specific and more in line with the *Gītā* and the BU in teaching merely acting without attachment to the fruits of action (BG 5.10, BU 4.4.5). It is far from clear to me that the verses are mostly meant to contrast ritual with renunciation, rather than, as in the first verse, to focus on the enlightened attitude in living life free from suffering.

Thieme reads, "do strive to live here (in this earthly world) a hundred years (that is, throughout your whole life) as one who is just (that is, without "attachment") doing his actions" (91). Thieme opines that this cannot easily be optative, since it then is **not** parallel to earlier verbs (enjoy, hold on) and would have a different accent—rather it is likely *jijīviṣa it* with *sandhi* combination. *It* is a vedic indeclinable meaning "only, just" which emphasizes acting without attachment, i.e., just doing them.

An alternate reading taking, Thieme into consideration and not Śaṅkara, might be: "even so, by simply performing actions here (without attachment) an ordinary person should live a hundred years; in this way, not otherwise, you will not be soiled by (unfortunate) fruits."

Thieme (90) notes that the concluding quarter (*pāda*) has ten rather than the eight syllables *anuṣṭubh* requires. This makes him suspicious of *nare*, thinking it was added later and is not needed, and that it was added to emphasize more strongly the difference in the smearability of the Self compared to the person (*nara*) or small self only when the small self has proper knowledge of the Owner and the requisite lack of attachment.

The *asti* Thieme suggests must be translated in the early Vedic usage as "actually," a way of emphasizing *na lipyate*, rather than just hanging there.

Study Questions

1. What is the doctrine of *karma* and where and when is it found first in Indian thinking? What different translations are possible for the term? How would it affect our understanding in each case?
2. Does this verse contradict verse one? Certainly this whole Upaniṣad is structured in binary oppositions and part of the point in gaining the "knowledge" is to be able to negotiate binaries. How does Śaṅkara see it? Do you necessarily agree?
3. To whom does "you" refer?
4. Compare Śaṅkara's commentary on this verse with that of Madhva (See Part V). Which do you find more helpful? Why? Śaṅkara understands this verse to be in opposition to Verse One, for those incapable of the renunciation and knowledge of the Self. Why?
5. As Ježić notes ChU 4.14.3 asserts the importance of the earlier verses in other Upaniṣads with similar wording to help interpret this: *yathā puṣkarapalāsa āpo na śliṣyanta evam evaṃvidi pāpaṃ karma na śliṣyate*. As Ježić notes: as water does not stick to the lotus leaf, so for one who knows this, *karma* does not stick. This is also very similar to BUK 4.4.23. What is the relationship between knowledge and the karmic fruit of action if this is true?
6. Restate the *mantra* in your own words and be prepared to explain your choices.

Mantra Three

Śaṅkara's Introduction to Mantra Three

atha idānīm avidvannindārtho'yaṃ mantra ārabhyate— Now then, this *mantra* is introduced to criticize the ignorant:

असुर्या नाम ते लोका
अन्धेन तमसावृताः।
तांस्ते प्रेत्याभिगच्छन्ति
ये के चात्महनो जनाः॥ ३॥

Veiled indeed are those worlds,
Infused with blind darkness,
To which they go after death
Those people who smother the Self || 3||

asuryā nāma te lokā
andhena tamasāvṛtāḥ|
tāṃste pretyābhigacchanti
ye ke cātmahano janāḥ|| 3||

असुर्या नाम ते लोका
अन्धेन तमसावृताः।
तांस्ते प्रेत्याभिगच्छन्ति
ये के चात्महनो जनाः॥ ३॥

असुर्या नाम ते लोका
asuryā nāma te lokā
Veiled indeed [are] those realities,

अन्धेन तमसावृताः।
andhena tamasā āvṛtāḥ|
Infused with blinding ignorance,

तांस्ते प्रेत्याभिगच्छन्ति
tāṃs te pretya ābhigacchanti
To which they go after death

ये के च आत्महनो जनाः॥ ३॥
ye ke ca ātma-hano janāḥ|| 3||
Those people who smother the Self.

asuryāḥ (m. nom. pl.) mfn. *asurya*: "demoniacal, belonging or relating to the Asuras," in the *Brāhmaṇas*, but originally in the Ṛg Veda: "incorporeal, spiritual, divine." Here: "veiled."[4]
nāma (ind.) from *nāman*, "by name, named, called." May also mean: "indeed, certainly, really, of course."
te (m. nom. pl.) dem. pron. *tad*: "those."
lokāḥ (m. nom. pl.) *loka*: "a tract, region, district, country, province, world."
andhena (adj. instr. sing.) *andha*: "blind, dark."
tamasā (n. instr. sing.) *tamas*: "darkness, gloom."
āvṛtāḥ (m. nom. pl.) mfn. p.p. of *ā* + $\sqrt{vṛ}$, "to cover, hide, conceal; to surround, enclose." Here: "covered, hidden, concealed, etc."
tān (m. acc. pl.) dem. pron. *tad* same as above. Here: "them."
te (m. nom. pl.) dem. pron. *tad*: "that, he, she." Here: "they."
pretya ger. of *pra* + $\sqrt{i}$ (cl. 2, P.) + *tya*: "to go out or away, depart (this life), die." Here: "after death (i.e., having departed this life)."
abhigacchanti (3rd pers. pl.) *abhi* + $\sqrt{gam}$: "to go near to, approach; to undertake; to get, gain, obtain." Here: "they go to; they obtain."
ye (m. nom. pl.) rel. pron. *yat*, "those who."
ke (m. nom. pl.) interrogative pron. *kim*: "who or what?" When used with the rel. pron. (as here) it becomes indefinite: "whoever or whatever."
ca (ind.) conjunctive partic.: "and, both, also, moreover, as well as."
ātma-hanaḥ (m. nom. pl.) from a comp. composed of *ātman*, "self," and the adj. (*han*) from $\sqrt{han}$ (cl. 2, P.): "to smite, slay, hit, kill, mar, destroy." Here: "smotherers of the self."
janāḥ (m. nom. pl.) *jana*: "living being, man, person, race." Here: "people."

[4]Probably from the Vedic word *asura* originally meaning: "a spirit, good spirit, supreme spirit (said of Varuṇa, for instance), but later meaning: " the chief of the evil spirits" (ṚV, 2.30.4 and 7.99.5) and "an evil spirit, demon, ghost, opponent of the gods" (ṚV, 8.96.9). We, however, take the alternate reading here, *asūrya*, "sunless," or, "veiled."

Veiled indeed are those worlds,
Infused with blind darkness,
To which they go after death,
Those people who smother the Self || 3||

Śaṅkara's Commentary

asuryāḥ *paramātmabhāvam advayam apekṣya devādayo'py asurāḥ, teṣāṃ ca svabhūtā lokā* **asuryā nāma** | *nāmaśabdo 'narthako nipātaḥ|*

Veiled—even the gods and others who do not see the non-dual nature of the supreme Self [can be considered] denizens of darkness. Their inherent realities are **veiled indeed**. The word *nāma* ["by name"] in the *mantra* is an

te lokāḥ *karma-phalāni| lokyante dṛśyante bhujyanta iti janmāni|* **andhena** *adarśana-ātmakena ajñānena* **tamasā āvṛtāḥ** *ācchāditāḥ|* **tān** *sthāvarān tān* **pretya** *tyaktvā imaṃ deham* **abhigacchanti** *yathā-karma yathā-śrutam|*

idiomatic usage not a technical name.[5]

Those realities (*loka*-s) are the results of *karma*. [They are called *loka*-s because] they are perceived (*lokyante*), seen, experienced. They are [really] births. **With blind** means "with unseeing ignorance"; **infused with darkness** means "enveloped by darkness." **Those** means [even] motionless beings [like plants]; **after death** means having let go of the body; [**to which they go means**] according to their *karma*, as it has been heard in the Veda.

ātmānaṃ ghnanti ity **ātmahanaḥ**| *ke te janāḥ ? ye 'vidvāṃsaḥ| kathaṃ te ātmānaṃ nityaṃ hiṃsanti ? avidyādoṣeṇa vidyamānasya ātmanas tiraskaraṇāt| vidyamānasya ātmano yatkāryaṃ phalam ajarāmaratvādisaṃvedanalakṣaṇaṃ taddhatasya iva tirobhūtaṃ bhavati iti prākṛtāvidvāṃso janā* **ātmahana** *ucyante| tena hy ātmahananadoṣeṇa saṃsaranti te || 3||*

Who smother the Self means who obstruct the Self. Who are those people? They are those ignorant [of the Self]. How can they wish to harm the eternal Self? Because, due to the darkness of ignorance, the reality of the truly existing Self is concealed [from them]. That which is the effect of the truly existing Self, awareness of being undying and free of aging, etc. is made to disappear, as if it were destroyed. Thus vulgar, ignorant people are said to be "**those who smother the Self**." By this darkness of smothering the Self they cycle through repeated births and deaths. (3)

[5]Lit. "The word *nāma* is a meaningless particle." (*nāmaśabdo'narthako nipātaḥ*). Śaṅkara means by this that the word *nāma* which often indicates a proper name should not be taken in that sense here. Thus, the realities to which the smotherers of the Self go are not called *asurya*; they are that way by nature.

Discussion

After reading Thieme it is less convincing that "hellish" is accurate here. Certainly in the Upaniṣadic view "hell(s)" are not a theological focus, as they become in the later Purāṇas, especially since in the BU *karma* only begins to be established, and once established, has no need to be buttressed by "hell" since suffering is basically the main concern. Suffering gets doled out by *karma* or the Lord or Lords of *karma* automatically—no special realm of punishment is needed as the religious stick. Suffering is always there and in ignorance (as Śaṅkara seems to point out) even the divine worlds (certainly the goal of the Ṛg Veda) are dark. The earliest Ṛg Vedic and ŚB meaning is "sunless." Yet the fact that Śaṅkara refers to divine worlds may imply the possibility of non-divine worlds, hells. It may also be seen as an attempt to head off the later (7th cent.) interpretations based on Purāṇas (not Brāhmaṇas?) of seven levels of hell, and punishment, of various exotic and scary types. The Christian tradition (not the Jewish) with an overemphasis on "not going to eternal damnation in hell" should not be allowed to influence the interpretation of this fairly early text.

Thieme asserts that the early Upaniṣads do **not** ever speak of "hell" as the result of ignorance—so irrespective of how things may have changed by Śaṅkara's time, *pace* Thieme this assertion would seem to undermine the translation here of "hell worlds." Seeing the worlds as joyless (*ananda*) is a matter of discrimination, and the KaU quote (1.3) is helpful, though it may not have influenced the Īśā. (Nakamura ranks the Īśā with the earliest pre-Buddhist Upaniṣads, and KaU as a middle period text.) Darkness, *tamas*, is consistently linked in the BU with this term. The difference between "darkness and light" easily parallels ignorance and knowledge and is metaphorically the more natural Vedic emphasis, to which comparison Śaṅkara is basically true. However, one must consider the possibility, which Thieme brings up, that what we have in Īśā 1-3 is a three part discussion (*pūrvapakṣa*, *uttarapakṣa*, and *siddhānta*). I see a logic in the text which is more inclusive rather than a debate between opposing sides. The possibility of both is also an alternative. Thieme focuses on "not robbing or killing" but this dramatizes the text beyond what is said, which seems to focus much more on not coveting or holding onto "experience (relative worlds)" in 1 and reiterates the same in 2 in terms of *naiṣkāmya-karma*—not a debate necessarily. It then seems natural to underpin the statement and restatement (not debate) of the first two verses with the importance of not smothering the light of the Self—bringing things back to a simplicity of light versus darkness. Even so, Śaṅkara seems a little bit of a fundamentalist in twisting his interpretation to devalue the worlds of light of the gods—somewhat brazen here. A more likely thrust is to value the movement toward self-knowledge and to link it to growing happiness and divine worlds (culminating in Brahma-loka or liberation [*mokṣa*]). In any case it is clear that verse 3 can be added to our growing list of verses that are taken from or adapted from the BU (BUK 4.4.11). Yet apparently the M version of BU (4.4.14) which uses the word *asurya* (Thieme thinks it is influenced by ĪU) is even closer, though according to Thieme out of context.

The Upaniṣadic worldview has taken up by this time the concept of *punar mṛtyu* (redeath) and the evils of the wheel of *saṃsāra*. Suffering has no end—one gets stuck in unhappiness through greedily holding on to false identity and changing objects of desire, now and potentially, forever. The pain in this world is infinitely enlarged by the threat of recurrence in even worse worlds infused with darkness rather than the Divine. The crux of the issue is now stated baldly: the problem of suffering is the problem of ignorance of one's true identity, Ātman.

The afterlife worlds of blinding ignorance and the attendant suffering is held up as the result of ignorant attached actions, actions which are tantamount to smothering the light of inner awareness which by implication is the very Lord or Owner of all. Some scholars read the term "infernal" (*asurya*, of or pertaining to the *asura*-s, demons) as *asūrya*, "sunless," which seems less dramatic and perhaps more fitting, given the Upaniṣad's emphasis on ignorance as darkness, and on the sun as a symbol of the Divine. Properly speaking, though, the word received in both is not sunless (*asūrya*), but "infernal" (*asurya*).

Restatement

The result of ignorant action is continuous rebirth in demonic worlds of suffering for the mistake of obscuring the true Self within.

Study Questions

1. Who are the *asura-s* in Vedic thinking?
2. How does the message of this verse emphasize earlier themes?
3. What do you think it means to smother or kill the Self?
4. Compare Śaṅkara's commentary with that of Madhva. Which seems to shed more light into the darkness? Why?
5. Restate the *mantra* making your own choices among the available translations of words and be prepared to explain your choices.

Mantra Four

Śaṅkara's Introduction to Mantra Four

yasya ātmano hananād avidvāṃsaḥ saṃsaranti, tadviparyayeṇa vidvāṃso janā mucyante| te na ātma-hanaḥ| tat-kīdṛśam ātma-tattvam ity ucyate—

Because of smothering the Self the ignorant [continue to] cycle through repeated births and deaths, the wise, on the other had are liberated [from such suffering]. [For] they do not smother the Self. What [then] is this true nature of the Self like? It is said:

अनेजदेकं मनसो जवीयो
नैनद्देवा आप्नुवन् पूर्वमर्षत्।
तद्धावतोऽन्यानत्येति तिष्ठत्
तस्मिन्नपो मातरिश्वा दधाति॥ ४॥

One, unmoving, faster than the mind,
It rushes ahead of the gods, [who are] unable to overtake it.
Though unmoving, it passes up the other runners.
In it, Life-energy generates all activity. (4)

anejadekaṃ manaso javīyo
nainaddevā āpnuvan pūrvamarṣat|
taddhāvato'nyānatyeti tiṣṭhat
tasminnapo mātariśvā dadhāti|| 4||

अनेजदेकं मनसो जवीयो
नैनद्देवा आप्नुवन् पूर्वमर्षत्।
तद्धावतोऽन्यानत्येति तिष्ठत्
तस्मिन्नपो मातरिश्वा दधाति॥ ४॥

अनेजदेकं मनसो जवीयो
anejad ekaṃ manaso javīyo
Unmoving, one, than the mind faster,

नैनद्देवा आप्नुवन् पूर्वमर्षत्।
na enad devā āpnuvan pūrvam arṣat|
Not this one the gods can catch, ahead it rushes.

तद्धावतोऽन्यानत्येति तिष्ठत्
tad dhāvato 'nyān atyeti tiṣṭhat
It running others passes up while standing.

तस्मिन्नपो मातरिश्वा दधाति॥ ४॥
tasminn apo mātariśvā dadhāti|| 4||
In it, activity Life-energy generates.[1]

[1] Though the Monier Williams dictionary glosses *mātariśvan* as Agni or Vāyu, the meaning of the term is uncertain. Śaṅkara says it means "it moves or blows (*śvayate*) in the atmosphere (*antarikṣe*)" making it, thus, the wind (*vāyu*), or, as we have given it here, the life-energy (or, life-breath). The word for activity is *apas* or waters. Thus, the image invoked (if Śaṅkara is correct) is of the wind bringing rain for crops or pastures. The word Śaṅkara glosses with atmosphere is *mātari* which could be the locative singular of *mātṛ*, "mother." That conjures up the image of the fetus moving inside the mother.

anejat (n. nom. sing., pres. part.,) $\sqrt{ej}$ (cl. 1, P. *ejati*): "to stir, move, tremble, shake." With neg. prefix *an*: "not to stir, not to move, not to tremble, not to shake," and therefore: "immovable" or "unmoving."

ekam (n. nom. sing.) mfn. *eka*: "one, alone, solitary, single."

manasas (n. abl. sing.) *manas*: "mind." Here: "than the mind."

javīyas (n. nom. sing.) compar. term. *īyas* + *java* from $\sqrt{j\bar{u}}$ (cl. 1, U, cl. 9. P): "to press forwards, hurry on, be quick." which means "speed, velocity, swiftness." The termination changes the meaning to the comparative "speedier, quicker, faster, etc."

na ind. Negative partic.: "not, no, nor, neither."

enat (n. acc. sing.) This *ena* form is a substitute form of *etad* ("this") and *idam* ("this") that occurs only in the acc. (s., du., and pl.), inst. (s.), gen. and loc. (du.). It generally occurs when its proper form has already been used in a previous clause.

devās (m. nom. pl.) "the gods."

āpnuvan (3rd. pers. pl. impf.) $\sqrt{\bar{a}p}$ (cl. 5, P.): "to reach, overtake, meet with, fall upon, obtain, gain, take possession." Here: "they overtake."

pūrvam ind.: "before, formerly, hitherto, previously."

arṣat (3rd. pers. sing. impf.) $\sqrt{ṛṣ}$ (cl. 1, P.): "to flow, flow quickly, glide, move with a quick motion."

tat (n. nom. sing.) Dem. pron.: "that."

dhāvatas (m. acc. pl., pres. part.) $\sqrt{dh\bar{a}v}$ (cl. 1, U): "to run, flow, stream, move, glide, swim."

anyān (m. acc. pl.) pronom. adj. *anya*: "other, different; other than, different from; another; another person"

ati-eti (3rd. pers. sing. pres.) *ati* ("beyond, over") + $\sqrt{i}$ (cl. 2, P.): "to pass by, elapse, pass over, overflow; to pass on; to get over."

tiṣṭhat (n. nom. sing., pres. part.) $\sqrt{sth\bar{a}}$ (cl. 1, U): "to stand, stand firmly, station one's self, stand upon, get upon, take up a position on." Here: "standing still."

tasmin (m. loc. sing.) Dem. pron. *tat*: "in that."

apas (n. acc. pl.) *apas*: "work, action, especially sacred act, sacrificial act." Or, from another root: "waters"

mātariśvā (m. nom. sing.) *mātariśvan*, name of Agni, god of fire. May also be a name of Vāyu, god of wind. (See fn. 1)

dadhāti (3rd. pers. sing.) $\sqrt{dh\bar{a}}$ (cl. 3, U; *dadhāti, dhatte*): "to make, produce, generate, create, cause, effect, perform, execute." Here: "It produces or generates."

One, unmoving, faster than the mind,
It rushes ahead of the gods, [who are] unable to overtake it.
Though unmoving, it passes up the other runners.
In it Life-energy (*mātariśvā*) generates all activity. (4)

Śaṅkara's Commentary

anejan *na ejat| ejṛ kampane| kampanaṃ calanaṃ svāvasthāpracyutis tadvarjitam sarvadā ekarūpam ity arthaḥ| tac ca* **ekaṃ** *sarvabhūteṣu|* **manasaḥ** *saṅkalpādilakṣaṇāj* **javīyo** *javavattaram|*

Unmoving means "not shaking." The root √*ej* is used in the sense of "trembling" or "shaking." Shaking means moving, departing from its original condition; [the Self] doesn't do that. It is always of one nature—this is the meaning. Moreover it is **one** in all beings. **Faster than the mind** means it is faster than thoughts, etc., the very fastest.

kathaṃ viruddham ucyate dhruvaṃ niścalam idaṃ manaso javīya iti ca?

[**Objection:**] How is it that it is said to be paradoxically [both] firmly stationary and yet faster than the mind?

na eṣa doṣaḥ| nirupādhyupādhimattvena upapatteḥ| tatra nirupādhikena svena rūpeṇa ucyate **anejad ekam** *iti| manaso'ntaḥkaraṇasya saṅkalpavikalpalakṣaṇasya upādher anuvartanād iha dehasthasya manaso brahmalokādidūragamanaṃ saṅkalpena kṣaṇamātrād bhavati ity ato manaso javiṣṭhatvaṃ loke prasiddham|*

[**Answer:**] This is not inconsistent since it is explained (demonstrated) by its being both with and without attributes. In this regard it is said to be **one**, and **unmoving**, [only] by reference to its inherent nature without attributes. Since the mind, the internal organ, characterized by [both] intention and hesitation etc. due to being conditioned by attributes, stationed in the body here in this world [is also known to] travel far to the world of Brahmā, etc. by mere intention in the blink of an eye—it is thus celebrated as the fastest thing in the world.

tasmin manasi brahmalokādīn drutaṃ gacchati sati prathamaṃ prāpta iva ātmacaitanyāvabhāso gṛhyate 'to manaso javīya ity āha| na **enad devāḥ** *dyotanād devāś cakṣurādīni indriyāṇy etatprakṛtam ātmatattvaṃ na āpnuvan na prāptavantaḥ| tebhyo mano javīyaḥ| manovyāpāravyavahitatvād ābhāsamātram apy ātmano na eva devānāṃ viṣayībhavati|*

In this case, while the mind is swiftly traveling to the world of Brahmā, etc., the manifestation of Self-awareness is perceived to have arrived first, as it were. Thus it says it is faster than the mind. **The gods** [*devas*, here meaning] those who illuminate, i.e., the sense organs such as the eyes, etc., do not catch up with **this** (*enat*), the true being of the Self, under discussion. The mind is faster than they are. The mind is faster than they are due to their separation [from the Self] by the mind's functioning. How much less even [does] the merest appearance, as it were, of the [unconditioned and immaterial] Self become an object of the senses (*devas*)?

yasmāj javanān manaso 'pi **pūrvam arṣat** *pūrvam eva gataṃ vyomavad vyāpitvāt| sarvavyāpi tadātmatattvaṃ sarvasaṃsāradharmavarjitaṃ svena nirupādhikena svarūpeṇa avikriyam eva sad-upādhikṛtāḥ sarvāḥ saṃsāravikriyā anubhavati ity avivekināṃ mūḍhānām anekam iva ca pratidehaṃ pratyavabhāsata ity etad āha taddhāvato drutaṃ gacchato 'nyān ātmavilakṣaṇān manovāgindriyaprabhṛtīn* **atyeti** *atītya gacchati iva| iva arthaṃ svayam eva darśayati* **tiṣṭhad** *iti| svayam avikriyam eva sad ity arthaḥ|*

It rushes ahead means it arrives even before the mind due to such speed, because [in reality] it pervades [everything] like space. This (Self) pervading all, unchanging, in its own inherent state without attributes, having none of the qualities of the relative world of birth and death, perceives all the transformations of this world of birth and death and appears as if it were the multiplicity, different in each body, of dull and undiscriminating people. As the verse related: **it passes up [all] the other runners** means it quickly, as it were, goes beyond the others, different from the Self, who are moving quickly, including mind, speech, and the senses. "As it were" is implied by the term **unmoving**, meaning being in itself without change.

tasminn *ātmatattve sati nityacaitanyasvabhāve* **mātariśvā** *mātary antarikṣe śvayati gacchati iti mātariśvā vāyuḥ sarvaprāṇabhṛt kriyātmako yadāśrayāṇi kāryakāraṇajātāni*

[**In it**] implies the inherent nature of the Self as eternal consciousness being there; *mātariśvan*, means **Life-energy**, because [from the etymology:] "it moves in the

yasminn otāni protāni ca yatsūtrasaṃjñakaṃ sarvasya jagato vidhārayitṛ sa mātariśvā|

atmosphere" (*mātari śvayati*); Life-energy is wind (*vāyu*), bearing all the life-energies (*prāṇa*), characterized by dynamism, on which all causes and effects are engendered, in which (they) are interwoven and [as it were] strung, and which is also called "the thread," since it is that which strings [together] the moving universe—this is what is meant by Life-energy (*mātariśvan*),

apaḥ *karmāṇi prāṇināṃ ceṣṭālakṣaṇāni agnyādityaparjanyādīnāṃ jvalanadahanaprakāśābhivarṣaṇādilakṣaṇāni* **dadhāti** *kartṛṣu vibhajati ity arthaḥ| dhārayati iti vā| bhīṣā 'smād vātaḥ pavate [tai. u. 2.8.1] ityādiśrutibhyaḥ| sarvā hi kāryakaraṇādivikriyā nityacaitanyātmasvarūpe sarvāspadabhūte saty eva bhavanti ity ādi || 4||*

Activity (*apas*) means the actions of living beings, meaning the behaviors of fire, sun, rain, etc., such as blazing, burning, illuminating, and raining; **bestows** means assigns the agents or supervises [them]. As we read in such Vedic texts as (TU 2.8.1) "From dread of it the wind blows." This means that all the transformations of cause and effects, etc., exist [only] so long as the inherent nature of the eternally conscious Self, the abode of everything, is present. (4)

Discussion

So what is the True Self really like? We wish to avoid the blind worlds at any cost. This knowledge of the infused Owner is paradoxical; it is not ordinary "knowledge" of things. It goes beyond the mind and cannot be reached by thought. It can be pointed to by mystical language which undermines the logical mind: echoing the assertion of contraries in the invocation and the balance (100) of the life lived in recognition of the Divine infusing all of the apparent non-divine relative world.

Restatement

The True Self, the Owner, is both fast and unmoving, beyond the divine powers of this world, the unchanging source of life, energy, and action.

Study Questions

1. The true nature of the Lord, as the Absolute, the Self, is discussed in the Upaniṣads in paradoxical terms, contrary binary oppositions. Why?
2. The understanding of the Lord as the Self is conveyed through these paradoxical statements: how would you summarize the points here describing the nature of the Divine, unpacking the paradoxes?
3. Compare Śankara's commentary with that of Madhva with special attention to their different understanding of the Lord.
4. Who is the Vedic deity Mātariśvan and how is this symbol to be interpreted in this context?
5. Restate the *mantra* in your own words and be prepared to explain your choices.

Mantra Five

Śaṅkara's Introduction to Mantra Five

na mantrāṇām jāmitā asti iti pūrva-mantra-uktam apy artham punar āha—

The mantras have no lack of repetition. Thus, the teaching presented by the previous mantra is repeated here:

तदेजति तन्नैजति
तद्दूरे तद्वन्तिके।
तदन्तरस्य सर्वस्य
तदु सर्वस्यास्य बाह्यतः॥ ५॥

It vibrates, it is still
It is far away, but it is near,
It is within everything,
But outside all of this too. (5)

tadejati tannaijati
taddūre tadvantike|
tadantarasya sarvasya
tadu sarvasyāsya bāhyataḥ|| 5||

तदेजति तन्नैजति
तद्दूरे तद्वन्तिके।
तदन्तरस्य सर्वस्य
तदु सर्वस्यास्य बाह्यतः॥ ५॥

तदेजति तन्नैजति
tad ejati tan na ejati
It vibrates; it not vibrates,

तद्दूरे तद्वन्तिके
tad dūre tad v antike
It is far away; it, too, is near,

तदन्तरस्य सर्वस्य
tad antar asya sarvasya
It is within, of this, of all,

तदु सर्वस्यास्य बाह्यतः
tad u sarvasya asya bāhyataḥ
It, too, of all, of this, outside.

tat (n. nom. sing.) Dem. pron. *tad*: "that" or "it."
ejati (3rd. pers. sing. pres.) $\sqrt{ej}$ "to stir, move, tremble, shake." Here: "it trembles or shakes."
tat See above.
na (ind.) negative partic., "not, no, nor, neither."
ejati See above.
tat See above.
dūre (ind.) from *dūra*: "distance, remoteness (in space and time), a long way." Here: "in a distant place, far, far away."
tat See above.
u (ind.) "on the other hand." This partic. may also serve to give emphasis as in "indeed" or "too."
antike (ind.) from *antika*: "vicinity, proximity, near." Here: "near, close by, in the proximity or presence of."
tat See above.
antar (ind.) "within, between, amongst, in the middle or interior."
asya (m./n. gen. sing.) of dem. pron. *idam* "this." Here: "of this."
sarvasya (m./n. gen. sing.) of the pronom. adj. *sarva* "all"
tat See above.
u See above.
sarvasya See above.
asya See above.
bāhyatas (ind.) *bāhya* + *tas*: "outside, externally, on the outside of."

It vibrates, it is still
It is far away, but it is near,
It is within everything,
But outside all of this too. (5)

Śaṅkara's Commentary

tad-ātma-tattvaṃ yat prakṛtaṃ **tad ejati** *calati* **tad** *eva ca* **na ejati** *svato na eva calati svato 'calam eva sac calati iva ity arthaḥ| kiṃca* **tad dūre** *varṣa-koṭi-śatair apy aviduṣām aprāpyatvād dūra iva| tad u antika iti cchedaḥ|* **tad v antike** *samīpe'tyantam eva viduṣām ātmatvān na kevalaṃ dūre'ntike ca|* **tad-antar** *abhyantare* **'sya sarvasya**| *ya ātmā sarvāntara iti śruteḥ|* **asya sarvasya** *jagato nāma-rūpa-kriyā-ātmakasya* **tad v** *api* **sarvasya asya bāhyato** *vyāpakatvād ākāśa-van niratiśaya-sūkṣmatvād antaḥ| prajñāna-ghana eva iti ca śāsanān nirantaraṃ ca|| 5||*

It means the true nature of the Self, which is being advanced [by saying], **in itself it is still** meaning in itself, stationary, it does not move; while however, **it vibrates** means it seems to move. That is the point. Moreover, **it is far away**, unattainable by the ignorant, as it were, even in hundreds of billions of years. The words *tadvantike* are to be divided as *tad u antike.* **But it is near**, absolutely close by, since it is the very Self of the wise—so it is both far away and near! **This is within everything** means inside of everything in this world (inside of all this). As the Veda says: "The Self is that which is within everything."[1] **Of all of this** means the world whose na-

[1]BU, 3.4.1.

ture is name, form, and action; **But (it) [is] outside all of this, too**, because of its pervasiveness, like space; [it is] within [all] because of its unsurpassed subtlety. Indeed, "[it is] a solid mass of consciousness," according to scripture,[2] absolutely undivided [in any way]. (5)

[2] ibid., 4.5.13.

Study Questions

1. How do the paradoxes introduced in this mantra contribute further to our understanding of the Self? Or is this a mere repetition of the same exact thoughts?
2. Compare Śankara's commentary with that of Madhva again with reference to their different understanding of the Lord.
3. Restate the *mantra* in your own words and be prepared to explain your choices.

Mantra Six

यस्तु सर्वाणि भूतानि
आत्मन्येवानुपश्यति।
सर्वभूतेषु चात्मानं
ततो न विजुगुप्सते॥ ६॥

But one who sees
All beings in this very Self
And this Self in all beings
Because of this does not recoil. (6)

yastu sarvāṇi bhūtāni
ātmanyevānupaśyati|
sarvabhūteṣu cātmānaṃ
tato na vijugupsate|| 6||

यस्तु सर्वाणि भूतानि
आत्मन्येवानुपश्यति।
सर्वभूतेषु चात्मानं
ततो न विजुगुप्सते॥ ६॥

यस्तु सर्वाणि भूतानि
yas tu sarvāṇi bhūtāni
One who, but, all beings,

आत्मन्येवानुपश्यति।
ātmany eva anupaśyati|
In this very Self, sees,

सर्वभूतेषु चात्मानं
sarva-bhūteṣu ca ātmānaṃ
In all beings, and, this Self

ततो न विजुगुप्सते
tato na vijugupsate
Because of this, not recoils.[1]

yas (m. nom. sing. rel. pron.) *yad*: "who, which, what, whichever, whatever, that."
tu (ind.) "but, however."
sarvāni (n. nom. pl.) adj. *sarva*: "whole, entire, all, every."
bhūtāni (n. nom. pl.) *bhūta*: "that which is or exists, any thing or living being (divine, human, animal, and even vegetable)."
ātmani (m. loc. sing.) *ātman*: "the soul, principle of life and sensation, the individual soul, self, abstract individual." Here: "in the self."
eva (ind.) "so, just so, exactly so, indeed, truly, really."
anupaśyati (3rd. pers. sing. pres.) *anu* + $\sqrt{\textit{paś}}$ (cl. 1, U., used only in the pres.): "to see, behold, look at, observe, perceive, notice."
sarva-bhūteṣu (n. loc. pl.) comp. *sarva-bhūta*: "all beings." Here: "in all beings."
ca (ind.) a conj. partic.: "and, both, also, moreover, as well as."
ātmānam (m. acc. sing.) See above. Here: "the self,"
tataḥ (ind.) used here as the abl. of the dem. pron. *tad*: "he, she, it, that, this." Here: "from this" or, "then, after that, because of that."
na (ind.) neg. partic.: "not, no, nor, neither."
vijugupsate (3rd. pers. sing. desid. Ā.) *vi* + $\sqrt{\textit{gup}}$ (cl. 1, Ā.): "to guard, defend, protect, preserve, hide, conceal." In the desid. (*jugups*): "to seek to defend one's self from, be on one's guard; to beware of, shun, avoid, recoil from, detest, spurn, despise."

[1] cf. BUK 4.4.15d, BUM 4.4.18d, KaU 4.5d,12d; M= *tato na vicikitsati||*

But one who sees
All beings in this very Self
And this Self in all beings
Because of this does not recoil. (6)

Śaṅkara's Commentary

yaḥ *parivrāḍ mumukṣuḥ* **sarvāṇi bhūtāny** *avyakta-ādīni sthāvarāntāny* **ātmany evānupaśyaty** *ātmavyatiriktāni na paśyati ity arthaḥ|* **sarva-bhūteṣu ca teṣv** *eva ca ātmānaṃ teṣām api bhūtānāṃ svam ātmānam ātmatvena yathā asya dehasya kārya-kāraṇa-saṅghātasya ātmā'haṃ sarva-pratyaya-sākṣi-bhūtaś cetayitā kevalo nirguṇo'nena eva sva-rūpeṇa avyakta-ādīnāṃ sthāvara-antānām aham eva ātmā iti sarva-bhūteṣu ca ātmānaṃ nirviśeṣaṃ yas tv anupaśyati sa* **tatas** *tasmād eva darśanān* **na vijugupsate** *vijugupsāṃ ghṛṇāṃ na karoti| prāptasya eva anuvādo'yam| sarvā hi ghṛṇā ātmano'nyad duṣṭaṃ paśyato bhavaty ātmānam eva atyanta-viśuddhaṃ nirantaraṃ paśyato na ghṛṇā-nimittam artha-antaram asti iti prāptam eva|* **tato na viju-**

One means a wandering ascetic, desirous of liberation; **all beings** means from the unmanifest [all the way to] the stationary beings [like trees etc.] **he sees in this very self**, meaning he does not see anything distinct from the self. And **in all beings [sees] the Self** means he [sees] indeed in all those beings his own Self, as the essence of those beings: [thinking as it were] "Just as I am the Self of this body (a [mere] collection of causes and effects), the witness of all mental states, the cause of consciousness, the singular one, beyond the three characteristics of matter, by this very Self-nature I myself am the very Self of all beings from the unmanifest [all the way to] the stationary beings [like trees etc.]"

gupsata *iti*|| *6*||

Moreover, one who sees this unconditioned Self in all beings, **because of this**, because of this very apprehension **does not recoil**, meaning does not experience aversion or anxiety, to reiterate an earlier idea. There is nothing but vexation for the one who sees [something] foreign as bad. However, for one who sees the Self as exceedingly pure and undivided, as generally found, there is nothing else that can cause aversion. Thus the meaning of **because of this does not recoil**. (6)

Discussion

Scholars are divided on reading the ambiguous construction of the last quarter (d) of the verse: *tato na vijugupsate*. This same construction is found in the last quarter of verses from the BU (4.4.15d)[2] and the KaU (4.5d, 12d),[3] which are probably earlier occurrences of the expression. The issue hinges on determining who is the subject, of the finite verb *vijigupsate*: who is it that is not recoiling or not hiding? The mystic seer who sees the Self in all beings and all beings in the Self, or the Self or Lord? The grammar of the verse seems to dictate that it is the Self or Lord who performs the action of the verb. This is because the relative pronoun *yas* which begins the verse should be connected with its co-relative *tatas* that begins the last quarter: "he who ... from him ... ." This would lead to the construction: the Self/Lord does not wish to hide (or recoil or) from the mystic seer who sees the Self in all beings and all beings in the Self.

Logic, however, seems to dictate that the grammatical reading produces a tautology: the first half of the verse asserts that the mystic has seen the Self inside and outside; the second half asserts that the Self does not hide from him. Hiding presupposes not having been seen. Therefore, most interpreters, including Śaṅkara and Madhva, take this to mean the mystic who sees the Self everywhere no longer fears or hates or recoils from anything. A similar idea is expressed already in the BU in which perceiving the Self is recognized as the basis of all forms of love whether one realizes it or not.[4]

Restatement

Since the True Self, the Owner, is both subjective and objective, both within and without all beings, the one who sees this is delivered from negativity: fear, hatred, despair, disturbance.

---

[2]4.4.15:

yadaitamanupaśyaty ātmānaṃ devamañjasā |
īśānaṃ bhūtabhavyasya na tato vijugupsate || *15* ||

"When one perceives the Self truly as the divine, the Lord of the past and future, because of this he does not recoil "

[3]4.5 (2.1.5):

ya imaṃ madhvadaṃ veda ātmānaṃ jīvamantikāt |
īśānaṃ bhūtabhavyasya na tato vijugupsate |
etadvai tat ||

"One who knows the experiencer (honey-eater) as the immanent living Self, the Lord of past and future, because of this he does not recoil. This verily is He." 4.12 (2.1.12):

aguṃṣṭhamātraḥ puruṣo madhya ātmani tiṣṭhati |
īśānaṃ bhūtabhavyasya na tato vijugupsate |
etadvai tat ||

"The thumb-sized person living within one, the Lord of past and future, from Him one does not recoil."

[4]See BU 4.5.6:

... na vā are bhūtānāṃ kāmāya bhūtāni priyāṇi bhavanti, ātmanas tu kāmāya bhūtāni priyāṇi bhavanti ...

"Indeed, it is not for love of creatures that creatures are dear, but for the love of the Self that creatures are dear."

Study Questions

1. The theology of the Ātman (Owner, Self, Lord) seems to come to a practical point in Mantra 6. What practical effect does this knowledge have for a wise person who sees the Ātman properly?

2. Compare Śaṅkara's commentary with that of Madhva in relation to the practical importance of right knowledge of the Ātman.

3. What does it mean to "recoil" from experiences? What might your life be like if you actually had such a perspective that you did not recoil from anything.

4. Referencing the discussion above, some scholars read this verse to mean that the Lord does not hide or shrink (recoil) from those who have proper knowledge. How does that change the meaning? Olivelle (quoted in Ježić p. 10) translates the last section, "it [the Self] will not hide from him." How does this change the meaning?

5. Restate the *mantra* in your own words and be prepared to explain your choices.

Mantra Seven

Śaṅkara's Introduction to Mantra Seven

imam eva artham anyo'pi mantra āha—

This same meaning is expressed by another *mantra*:

यस्मिन् सर्वाणि भूतान्य्
आत्मैवाभूद्विजानतः।
तत्र को मोहः कः शोक
एकत्वमनुपश्यतः॥ ७॥

When one realizes "the Self
Has become all beings,"
Then for the seer of oneness
What delusion and sorrow can there be? (7)

yasmin sarvāṇi bhūtāny
ātmaivābhūdvijānataḥ|
tatra ko mohaḥ kaḥ śoka
ekatvamanupaśyataḥ|| 7||

यस्मिन् सर्वाणि भूतान्य्
आत्मैवाभूद्विजानतः।
तत्र को मोहः कः शोक
एकत्वमनुपश्यतः॥ ७॥

यस्मिन् सर्वाणि भूतानि
yasmin sarvāṇi bhūtāni
When all living beings,

आत्मैवाभूद् विजानतः
ātmā eva abhūd vijānataḥ
The Self itself has become for one who knows,

तत्र को मोहः कः शोक
tatra ko mohaḥ kaḥ śokaḥ
Then, what delusion, what sorrow,

एकत्वमनुपश्यतः
ekatvam anupaśyataḥ
Oneness for one who perceives?

yasmin (m. loc. sing. rel. pron.) *yad*: "who, which, what, whichever, whatever, that." Here: "when" or "in which."
sarvāṇi (n. nom. pl.) adj. *sarva*: "whole, entire, all, every." Here: "all."
bhūtāni (n. nom. pl.) *bhūta*: "that which is or exists, any living being (divine, human, animal, and even vegetable)." This word also means in its broadest sense an element or thing, one of the five elements (esp. a gross element or *mahābhūta*, but also a subtle element or *tan-mātra*). Here: "beings."
ātmā (m. nom. sing.) *ātman*: "the soul, principle of life and sensation, the individual soul, self, abstract individual." Here: "the Self."
eva (ind.) "so, just so, exactly so, indeed, truly, really." Here: "itself."
abhūt (3rd. pers. sing. aor. 1) $\sqrt{bhū}$: "to become, be." Here: "has become."
vijānataḥ (m. gen. sing. pres. part.) *vi* + $\sqrt{jñā}$ (cl. 9, U.): "to know, have knowledge, become acquainted with, perceive, apprehend, understand." Here: "for the wise, that is, of one who knows."
tatra (m. loc. sing.) dem. pron. *tad*: "he, she, it, that, this." Here: "in this, then."
kaḥ (m. nom. sing. interr. pron.) *kim*: "what, how, whence, wherefore, why." Here: "what?"
mohaḥ (m. nom. sing.) *moha*: "loss of consciousness, bewilderment, perplexity, distraction, infatuation, delusion, error, folly." Here: "delusion."
kaḥ See above.
śokaḥ (m. nom. sing.) *śoka*: "sorrow, affliction, anguish, pain, trouble, grief." Here: "sorrow."
ekatvam (n. acc. sing.) *ekatva*: "oneness."
anupaśyataḥ (m. gen. sing. pres. part.) *anu* + $\sqrt{paś}$ (cl. 1, U., used only in the pres.): "to see, behold, look at, observe, perceive, notice." Here: "who perceives, that is, of one who sees."

When one realizes "the Self
Has become all beings,"
Then for the seer of oneness
What delusion and sorrow can there be? (7)

Śaṅkara's Commentary

yasmin *kāle yathā ukta-ātmani vā tāny eva* **bhūtāni sarvāṇi** *parama-artha-ātma-darśanād* **ātmā eva abhūd** *ātmaiva saṃvṛttaḥ parama-artha-vastu vijānataḥ tatra tasmin kāle tatra ātmani vā* **ko mohaḥ kaḥ śokaḥ|** *śokaś ca mohaś ca kāma-karma-bījam ajānato bhavati| na tv ātma-ekatvaṃ viśuddhaṃ gaganā-upamaṃ paśyataḥ* **ko mohaḥ kaḥ śoka** *iti śokamohayor avidyākāryayor ākṣepeṇāsambha-*

The word *yasmin*, **when**, means either **when** or **in** the previously mentioned Self. Due to the apprehension of the supreme Self by the one who has perceived the supreme reality, **the Self itself has become all beings**, meaning the Self alone is the supreme reality for the wise. Then, at that time, or in that Self, **what delusion or sorrow can there be?** For one ignorant of the

vapradarśanāt sakāraṇasya saṃsārasya atyantam eva ucchedaḥ pradarśito bhavati|| 7||

seed of action and desire, there is delusion and sorrow, but not **for the seer of oneness** of the self, pure like the sky. By raising the question, "**What delusion or sorrow can there be?**" the impossibility of delusion and sorrow, [which are] the effects of ignorance, is implied, and, indeed, the total annihilation of the relative world of birth and death along with its cause is demonstrated. (7)

Restatement

Realizing, actually seeing that, the true Self, the Spirit, is non-dual and is both the Absolute unchanging and the changing relative world of beings, frees one from ignorance and suffering.

Study Questions

1. This verse seems to interpret the earlier verse, or at least again state a great advantage of knowing the Self and the world as non-dual (a-dvaita). Explain the thought in your own words.
2. What does it mean for the Self to become all beings? Can you relate this to ethics? How might one automatically behave if one saw the world and all creatures as the Self?
3. Compare Śaṅkara's commentary with that of Madhva, who each have their own understanding of what Advaita (not-two) Vedānta means.
4. Restate the *mantra* in your own words and be prepared to explain your choices.

Mantra Eight

Śaṅkara's Introduction to Mantra Eight

yo'yam atītair mantrair ukta ātmā sa svena rūpeṇa kiṃ lakṣaṇa ity āha ayaṃ mantraḥ—

What is the nature of the Self just mentioned in the earlier *mantra* in its own inherent state? This *mantra* explains:

स पर्यगाच्छुक्रमकायमव्रणम्
अस्नाविरं शुद्धमपापविद्धम्।
कविर्मनीषी परिभूः स्वयम्भूर्
याथातथ्यतोऽर्थान् व्यदधाच्छाश्वतीभ्यः
समाभ्यः॥ ८॥

He permeates everything, luminous,
Incorporeal, flawless, without nerves,
Immaculate, impervious to evil,
Enlightening, sage, all-encompassing,
Self-sufficient; he allots all things
As needed for aeons eternal. (8)

sa paryagācchukramakāyamavraṇam
asnāviraṃ śuddhamapāpaviddham|
kavirmanīṣī paribhūḥ svayambhūr
yāthātathyato'rthān vyadadhācchāśvatībhyaḥ samābhyaḥ|| 8||

स पर्यगाच्छुक्रमकायमव्रणम्
अस्नाविरं शुद्धमपापविद्धम्।
कविर्मनीषी परिभूः स्वयम्भूर्
याथातथ्यतोऽर्थान् व्यदधाच्छाश्वतीभ्यः समाभ्यः॥ ८॥

स पर्यगाच्छुक्रमकायमव्रणम्
sa paryagāc chukram akāyam avraṇam
He permeates everything, resplendent, incorporeal, flawless

अस्नाविरं शुद्धमपापविद्धम्
asnāviraṃ śuddham apāpaviddham
Without nerves, immaculate, impervious to evil

कविर्मनीषी परिभूः स्वयम्भूर्
kavir manīṣī paribhūḥ svayambhūr
Perceptive, sage, transcendent, self-sufficient,

याथातथ्यतोऽर्थान् व्यदधाच्छाश्वतीभ्यः समाभ्यः
yāthātathyato'rthān vyadadhāc chāśvatībhyaḥ samābhyaḥ
As needed things he allots for eternal aeons.[1]

[1]cf. KaU 5.13, SU 6.13.

saḥ (m. nom. sing.) dem. pron. *tad*: "he, she, it, that, this." Here: "he."
paryagāt (3rd. pers. sing. aor. 1) *pari* + $\sqrt{gā}$: "to go round or through, circumambulate, permeate; to enter; to come near, approach, reach, visit." Here: "has permeated."[1]
śukram (n./m. nom./acc. sing.) mfn. *śukra* "bright, resplendent; clear, pure; light-coloured, white; brightness, clearness, light; seed, semen, ."
akāyam (n./m. nom./acc. sing.) mfn. *akāya*: "without body, bodiless, incorporeal."
avraṇam (n./m. nom./acc.) mfn. *avraṇa*: "without wound, flawless."
asnāviram (n./m. nom./acc sing.) mfn. *asnāvira*: "without nerves, veins, or sinews."
śuddham (n./m. nom./acc. sing.) mfn.*śuddha*: "cleansed, cleared, clean, pure, immaculate."
apāpa-viddham (n./m. nom./acc. sing.) mfn. *a* ("not") + *pāpa* ("evil, sin") + *viddha* ("pierced, perforated, penetrated"): "impervious to evil."
kaviḥ (m. nom. sing.) mfn. *kavi*: "gifted with insight, intelligent, knowing, enlightened, wise, sensible, prudent, skilful , cunning." Here: "perceptive."
manīṣī (m. nom. sing.) mfn. *manīṣin*: "thoughtful, intelligent, wise, sage, prudent." Here: "sage."
paribhūḥ (m. nom. sing.) mfn. *pari* + *bhū*: "surrounding, enclosing, containing, pervading, guiding, governing." Here: "transcendent."
svayambhūḥ (m. nom. sing. masc.) mfn. *svayam* + *bhū*: "self-existing, self-sufficient."
yāthātathyataḥ (ind.) *yāthātathya* + *tas*: "from the truth, truly, really." Here: "as needed."
arthān (m. acc. pl.) *artha*: "aim, purpose; cause, motive, reason; thing, object." Here: "things."
vyadadhāt (3rd. pers. sing. impf.) *vi* + $\sqrt{dhā}$ (cl. 3, U.): "to distribute, apportion, grant, bestow."
śāśvatībhyaḥ (f. dat. pl.) mfn. *śāśvatī*: "eternal, constant, perpetual, all." Here: "for ... eternal. "
samābhyaḥ (f. dat. pl.) *samā*: "years." Here: "aeons."

[1]Or, it may be taken to mean: "has reached or entered" the objects of the sentence *śukra*, etc. It is a way of saying the self possesses or has assumed those traits.

He permeates everything, luminous,
Incorporeal, flawless, without nerves,
Immaculate, impervious to evil,
Enlightening, sage, all-encompassing,
Self-sufficient; he allots all things
As needed for aeons eternal. (8)

Śaṅkara's Commentary

sa yathā ukta ātmā **paryagāt** *pari samantād agād gatavān ākāśa-vad vyāpī ity arthaḥ|* **śukraṃ** *śuddhaṃ jyotiṣmad dīptimān ity arthaḥ|* **akāyam** *aśarīro liṅga-śarīra-varjita ity arthaḥ|* **avraṇam** *akṣatam|* **asnāviraṃ** *snāvāḥ śirā yasmin na vidyanta ity asnāviram| avraṇam asnāviram ity ābhyāṃ sthūla-śarīra-pratiṣedhaḥ|* **śuddhaṃ** *nirmalam avidyā-mala-rahitamiti kāraṇaśarīrapratiṣedhaḥ|* **apāpa-viddhaṃ** *dharma-adharma-ādi-pāpavarjitam|* **śukram** *ityādīni vacāṃsi pul-liṅgatvena pariṇeyāni| sa paryagād ity upakramya* **kavir manīṣī** *ity ādinā pul-liṅgatvena upasaṃhārāt|*

kaviḥ *krānta-darśī sarvā-dṛk| na anyo'to'sti draṣṭā (bṛ.u. 3.8.11) ity-ādi-śruteḥ|* **manīṣī** *manasa iṣitā sarva-jña īśvara ity arthaḥ|* **paribhūḥ** *sarveṣāṃ pary upari bhavati iti paribhūḥ|* **svayam-bhūḥ** *svayam eva bhavati iti| yeṣām upari bhavati yaś ca upari bhavati sa sarvaḥ svayam eva bhavati iti svayam-bhūḥ|*

sa nityamukta īśvaro **yāthātathyataḥ** *sarva-jñatvādyathā-tathā-bhāvo yāthātathyaṃ tasmād yathā-bhūta-karma-phala-sādhanato 'rthān kartavya-pada-arthān* **vyadadhād** *vihitavān yathā anurūpaṃ vyabhajad ity arthaḥ,* **śāśvatībhyo** *nityābhyaḥ* **samābhyaḥ** *saṃvatsarākhyebhyaḥ prajāpatibhya ity arthaḥ|| 8||*

That Self just mentioned, **permeates everything**, that is, has spread out universally everywhere, like space itself. **Resplendent**, means luminous, bright. **Incorporeal** means without a body,[that is], without a subtle body).[2] **Flawless** means uninjured. **Without nerves** means within it bodily channels are not to be found. The two negations (flawless, without nerves) thus negate a gross physical body. **Immaculate** means unsullied, without the taint of ignorance, thus without a causal body.[3] **Impervious to evil**, means without the trouble of virtue and vice. Neuter-gendered words like **resplendent** *śukra* and the others should be transformed into masculine-gendered words because beginning with the pronoun *saḥ* "**he**" and continuing with **perceptive**, and **sage**, the masculine gender is used.

Perceptive means having transcendent vision, all-seeing. "There is no other seer than this."[4] **Sage** means owner of the mind, omniscient lord. **Transcendent** means above all. **Self-sufficient** means one who exists [entirely] on his own. He is everything: both all [relative existence] which he surpasses and the transcendent itself; he exists entirely on his own, thus is **Self-sufficient**.

Because of his omniscience he, the eternally free Owner (*īśvara*), **allots**, distributes, divides accordingly, **as needed**, that is, according to performance and the fruits of actions of [all] beings, all things ordained to be done **for aeons eternal**, meaning the immortal Lords of Progeny (*prajāpati*) called "**aeons**" (*saṃvatsara*). (8)

---

[2]The subtle body or *liṅga-sarīra* is one of the three bodies attributed to the individual in Vedāntic texts. The subtle body is the body in which the living being transmigrates to another physical body. There are seventeen constituents of the subtle body: the five knowledge-gathering senses, the intellect, the mind, the five actions senses, and the five vital breathes. See the *Vedānta-sāra* of Sadānanda (15th cent.), paras. 57-72, in Delmonico, ed. and trans., *The Fundamentals of Vedānta: Vedāntic Texts for Beginners*, 87-89 (Kirksville: Blazing Sapphire Press, 2006).

[3]The causal body or *kāraṇa-śarīra* is the third body recognized in Vedānta. The causal body is also described in the *Vedānta-sāra* (para 44). It is the cause of the ego or *ahaṅkāra*, it is blissful and is thus the "joyful wrapping" (*ānanda-kośa*) and it is the place of the dissolution of all things called deep sleep (*suṣupti*). Into it dissolve the gross and subtle bodies as well as the manifest world. See the *Vedānta-sāra* in *The Fundamentals of Vedānta*, 77.

[4]BUK 3.8.11: *nānyad ato'sti draṣṭṛ*.

Discussion

Here, the masculine pronoun *saḥ* is used, according to Śaṅkara, to refer to the Self (*ātman*) which is appropriate, since *ātman* is a masculine noun. Sometimes, however, the neuter pronoun *tat* is used (as in Mantra 4, for instance). In Śaṅkara's view this Upaniṣad uses them both interchangeably. However, the closest and most likely referent of the *saḥ* is the person in the previous *mantra*, the person who sees that the Self has become all beings, who thus sees oneness, and who is free of delusion and sorrow. Madhva, for instance, also takes it in this way, as a description of what happens to someone who gains salvific knowledge or experience of the Self or, in his case, the Lord and returns to the Lord. Such a reading fits the grammar of the *mantra* better since it takes *saḥ*, "he," as the subject of a transitive verb, *paryagāt*, "reached or attained or returned to," a verb in the aorist tense (like the present perfect in English). *Śukram* and the rest of the words ending in *m* are objects of the verb or modifiers of the object of the verb. *Śukra* is the only substantive in the *mantra* that can function as an object. The other words ending in *m* are clearly adjectives. So, another, more grammatically correct way of translating this verse would be: "He has fully attained to the seed [of existence, Ātman or Viṣṇu], who is bodiless, woundless, without nerves or tendons, pure, unpierced by sin. As poet, wise man, self-governing, self-born, he created appropriately objects for the eternal ages [or, he has set his affairs in proper order for the rest of time]."[2] Thus, though it is certainly about the Self, the *mantra* signals the return of the knower, through seeing that the Self has become all beings as described in the previous *mantra*, to a primordial state of purity, unity, and power. The question is: why does Śaṅkara want to force his ungrammatical interpretation on this *mantra* and tell us to ignore the accusative case endings on the words *śukra* and the rest? What is it about this interpretation that Śaṅkara doesn't like?

With respect to the eternal "years" (*samāḥ*) interpreted by Śaṅkara as Prajāpati-s, which seem to act as demi-urges or lords of *karma*, the second century gnostic sects of Christianity seem to have a parallel concept of Aeons, (*ho aion* sg.) divine primordial beings which emanate from the One. Brahminical or Buddhist influence on the mysticism of the Hellenistic mystery religions and early Christian sects seems possible, though textual evidence is lacking. In the Indian context it is interesting to see how important the "year" is as a divine entity in Ṛg-vedic thinking, as well as the huge number of synonyms in Sanskrit for "year." (Note that year (*samaḥ*) occurs earlier in verse two.) Śaṅkara's reference to Prajāpati-s is far from clear; Prajāpati singular is one of the names of the primordial creator god, sometimes identified with Hiraṇyagarbha (RV 10.121.10a) and Viśvakarman and Brahmā. Later traditions increase the number of Prajāpati-s to sixteen (parts of the year) in BU 1.5.14, the most likely reference, and PU 1.9 (as the sixteenfold *puruṣa*). Later still they are either the ten sons of Brahmā (*Manu-smṛti*), eleven in number in the *Mahābhārata, Śānti-parvan,*or twenty-one in number found in the *Bhāgavata Purāṇa*, 8.8.16, and so forth.[3]

Restatement

The True Self is all-pervasive, luminous, perfect, incorporeal, transcendent, autonomous, and supreme — yet the reliable source of true wisdom, enlightenment, and order in the world.

Study Questions

1. This verse continues to flesh out the theological description of the Lord as the Self of all in Mantras Six and Seven. What new is added to our understanding?
2. How do Śaṅkara and Madhva interpret the new descriptions?
3. This verse for once goes beyond paradoxical riddles of Mantras Six and Seven—how would you characterize this different use of language? What different effect does it have? Do you note an element of *bhakti*?
4. With reference to the above discussion we have chosen to translate the term *samābhyaḥ* as Aeons. Research the term in its Western uses, especially in Plato, Gnosticism, and in the Bible. Is there any parallel with Śaṅkara's interpretation of the term, basically a word for "year," as the eternal Prajāpati-s? Who are they? Who is Prajāpati in Vedic thinking?
5. Restate the *mantra* in your own words and be prepared to explain your choices.

---

[2]See Thieme's translation of this verse, 94.

[3]See *http://en.wikipedia.org/wiki/Prajapati* and the *Pūranic Encyclopedia* under the heading "Prajapati."

Mantra Nine

Śaṅkara's Introduction to Mantra Nine

atra ādyena mantreṇa sarva-eiṣaṇāparityāgena jñāna-niṣṭhā-uktā prathamo veda-arthaḥ **īśā āvāsyam idaṃ sarvaṃ ... mā gṛdhaḥ kasya-svid dhanam** *iti| ajñānāṃ jijīviṣūṇāṃ jñāna-niṣṭhā-asambhave* **kurvann eva iha karmāṇi ... jijīviṣed** *iti karma-niṣṭhā-uktā dvitīyo veda-arthaḥ|*

In this Upaniṣad with the first mantra (ĪU 1) "**By the Owner infused / Is all this ... Don't hold on; Who's property is it?**" the first goal of the Veda, the path of wisdom by total renunciation of all obsessions is enunciated. The second goal of the Veda with reference to those without knowledge who hope to live [a hundred years] and for whom the path of knowledge is impossible, the path of action is enunciated [in the following mantra (ĪU 2)]: "**Just by performing actions here, one should live ... ..**

anayoś ca niṣṭhayor vibhāgo mantrapradarśitayor bṛhad-āraṇyake'pi pradarśitaḥ so 'kāmayata jāyā me syāt (bṛ.u. 1.4.17) ity ādinā ajñasya kāminaḥ karmāṇi iti| mana eva asya ātmā vāg jāyā (bṛ.u. 1.4.17) ity-ādi-vacanād ajñatvaṃ kāmitvaṃ ca karma-niṣṭhasya niścitam avagamyate| tathā ca tat-phalaṃ sapta-anna-sargas teṣv ātma-bhāvena ātma-sva-rūpa-avasthānam|

Moreover, the distinction between these two paths taught in the *mantra* is also taught in the *Great Forest Upaniṣad* (BU, 1.4.17):"he desired: 'May I have a wife.'" etc.—[the viewpoint] of an ignorant person desiring ritual actions. From the expression: "the mind is his Self, speech his wife" (BU 1.4.17) and others, the ignorance and desire of the path of ritual action is clearly understood. And so are its consequences, the generation of the [so-called] "seven foods"[1] and the [erroneous] identification of the Self as their essential nature.

jāyā-ādy-eṣaṇā-traya-saṃnyāsena ca ātma-vidāṃ karma-niṣṭhā-prātikūlyena ātma-svarūpa-niṣṭhā eva darśitā kiṃ prajayā kariṣyāmo yeṣāṃ no'yam ātmāyaṃ lokaḥ (bṛ.u. 4.4.22) ity-ādinā| ye tu jñāna-niṣṭhāḥ saṃnyāsinas tebhyo **asuryā nāma ta** *ity-ādinā avidvan-nindā-dvāreṇa ātmano yāthātmyaṃ sa* **paryagād** *ity-etad-antair mantrair upadiṣṭam| te hy atra adhikṛtā na kāmina iti| tathā ca śvetāśvatarāṇāṃ mantra-upaniṣadi aty-āśramibhyaḥ paramaṃ pavitraṃ pravāca samyag-ṛṣi-saṅgha-juṣṭam (śve.u. 6.21) ity ādi vibhajya uktam| ye tu karmiṇaḥ karma-niṣṭhāḥ karma kurvanta eva jijīviṣavas tebhya idam ucyate—*

The commitment of those who know the true nature of the Self is demonstrated both by the renunciation of the three obsessions, beginning with desire for a wife, and by their disinclination to action. Thus, (BU, 4.4.22): "What shall we do with children—we for whom this Self is [our true] Reality?" The [third] *mantra* (ĪU 3): "**Veiled indeed ...** " is to criticize the ignorant, but by [the next] *mantras* ending with the eighth: "**It permeates everything,**" those who are committed to knowledge,

[1] BU, 1.5.1-3. The seven foods are:

> One was common to all here.
> Two he gave to the gods.
> Three he kept for himself.
> One he gave to the beasts.

He, here, is "the father." The common food is just what people eat here. The two foods of the gods are burnt and non-burnt ritual offerings. The three foods he kept are mind, speech, and breath. And the one he gave to the beasts is milk. The generation and acquisition of these seven foods is clearly connected to the path of action and to one's superimposing the Self on them.

renunciants, are taught the reality of the Self, since they [alone] are qualified for it, not those filled with longing. For instance, it is said in the *Owner of White Mules Upaniṣad* (ŚU, 6.21): "To those beyond all the stages of life he declared the highest teaching which purifies, welcomed by the righteous assembly of seers." But to those ritualists, committed to action, filled with desires, desiring a full life, this is said:

अन्धं तमः प्रविशन्ति
येऽविद्यामुपासते।
ततो भूय इव ते तमो
य उ विद्यायां रताः॥ ९॥

They enter into blind darkness
Who devote themselves to ignorance;
To greater gloom than that go they
Who desire knowledge. (9)

andhaṃ tamaḥ praviśanti
ye 'vidyāmupāsate|
tato bhūya iva te tamo
ya u vidyāyāṃ ratāḥ|| 9||

अन्धं तमः प्रविशन्ति
ये ऽविद्यामुपासते।
ततो भूय इव ते तमो
य उ विद्यायां रताः॥ ९॥

अन्धं तमः प्रविशन्ति
andhaṃ tamaḥ praviśanti
Blind darkness they enter,

ये ऽविद्यामुपासते।
ye 'vidyām upāsate|
Who to ignorance devote themselves,

ततो भूय इव ते तमो
tato bhūya iva te tamo
Than that greater even they gloom,

य उ विद्यायां रताः
ya u vidyāyāṃ ratāḥ
Who knowledge desire.

andham (n. acc. sing.) mfn. *andha*: "blind; dark." As a noun (n.): "darkness; turbid water, water."
tamaḥ (n. acc. sing.) *tamas*: "darkness, gloom; the darkness of hell, hell or a particular division of hell."
praviśanti (3rd pers. pl. pres.) *pra* + $\sqrt{viś}$ (cl. 6, P.): "to enter, enter in or settle down on, go into." Here: "they enter."
ye (m. nom. pl.) rel. pron. *yad*: "who, which, what, whichever, whatever, that." Here: "they who, or, whoever."
avidyām (f. acc. sing.) *avidyā*: "ignorance, spiritual ignorance."
upāsate (3rd pers. pl. pres.) *upa* + $\sqrt{ās}$ (cl. 2, Ā.): "to wait upon , approach respectfully, serve, honor, revere, respect, acknowledge, do homage, worship, be devoted or attached to." Here: "they revere."
tataḥ ind. an abl. form of the dem. pron. *tad*: "he, she, it, that, this." Here: "than that."
bhūyaḥ ind. *bhūyas*: "more, most, very much, exceedingly; still more, moreover, besides, further on."
iva ind.: "like, in the same manner as."[2] Here: "in some indefinite way."
te (m. nom. pl.) dem. pron. *tad*: "he, she, it, that, this." Here: "they."
tamaḥ (n. acc. sing.) *tamas*: "darkness, gloom; the darkness of hell, hell or a particular division of hell."
ye (m. nom. pl.) rel. pron. *yad*: "who, which, what, whichever, whatever, that." Here: "they who, or, whoever."
u ind. partic.: "on the other hand," esp. when used as it is here with *yad* (*ya u*).
vidyāyām (f. loc. sing.) *vidyā*: "knowledge; science, learning, scholarship, philosophy."
ratāḥ (m. nom. pl.) p.p. from $\sqrt{ram}$: "pleased, amused, gratified; delighting in, intent upon, fond or enamoured of, devoted or attached or addicted or disposed to."

[2] See Brereton's "The Particle Iva in Vedic Prose" on the uses of *iva* in Vedic language here.

They enter into blind darkness
Who devote themselves to ignorance;
To greater gloom than that go they
Who desire knowledge. (9)

Śaṅkara's Commentary

kathaṃ punar evam avagamyate na tu sarveṣām iti|

ucyate akāminaḥ sādhya-sādhana-bheda-upamardena

[Objection:] How again is it thus understood that this [path] is not for all?

[Answer:] Apropos of this it is said— by the erasure, for those free of desire, of the [false] distinction between the means and the goal of action:

yasmin sarvāṇi bhūtāny
ātmā eva abhūd vijānataḥ|
tatra ko mohaḥ kaḥ śoka
ekatvam anupaśyata iti

When one realizes "the Self
Has become all things"
Then for the seer of oneness
What delusion and sorrow can there be?
(Mantra 7)

yad ātma-ekatva-vijñānam uktaṃ tan na kena-cit karmaṇā jñāna-antareṇa vā hy amūḍhaḥ samuccicīṣati| iha tu samuccicīṣayā avidvad-ādi-nindā kriyate| tatra ca yasya yena samuccayaḥ sambhavati nyāyataḥ śāstrato vā tad iha ucyate yad daivaṃ vittaṃ devatā-viṣayaṃ jñānaṃ karma-sambandhitvena upanyastaṃ na parama-ātma-jñānam| vidyayā deva-lokaḥ (bṛ.u. 1.5.16) iti pṛthak-phala-śravaṇāt| tayor jñāna-karmaṇor iha eka-eka-anuṣṭhāna-nindā samuccicīṣayā na nindā-parā eva eka-ekasya pṛthak-phala-śravaṇād vidyayā tad ārohanti, vidyayā deva-lokaḥ (bṛ.u. 1.5.16) na tatra dakṣiṇā yanti, karmaṇā pitṛ-lokaḥ (bṛ.u. 1.5.16) iti| na hi śāstra-vihitaṃ kiñcid akartavyatām iyāt|

None but fools would wish to combine this [precious] knowledge of the unity of the Self just mentioned with any ritual action or with any other kind of knowledge. But here the unwise, etc. are being criticized for this wish to combine [them]. Here that with which the combination could be put together, whether by reason or scripture, is discussed. That divine asset, knowledge whose object is the divinities, placed in combination with ritual action is not the knowledge of the supreme Self, since one [actually] hears of different consequences [of that knowledge] in [the statement that] "by knowledge the world of the gods [is achieved]" (BU, 1.5.16). Criticism of the separate performance of these two, knowledge and ritual action, is here due to the wish to combine them [as explained in Mantra Eleven], not mainly for criticism [of either one separately], because one hears of different consequences for each. [For example] they ascend to it [the world of the gods] by knowledge: "by knowledge the world of the gods [is achieved]" (BU, 1.5.16). They do not go there on the southern [path]:[3] "by ritual action they go to the world of the ancestors" (BU, 1.5.16). Since nothing at all commanded by scripture (Veda) should lack consequence.

tatra **andhaṃ tamaḥ** *adarśana-ātmakaṃ tamaḥ* **praviśanti**| *ke ye'vidyāṃ vidyāyā anyā avidyā tāṃ karma ity arthaḥ karmaṇo vidyā-virodhitvāt| tām* **avidyām** *agni-hotra-ādi-lakṣaṇām eva kevalām* **upāsate** *tat-parāḥ santo 'nutiṣṭhanti ity-abhiprāyaḥ|* **tatas** *tasmād andha-ātmakāt tamaso* **bhūya iva** *bahutaram eva* **te tamaḥ praviśanti**| *ke karma hitvā ye u ye tu* **vidyāyām** *eva devatā-jñāna eva* **ratā** *abhiratāḥ| tatrāvāntaraphalabhedaṃ vidyākarmaṇoḥ samuccaya-kāraṇam āha| anyathā phala-vad-aphalavatoḥ sannihitayor aṅga-aṅgitā eva syād ity arthaḥ|| 9||*

Here **they enter into blind darkness**, whose nature is undiscerning. Who? Those **who devote themselves to ignorance**; for knowledge is different from ignorance, which thus means ritual action since ritual action is op-

[3]The southern and northern paths are described at BU, 6.2.15-16. The southern and northern paths are an early expression of the ideas of liberation and reincarnation that later became major parts of the Hindu worldview. If after death one travels by the northern path, one goes to the world of the gods and then on to the sun and from there to the worlds of Brahman from which one never returns. If after death one travels by the southern path, one goes to the worlds of the forefathers and from there to the moon where the gods enjoy them as food. When their good works are exhausted they return to the earth in the rain, become food, are eaten by men and born again through women. The qualifications for traveling the northern path are knowledge of and meditation on the Truth and the qualifications for traveling the southern path are having performed sacrifices, charity, and austerity.

posed to it [knowledge]. **They devote themselves,** i.e., being totally intent on that ignorance alone, meaning the ritual invocation of fire (*agni-hotra*), etc. This is the intention. **Than that**, i.e. than the darkness which is deep, **to greater gloom than that go they**, i.e., into much deeper gloom do they enter. Who? **They** means those who have given up ritual action, **But those who desire**, are happy with, **knowledge**, knowledge of the divinities. In this regard he says the respective disparity in inferior consequences of ritual action and knowledge are the reason why they are combined [in the first place]. Otherwise, the combination of one which is effective with another which is ineffective would subordinate one to the other [which would contradict Vedic usage].[4] (9)

[4]They are different because there would be no reason to combine them logically if they were not mutually exclusive, i.e. if they actually already included each other

Discussion

Mantra Nine seems reasonably easy to understand. There are many references to intellectual arrogance in the Upaniṣads (BU 4.4.22) and here it makes sense to see this first reference to "knowledge" (*vidyā*) as the kind that one might well get from reading this concise account of Self and Owner in ĪU. Getting the idea intellectually is different from realizing the Self phenomenologically in non-dual intuition.

Blind darkness, *andhaṃ tamaḥ* occurs thrice in the ĪU 3, 9, and 12. This makes *tamas* vs. *sattva* a major thematic contrast for the text. This recalls, of course, the famous *Śānti mantra* from BU 1.3.28 also called the *Pavamāna mantra*: *asato mā sadgamaya, tamaso mā jyotirgamaya, mṛtyormāmṛtaṃ gamaya*, "from the unreal lead me to the real; from darkness lead me to the light; from death lead me to immortality." This *mantra* with tripart parallel structure seems to equate *asat, tamas*, and *mṛtyu*, non-being (non-truth), darkness, and death, imploring to be led from these to the *sat, jyotis*, and *amṛta*, or, being (truth), light, and immortality. This is not too divergent from the sentiment at the end of the ĪUK 15-18. Olivelle notes the point of much Vedic religion is not to be left without a world, but rather to conquer a world (*loka*), to have a space to exist in—especially after death—assured by doing proper rituals, having knowledge of the rituals, and having a son (to do funeral rituals after death).[1] In BU 1.4.16 the Self (*ātman*) is acknowledged above all to be the *loka* or "dwelling space" of all beings (*atho ayaṃ vā ātmā sarveṣām bhūtānām lokaḥ*). The space of the supreme Self is the thrust of the ĪU whether understood as infusing or enveloping all. Suddenly Mantras 9-14 confront us with an unexpected contrast: the usual means of attaining some kind of suitable *loka* after death is flatly rejected. Here this rejection focuses on devotion to ignorance (*avidyā*). And much worse (and much more perplexing and paradoxical) delight in "knowledge" (*vidyā*). BU seems very much relevant since Mantra Nine appears there as 4.4.10![2]

Andhaṃ tamaḥ (blind darkness) is adumbrated in a number of other texts later: Vyāsa's commentary on the *Yoga-sūtra* (YS) 3.26 describes *andha-tāmisra* as one of the seven great hell worlds that make up part of the *bhū-loka* (Earth-world), upon which are stacked another seven netherworlds (*tala*-s), which reach up to the Earth we know, as the eighth, reaching up to Mt. Meru. The *Bhāgavata* at 1.2.3 mentions the term in the context of what worldly people seek to overcome.

So the big question is what is meant by knowledge and ignorance. One clue would be to read it in parallel with Mantras Eleven and Twelve, since there is parallel structure, such that Nine and Eleven explain each other. Using this hermeneutic, devotion to ignorance is linked

[1]Olivelle, 296.

[2]BU, however, reads *tamaḥ* not *tamo*. And Mantra Ten appears also as KU 1.4 with some slightly different words: *viditād, aviditād*, and *pūrveṣām*

with regression (return to the unmanifest) and focus on knowledge linked to progression (evolution toward manifestation). The final explanations are not binary exclusions: Mantras Eleven and Fourteen in parallel enjoin combining both for the ultimate good. Here we have a common trope—that the Ultimate is not to be found in the realm of binary oppositions, but is quite beyond it. This is a very common Upaniṣadic message.

Study Questions

1. Blind darkness, *andhaṃ tamaḥ* occurs thrice in the ĪUK 3, 9, and 12. What does the term imply? Can you use BUK 4.4.10 (its origin) and surrounding passages to contextualize it more? How so?

2. We are clearly back to paradox and picking up the thread of threat that began in ĪU 3. This paradox becomes more and more difficult in the third part of the triplet 9,10,11 (ĪUM 12,13,14). Start an analysis of the meanings possible by making a list of possible meanings for *vidyā* and *avidyā*. How do Śaṅkara and Madhva interpret the terms? What other possibilities strike you?

3. Restate the *mantra* in your own words and be prepared to explain your choices.

Mantra Ten

अन्यदेवाहुर्विद्ययान्यदाहुरविद्यया।
इति शुश्रुम धीराणां ये नस्तद्विचचक्षिरे॥ १०॥

They say one thing indeed results from knowledge.
Another from ignorance, they say.
Thus have we heard from the wise,
Those who have perceived it for us. (10)

anyadevāhurvidyayānyadāhuravidyayā|
iti śuśruma dhīrāṇāṃ ye nastadvicacakṣire|| 10||

अन्यदेवाहुर्विद्ययान्यदाहुरविद्यया।
इति शुश्रुम धीराणां ये नस्तद्विचचक्षिरे॥ १०॥

अन्यदेवाहुर्विद्यया
anyad eva āhur vidyayā
One thing, indeed, they say from knowledge,

अन्यदाहुरविद्यया
anyad āhur avidyayā
Another they say from ignorance.

इति शुश्रुम धीराणाम्
iti śuśruma dhīrāṇām
Thus we have heard from the wise,

ये नस्तद्विचचक्षिरे
ye nas tad vicacakṣire
Those who for us it have perceived.[1]

[1]Alternative trans.: Those who have told us about it.

anyat (n. sing. acc.) pronom. adj. *anya*: "other, different; other than, different from, opposed to." The use of two *anyat*-s together means: "one thing [and] another."
eva ind.: "so, just so, exactly so, indeed, truly, really."
āhuḥ (3rd pers. pl. pf.) This verb ($\sqrt{ah}$) only has forms in the pf., most commonly the two: *āha* "he or she said" and *āhuḥ* "they said." Meanings: "to say, speak; to express, signify; to call (by name)."
vidyayā (f. sing. instr.) *vidyā*: "science, learning, scholarship, philosophy; knowledge of soul or of spiritual truth."
anyat See above.
āhuḥ (3rd. pers. pl. pf.) . See above.
avidyayā (f. sing. instr.) *a* + *vidyā* the opposite or absence of *vidyā* (see above): "ignorance, spiritual ignorance; illusion."
iti ind. from the pronom.l base *i*) "in this manner, thus."[5]
śuśruma (1st pers. pl. pf.) $\sqrt{śru}$ (cl. 5, P.): "to hear, listen or attend to anything (acc.), give ear to anyone, hear or learn anything about." Here: "We heard."
dhīrāṇām (m. gen. pl.) *dhīra*: "intelligent, wise, skillful, clever, familiar with, versed in; steady, constant, firm, resolute, brave, energetic, courageous, self-possessed, composed, calm, grave."
ye (m. nom. pl.) rel. pron. *yad*: "who, which, what, whichever, whatever, that." Here: "They who, or, whoever."
nas (1st pers. acc. pl.) *nas* is a substitute for the pers. pron. *asmat* ("I") in the acc., dat., and gen. pl. Here ii means, "us."
tat (n. nom. sing.) dem. pron. tad: "that" or "it."
vicacakṣire (3rd. pers. pl. pf.) *vi* + $\sqrt{cakṣ}$ (cl. 2, Ā.): "to see, look at, observe, notice; to tell, inform."

[5]*Iti* refers to something that has been said or thought, or lays stress on what immediately precedes it. It is used to close quotations of every kind and thus is like a pair of quotation marks.

They say one thing indeed results from knowledge.
Another from ignorance, they say.
Thus have we heard from the wise,
Those who have perceived it for us.[2] (10)

[2]The verb root $\sqrt{cakṣ}$ means either "to perceive" or "to tell." We have taken it as the former.

Śaṅkara's Commentary

anyat *pṛthag* **eva vidyayā** *kriyate phalam ity* **āhur** *vadanti vidyayā deva-lokaḥ (bṛ.u. 1.6.16), karmaṇā kriyate karmaṇā pitṛ-lokaḥ (bṛ.u. 1.5.16) iti śruteḥ|* **ity** *evaṃ* **śuśruma** *śrutavanto vayaṃ* **dhīrāṇāṃ** *dhīmatāṃ vacanam|* **ye** *ācāryā* **no** *'smabhyaṃ* **tat** *karma ca jñānaṃ ca* **vicacakṣire** *vyākhyātavantas teṣām ayam āgamaḥ pāramparyāgata ity arthaḥ|| 10||*

"**One thing indeed [results] from knowledge**" means a separate result is produced; **they say** means it is proclaimed in the Veda (BU, 1.5.16), "from knowledge the world of the gods [is attained]." By ritual action [a different result] is accomplished, " ... by ritual action the world of the ancestors [is attained]" (ibid.) **So we have heard**—it is heard by us; **from the wise** means it is an utterance from the those of exalted intellect. **Those** means the masters (*ācāryas*), "**us** (*nas*)" means for us (*asmabhyam*); "**it**" means both ritual action and knowledge; "**who have perceived**" means they have explained it; i.e., that this was passed down as received scripture. This is the meaning. (10)

Discussion

So the argument is put forward in terms of the different results from the opposing principles, knowledge vs. ignorance. Here the idea of *karma* is clearly in the background.

Study Questions

1. Verses IUK 10 and IUK 13 both focus on the results of knowledge and ignorance and the results of the manifest and unmanifest. How does this move the train of thought forward?
2. Look up Kena Upaniṣad 2 and 4 and BUK 4.4.18, and BUK 4.4.14c-17d which have similar verses ... does this help to interpret the thought?
3. Again compare Śankara and Madhva interpretations of the two verses.
4. Focus on the results means focus on what particular philosophical doctrine?
5. Who are the wise, those who have perceived It for us? Why is this thought brought in?

Mantra Eleven

Śaṅkara's Introduction to Mantra Eleven

yata evam ataḥ	Indeed, since this is true, thus [it follows]:

विद्यां चाविद्यां च यस्
तद्वेदोभयं सह ।
अविद्यया मृत्युं तीर्त्वा
विद्ययामृतमश्नुते ॥ ११॥

Knowledge and ignorance,
One who knows both together
Crossing death by ignorance,
Gains immortality by knowledge. (11)

vidyāṃ cāvidyāṃ ca yas
tadvedobhayaṃ saha|
avidyayā mṛtyuṃ tīrtvā
vidyayāmṛtamaśnute|| 11||

विद्यां चाविद्यां च यस्
तद्वेदोभयं सह।
अविद्यया मृत्युं तीर्त्वा
विद्ययामृतमश्नुते॥ ११॥

विद्यां चाविद्यां च यस्
vidyāṃ ca avidyāṃ ca yas
Knowledge and ignorance, one who

तद्वेदोभयं सह
tad veda ubhayaṃ saha
That knows both together

अविद्यया मृत्युं तीर्त्वा
avidyayā mṛtyuṃ tīrtvā
By ignorance crossing death,

विद्ययामृतमश्नुते
vidyayā amṛtam aśnute
By knowledge immortality gains.

vidyām (f. acc. sing.) *vidyā*: "knowledge; science, learning, scholarship, philosophy."
ca ind. a conj. partic.: "and, both, also, moreover, as well as."
avidyām (f. acc. sing.) *a* + *vidyā*: "ignorance, spiritual ignorance."
ca See above.
yas (m. nom. sing.) rel. pron. *yad*: "who, which, what, whichever, whatever, that." Here: "he who, or whoever."
tat (n. acc. sing.) dem. pron. *tad*: "he, she, it, that, this." Here: "those [two]."
veda (3rd pers. sing. pf.) $\sqrt{vid}$ (cl. 2, P.): "to know, understand, perceive, learn, become or be acquainted with, be conscious of, have a correct notion of." Here: "he/she/it knows." [1]
ubhayam (n. acc. sing.) mfn. (*ubhaya*): "both, of both kinds, in both ways, in both manners." Here: "both."
saha ind.: "in common, in company, jointly, conjointly, in concert." Here: "together."
avidyayā (f. instr. sing.) See above. Here: "by or through or from ignorance."
mṛtyum (m. acc. sing.) *mṛtyu*: "death, dying."
tīrtvā ger. (with the suffix *tvā*) of $\sqrt{\text{tṝ}}$ (cl. 1, P.): "to pass across or over, cross over (a river); to surpass, overcome, subdue, escape." Here: "having crossed over or having crossed beyond."
vidyayā (f. instr. sing.) See above. Here: "by or through or from knowledge."
amṛtam (n. acc. sing.) *a* + *mṛta* (lit. "not dead;" the p.p. of $\sqrt{\text{mṛ}}$ [cl. 6, Ā. and cl. 1, U.]: "to die." As a n. noun (*amṛta*): "collective body of immortals; world of immortality, heaven, eternity; immortality; final emancipation."
aśnute (3rd pers. sing. pres.) $\sqrt{\text{aś}}$ (cl. 5, Ā.): "to reach, come to, arrive at, get, gain, obtain." Here: "he/she attains."

[1] Though this is a pf. which should indicate an action in the past, it often replaces the present form (*vetti*), as it does here, and has a present meaning.

Knowledge and ignorance,
One who knows both together
Crossing death by ignorance,
Gains immortality by knowledge. (11)

Śaṅkara's Commentary

vidyāṃ ca avidyāṃ *ca devatā-jñānaṃ karma ca ity arthaḥ|* **yas tad** *etad* **ubhayaṃ saha** *ekena puruṣeṇa anuṣṭheyaṃ* **veda** *tasya evaṃ samuccaya-kāriṇa eva eka-puruṣa-artha-sambandhaḥ krameṇa syād ity ucyate|*

Both knowledge and ignorance means knowledge of the gods and ritual action. **One who knows both together** means that this knowing is to be done by one person; the one combining both together—will get one of the achievements at a time, in succession, [i.e., crossing death and gaining immortality]. Thus is it explained.

avidyayā *karmaṇā agni-hotra-ādinā* **mṛtyuṃ** *svābhāvikaṃ karma jñānaṃ ca mṛtyu-śabda-vācyam* **ubhayaṃ** *tīrtvātikramya* **vidyayā** *devatājñānena* **amṛtaṃ** *devatā-ātma-bhāvam* **aśnute** *prāpnoti| tad dhy* **amṛtam** *ucyate yad devatā-ātma-gamanam|| 11||*

By ignorance means by ritual actions such as the Fire invocation (*agni-hotra*) etc.; **death** means rituals and knowledge according to one's common proclivities; **both of them** [together] are expressed by the word **death**; crossing means having passed beyond [ritual and knowledge]; **by knowledge** means by knowledge of the gods (*devatā*); **immortality** means becoming a god onself; **attains** means arrives at. This very **immortality** is explained as being transformed into a god oneself. (11)

Discussion

What kind of immortality is meant by the Upaniṣad here? The Upaniṣad probably means the absolute immortality described in an important passage in the BUK (1.4.10). There it is said that one who knows "I am Brahman" becomes all this and not even the gods (*deva*) are able to unmake him. He has become the very Self of the gods.[1] Moreover, one who worships the gods as different from himself and thinks "he is one and I am another" does not know [the truth]. He is like a domesticated animal of the gods. Just as many domesticated animals are exploited by humans, so too is each human exploited by the gods. And as when with the loss of even one animal, its owner is distressed, how much more so when many are lost? Therefore, it is not pleasing to these gods that humans come to know this.[2] Śaṅkara points out in his commentary on this passage in the BUK that one who knows does not "become" Brahman or all this or the Self of the gods. Knowledge of Brahman destroys the ignorance that makes one think one is not Brahman or all this or the Self of the gods. One is always already Brahman or all this or the Self of the gods.

Study Questions

1. What could it possibly mean to know knowledge and ignorance at the same time?
2. The last half of this mantra and the parallel Mantra Fourteen seems to be the most difficult paradox in the whole Upaniṣad—What does it mean in the early time it was written? Why this strange insistence on going beyond the traditional binaries by knowing both together?
3. What does the last half mean according to Śaṅkara and Madhva?

---

[1] *ya evaṃ vedāhaṃ brahmāsmīti sa idaṃ sarvaṃ bhavati, tasya ha na devāś canābhūtyā īśate| ātmā hy eṣāṃ sa bhavati|*

[2] *atha yo 'nyāṃ devatām upāste 'nyo 'sāv anyo 'ham asmīti na sa veda yathā paśur evaṃ sa devānām| yathā ha vai bahavaḥ paśavo manuṣyaṃ bhuñyur evam ekaikaḥ puruṣo devān bhunakty ekasminn eva paśāv ādīyamāne 'priyaṃ bhavati kim u bahuṣu tasmād eṣāṃ tan na priyaṃ yad etan manuṣyā vidyuḥ*

Mantra Twelve

Śaṅkara's Introduction to Mantra Twelve

adhunā vyākṛtāvyākṛtopāsanayoḥ samuccicīṣayā pratyekaṃ nindā ucyate|

Now, out of a desire to combine the worship of both the developed and the undeveloped, each is being criticized separately:

अन्धं तमः प्रविशन्ति
येऽसम्भूतिमुपासते।
ततो भूय इव ते तमो
य उ सम्भूत्यां रताः॥ १२॥

They enter into blind darkness
Who devote themselves to regression.
To greater gloom than *that* go they
Who desire progression. (12)

andhaṃ tamaḥ praviśanti
ye'sambhūtimupāsate|
tato bhūya iva te tamo
ya u sambhūtyāṃ ratāḥ|| 12||

अन्धं तमः प्रविशन्ति
येऽसम्भूतिमुपासते।
ततो भूय इव ते तमो
य उ सम्भूत्यां रताः॥ १२॥

अन्धं तमः प्रविशन्ति
andhaṃ tamaḥ praviśanti
Blind darkness they enter

ye 'sambhūtimupāsate|
ye 'sambhūtim upāsate|
Who to regression they devote.

ततो भूय इव ते तमो
tato bhūya iva te tamo
Than that greater even their gloom

य उ सम्भूत्यां रताः॥
ya u sambhūtyāṃ ratāḥ||
Who progression desire.

andham (neut. acc. sing.) adj. *andha*: "blind; dark." As a noun (neut.): "darkness; turbid water, water."
tamaḥ (neut. acc. sing.) noun *tamas*: "darkness, gloom; the darkness of hell, hell or a particular division of hell."
praviśanti (3rd. pers. plu. pres.) *pra* + $\sqrt{viś}$ (cl. 6 P.): "to enter, enter in or settle down on, go into." Here: "they enter."
ye (masc. nom. plu.) rel. pron. *yad*: "who, which, what, whichever, whatever, that." Here: "they who, or, whoever."
asambhūtim (fem. acc. sing) *asambhūti*: "non-being, non-existence, destruction." Here: "regression."
upāsate (3rd. pers. plu. pres.) from *upa* + $\sqrt{ās}$ (cl. 2, Ā): "to sit by the side of, sit near at hand (in order to honour or wait upon); to wait upon, approach respectfully, serve, honor, revere, respect, acknowledge, do homage, worship, be devoted or attached to."
tataḥ (ind.) *tatas* used here as the abl. of the demonstrative pronoun *tad*: "he, she, it, that, this." Here: "than that."
bhūyaḥ (ind.) *bhūyas*: "more, most, very much, exceedingly; still more, moreover, besides, further on."
iva (ind.) "like, in the same manner as." Here it most likely has the same force as *eva*: "indeed, truly, really."
te (masc. nom. plu.) demonstrative pronoun *tad*: "he, she, it, that, this." Here: "they."
tamaḥ (neut. acc. sing.) noun *tamas*: "darkness, gloom; the darkness of hell, hell or a particular division of hell."
ye See above.
u (ind.) particle: "on the other hand," esp. when used as it is here with *yad* (*ya u*).
sambhūtyām (fem. loc. sing.) *sambhūti*: "becoming, birth, origin, production; growth, increase." Here: "progression."
ratāḥ (masc. nom. plu.) adj. *rata*, the past part. of the root $\sqrt{ram}$ (cl.1, Ā): "to delight, make happy, enjoy carnally." As pp it means: "pleased, amused, gratified; delighting in, intent upon, fond or enamoured of, devoted or attached or addicted or disposed to." Here: "who desire."

They enter into blind darkness
Who devote themselves to regression.
To greater gloom than *that* go they
Who desire progression. (12)

Śaṅkara's Commentary

andhaṃ tamaḥ praviśanti ye asambhūtiṃ *sambhavanaṃ* **sambhūtiḥ** *sā yasya kāryasya sā sambhūtiḥ tasyā anyā* **asambhūtiḥ** *prakṛtiḥ kāraṇam avidyā avyākṛta-ākhyā tām asambhūtim avyākṛta-ākhyāṃ prakṛtiṃ kāraṇam avidyāṃ kāma-karma-bīja-bhūtām adarśana-ātmikām* **upāsate ye** *te tad-anurūpam eva andhaṃ tamo adarśanātmakaṃ*

They enter into blind darkness [who devote themselves to] regression. Being produced is **progression** as also the producing of an effect; the opposite of that is **regression**, primordial nature (*prakṛti*), the underlying cause, and ignorance, which is called the undeveloped. **Those who devote themselves** to that **regres-**

praviśanti| **tatas** *tasmādapi* **bhūyo** *bahutaram* **iva tamaḥ praviśanti ya u sambhūtyāṃ** *kāryabrahmaṇi hiraṇya-garbha-ākhye* **ratāḥ**|| *12*||

sion, called the undeveloped, primordial nature, the cause, and ignorance, which is the seed of desire and ritual and whose essence is non-perception—**they enter** into a similar **deep darkness** whose essence is also non-perception. **Than that**, even more than that, **to a greater gloom than that go they who desire progression**, that is, who desire the [lower] effect-Brahman (*kārya-brahman*), called Hiraṇya-garbha, the Golden Embryo. (12)

Discussion

Sambhūti is difficult to translate. We translate it as progression which is opposed to regression (*asambhūti*). Śaṅkara takes *sambhūti* as Hiraṇya-garbha, the Sun, the Creator, or lower or effect-Brahman; regression *asambhūti*, he takes as undeveloped matter *prakṛti* leading to dissolution into primordial matter (*prakṛti-laya*). Worship of progression leads to supernormal powers like the gods (*devas*) have, whereas renunciation of desires leads to *prakṛti-laya*, merging with unconscious, primordial matter.

Olivelle thinks *asambhūti* is suicide and *sambhūti* is rebirth.

In any case, somehow the desired goal, immortality, is beyond (according to Ježić) both *sambhūti* and *asambhūti*, beyond both good reincarnation and temporary but lengthy merging into nonconscious matter (or *prakṛti-laya*).

Study Questions

1. What is meant by *asaṃbhūti* and *saṃbhūti* (translated here as regression and progression, or often as unmanifest and manifest respectively? Look up the philosophical system of Sāṃkhya, (a system parallel with Yoga philosophy) and explain how the concepts *manifest* and *unmanifest* (*vyakta* and *avyakta*) with respect to primordial matter, might relate to this ancient dualistic philosophy which aims to explain the Upaniṣads. You will need to understand the terms *puruṣa* and *prakṛti*, pure consciousness and primordial matter, the basic binary opposition that all boils down to in dualistic Sāṃkhya and Yoga systems.

2. Research the Sāṃkhya/Yoga term *prakṛti-laya*, one "dissolved into primordial matter," found in *Yoga-sūtra* (YS) 1.19 with reference to the fate of those who devote themselves to the lower form of meditative absorption (*saṃprajñāta-samādhi*).

3. How do Śankara and Madhva differ in their explanations of ĪU 12?

4. Does the exactly parallel structure of the two triplets, 9,10, 11 and 12,13,14, seemingly equating ignorance/knowledge with the regression/progression, sequentially reveal something new about the nature of ignorance and knowledge?

5. The earliest version of ĪU is probably ĪUM. Notice that both ĪUK and ĪUM have two sets of paradoxical triplets with a binary opposition in each triplet that in the third verse (ĪU 11 and 14) is resolved by a strange and mysterious conjunction of the two. However, ĪUM, the earlier version, starts with the opposition of *asambhūti* and *sambhūti* regression/progression, and then contrasts it with ignorance (*avidyā*) and knowledge (*vidyā*) in the second triplet—while ĪUK version has the triplets in the opposite order (ignorance/knowledge first and regression/progression second). What different effect is created by switching the order of presentation? If the M version is oldest, what might that mean for interpreting these difficult verses?

Mantra Thirteen

Śaṅkara's Introduction to Mantra Thirteen

adhunā ubhayor upāsanayoḥ samuccaya-kāraṇam ava-yava-phala-bhedam āha—

Now with respect to the worship of both, the reason for combining them, the difference in the results of the two components is explained.

अन्यदेवाहुः संभवाद्
अन्यदाहुरसंभवात्।
इति शुश्रुम धीराणां
ये नस्तद् विचचक्षिरे॥ १३॥

They say one thing indeed
Results from progression,
Another from regression, they say.
Thus have we heard from the wise,
Those who have perceived it for us. (13)

anyadevāhuḥ saṃbhavād
anyadāhurasaṃbhavāt|
iti śuśruma dhīrāṇāṃ
ye nastadvicacakṣire|| 13||

अन्यदेवाहुः संभवाद्
अन्यदाहुरसंभवात्।
इति शुश्रुम धीराणां
ये नस्तद्विचचक्षिरे॥ १३॥

anyadevāhuḥ saṃbhavād
anyad eva āhuḥ saṃbhavād
One thing indeed they say from progression,

अन्यदाहुरसंभवात्।
anyad āhur asaṃbhavāt|
Another thing they say from regression.

इति शुश्रुम धीराणां
iti śuśruma dhīrāṇāṃ
Thus have we heard from the wise.

ये नस्तद्विचचक्षिरे॥
ye nas tad vicacakṣire||
Those who for us it have perceived.

anyat (neut. sing. acc.) From the pron. adj., *anya*: "other, different; other than, different from, opposed to." The use of two *anyat*-s together means: "one thing [and] another."

eva (ind.) "so, just so, exactly so, indeed, truly, really."

āhuḥ (3rd plu. perf.) This verb (√*ah*) only has forms in the pf., most commonly the two: *āha* "he or she said" and *āhuḥ* "they said." Meanings: "to say, speak; to express, signify; to call (by name)."

sambhavāt (masc. sing. abl.) *sambhava*: "birth, production, origin, source, being, existence." Here: "progression."

anyat See above.

āhuḥ See above.

asamabhavāt (masc. sing. abl.) *a* + *sambhava* the opposite or absence of *sambhava* (see above): "non-existence, destruction, non-happening, cessation, interruption." Here: "regression."

iti (ind.) (from the pronomial base *i*) "in this manner, thus." *Iti* refers to something that has been said or thought, or lays stress on what immediately precedes it. It is used to close quotations of every kind and thus is like a pair of quotation marks.

śuśruma (1st pers. plu. perf.) √*śru* (cl. 5, P): "to hear, listen or attend to anything (acc.), give ear to any one (acc. or gen.), hear or learn anything about." Here: "We heard."

dhīrāṇām (masc. gen. plu.) *dhīra*: "intelligent, wise, skillful, clever, familiar with, versed in; steady, constant, firm, resolute, brave, energetic, courageous, self-possessed, composed, calm, grave."

ye (masc. nom. plu.) rel. pron. *yad*: "who, which, what, whichever, whatever, that." Here: "They who, or, whoever."

nas (1st. pers. acc. plu.) *nas* is a substitute for the pers. pron. *asmat* ("I") in the acc., dat., and gen. plurals. Here it means, "us."

tat (neut. nom. sing.) Demonstrative pronoun: "that" or "it."

vicacakṣire (3rd plu. perf.) *vi* + √*cakṣ* (cl. 2, Ā.): "to see, look at, observe, notice; to tell, inform."

They say one thing indeed
Results from progression,
Another from regression, they say.
Thus have we heard from the wise,
Those who have perceived it for us. (13)

Śaṅkara's Commentary

anyad eva *pṛthag eva* **āhuḥ** *phalaṃ* **sambhavāt** *sambhūteḥ kārya-brahma-upāsanād aṇimā-ādy-aiśvarya-lakṣaṇaṃ vyākhyātavanta ity arthaḥ*|

tathā ca **anyad āhur asambhavād** *asambhūter avyākṛtād avyākṛta-upāsanād yad-uktam* **andhaṃ tamaḥ praviśanti** *iti prakṛti-laya iti ca paurāṇikair ucyata* **iti** *evaṃ* **śuśruma dhīraṇāṃ** *vacanaṃ* **ye nas tad vicacakṣire** *vyākṛtāvyākṛtopāsana-phalaṃ vyākhyātavanta ity arthaḥ*|| *13*||

One thing, indeed, means separate (singly) indeed; **they say,** is the result **from progression,** i.e., from the manifest, from the meditation on manifest *brahman* (*kārya-brahma*), namely, supernormal powers such as minification, etc.;[2] **they say**, they explain. This is the point.

Thus, **another, they say, from regression,** i.e., from the unmanifest, from the unexpressed, from meditation on the undeveloped, speaking of which it is said **"They enter into blind darkness"** (Mantra 12), which is described in the *Purāṇas* as "merging into primordial mat-

[2]These supernormal powers are first mentioned in *Yoga-sūtra* 3.45 with the *Vyāsa-bhāṣya*, Pflueger translation:

tato 'ṇimādi-prādurbhāvaḥ kāya-sampat-tad-dharmānabhighātaś ca

From this arises [the supernormal powers of] miniaturization, etc. and [there is] perfection of the body and invulnerability to the properties (*dharmas*) of these [earlier mentioned elements].

Of these: (1) **miniaturization** (*animan*) [means] one becomes minute; (2) levitation (*laghiman*) [means] one becomes light; (3) magnification (*mahiman*) [means] one becomes huge; (4) extension (*prāpti*) [means] one touches the moon with one's fingertips themselves; (5) irresistible desire (*prākāmya*) [means] the lack of opposition to one's wishes—one dives into the earth and emerges as [if] in water; (6) mastery (*vaśitva*) means one masters the elements and material things, but is not mastered by others; (7) command (*īśitṛtva*) [means] to govern manifestation, disappearance, and disposition [of the elements etc.]; (8) wish realization (*yatrakāmāvasāyitva*) [means] making whatever is desired real—as one desires, so the gross elements and their natures (*prakṛtis*) arrange themselves. Although one is able, one does not radically reverse the nature of things. Why not? Due to the intention of Another One, previously perfected, who has [already] realized his desires with respect to the elements as they are. These are the eight powers (*aiśvaryāṇi*). The perfection of the body will be described [later]).

[As to the phrase:] ... **and invulnerability to the properties of these [elements]**—[it means] the earth [element] does not obstruct the activity of the yogin's body etc. with its solidity; he [even] enters rock; water adhesive as it is, does not wet [him]; nor does fire, hot as it is, burn [him], nor does the wind, forceful as it is, move him. Even in space, which is by nature transparent, he remains concealed, invisible even to [other] Perfected Ones.

ter (*prakṛti-laya*)."[3] **Thus have we heard from the wise. Those who have perceived it for us.** They described the results of meditation on the manifest and the unmanifest—this is what it means. (13)

[3]One of the earliest philosophical references to *prakṛti-laya* state is in *Yoga-sūtra* 1.19. Here Patañjali differentiates *asamprajñāta samādhi*—the state of total mental quiescience which brings liberation—from the similar state of merely merging mentally with *prakṛti*, which brings temporary mental peace only until *karma* in the form of mental impresson brings the individual mind back into activity.

The thought that immersion in (regression or dissolution back into) *prakṛti* is described as like *kaivalya* is interesting. The only difference pointed at here is the eventual return to ordinary existence due to the force of unsatisfied strivings latent in the mind. Yet it is curious that this might even be described as similar to *kaivalya*, since it does not involve the isolation of pure consciousness, but merely the temporary cessation presumably of only the gross operations of awareness—the subtle remnant still exists. However, the intention of the authors is mysterious. It may actually be that the state of the so-called *prakṛti-laya* is phenomenologically the same as the yogin experiencing non-percipient coherence, only it is not final. This raises several problems which cannot be discussed in the more narrow confines of this essay.

Here is the actual *Yoga-sūtra* 1.19 with the *Vyāsa-bhāṣya*, Pflueger translation:

bhava-pratyayo videha-prakrtilayānām

For the discarnate and those dissolved into *prakṛti* [coherence depends on] the experience of relative existence.

The experience of relative existence (*bhava*) is for the gods and the discarnate. Indeed, those who experience a state of awareness like *kaivalya*, experiencing only their own impressions, [eventually] move along to the [experience] of the results corresponding to their own impressions. So also those dissolved into *prakṛti*, their awareness along with its [unsatisfied] striving (*adhikāra*) [for liberation also] dissolved into *prakṛti*, do experience a state like *kaivalya* (liberation), but only so long as the awareness does not return by force of its [unsatisfied] striving.

Discussion

There is weird irony here: the state of the liberated is very similar to *asambhūti*, since individuality and materiality, the pleasures of creation, are renounced by going beyond both progression and regression. This may imply a third entity such as *puruṣa* in YS and *Sāṃkhya-kārikā* (SK).

Study Questions

1. What do you think is the importance of differentiating the two results Śaṅkara outlines: attaining super normal powers, and merging into primordial matter?[1]
2. How do Śaṅkara and Madhva differ in their explanations of ĪU 13?
3. The received "scientific" viewpoint on the mechanics of creation in Indian philosophy concerns a material universe woven and built up out of three primary threads of being or *guṇa*-s, namely *sattva, rajas,* and *tamas* (purity, energy, and solidity). This concept, elaborated from the Upaniṣads in later Sāṃkhya/Yoga philosophy, is perhaps adumbrated here. Explain the basic concepts of periodic creation and dissolution of the

[1]Some sources indicate that after merging into primordial matter (*prakṛti-laya*) one reappears after dissolution as *iśvara*, the yogic God. See, for instance, Vijñāna-bhikṣu's commentary *Yoga-vārtika* on YS 1.19 and specially his commentary on *Sāṃkhya-sūtra* 3.56.

universe in Indian philosophy. The YS and the SK are important texts in this regard. (See, for example, YS 4.34. which relates the achievement of liberation (*kaivalya*) spiritually to the material *pratiprasava*, or regression/reabsorption of the mind/body complex made of *guṇa*-s.)

Mantra Fourteen

Śaṅkara's Introduction to Mantra Fourteen

yata evamataḥ samuccayaḥ sambhūtyasambhūtyupāsanayor yukta eva eka-puruṣa-arthatvācca ity āha—

Indeed, because of this, the combination of meditation on progression and regression is appropriate and because of [both] being the concern of just a single human, thus he says:

संभूतिं च विनाशं च
यस्तद् वेदोभयं सह।
विनाशेन मृत्युं तीर्त्वा
संभूत्यामृतमश्नुते॥ १४॥

Progression and destruction,
One who knows both together
Crossing death by destruction
Gains immortality by progression. (14)

saṃbhūtiṃ ca vināśaṃ ca
yastadvedobhayaṃ saha|
vināśena mṛtyuṃ tīrtvā
saṃbhūtyāmṛtamaśnute|| 14||

संभूतिं च विनाशं च
यस्तद्वेदोभयं सह।
विनाशेन मृत्युं तीर्त्वा
संभूत्यामृतमश्नुते॥ १४॥

संभूतिं च विनाशं च
saṃbhūtiṃ ca vināśaṃ ca
Progression and destruction,

यस्तद्वेदोभयं सह।
yas tad veda ubhayaṃ saha|
One who that knows, both together,

विनाशेन मृत्युं तीर्त्वा
vināśena mṛtyuṃ tīrtvā
By destruction crossing death,

संभूत्यामृतम् अश्नुते॥
saṃbhūtyā amṛtam aśnute||
By progression gains immortality.

sambhūtim (fem. acc. sing.) noun *sambhūti*: "birth, origin, production; growth, increase." Here: "progression."

ca (ind.) a conjunctive particle meaning "and, both, also, moreover, as well as."

vināśam (masc. acc. sing.) noun *vināśa*: "utter loss, annihilation, perdition, destruction, decay, death, removal." Here: "destruction."

ca See above.

yas (masc. nom. sing.) rel. pron. *yad*: "who, which, what, whichever, whatever, that." Here: "he who, or whoever."

tat demonstrative pronoun *tad*: "he, she, it, that, this." Here: "those [two]."

veda (3rd pers. sing. perf.) from $\sqrt{vid}$ (cl. 2 P.): "to know, understand, perceive, learn, become or be acquainted with, be conscious of, have a correct notion of." Here: "he/she/it knows." Note: though this is a perfect form which should indicate an action in the past, it often replaces the present form (*vetti*), as it does here, and has a present meaning.

ubhayam (neut. acc. sing.) adj. (*ubhaya*): "both, of both kinds, in both ways, in both manners." Here: "both."

saha (ind.) "in common, in company, jointly, conjointly, in concert." Here: "together."

vināśena (masc. instr. sing.) See *vināśa* above. Here: "by or through destruction."

mṛtyum (masc. acc. sing.) *mṛtyu*: "death, dying."

tīrtvā gerund with the suffix *tvā* of the root $\sqrt{tṝ}$ (cl. 1, P): "to pass across or over, cross over (a river); to surpass, overcome, subdue, escape." As a gerund it means: "having crossed over or beyond."

sambhūtyā (fem. instr. sing.) See *sambhūti* above. Here: "by or through progression."[4]

amṛtam (neu. acc. sing.) *amṛta* (lit. not dead; the passive participle of the verb $\sqrt{mṛ}$ [cl. 6, A and cl. 1, U.]: "to die," with the negative prefix *a*: not dead, undead). As a neuter noun it means: "collective body of immortals; world of immortality, heaven, eternity; immortality; final emancipation."

aśnute (3rd. pers. sing. pres.) $\sqrt{aś}$ (cl. 5, A): "to reach, come to, arrive at, get, gain, obtain." Here: "he/she attains."

[4] Śaṅkara claims this is *a-sambhūti*, the "a" combining with the final "ā" of the previous word (*tīrtvā*), in which case it means regression. Thus, it stands for *prakṛti* or primordial matter, the meditation on which leads to a kind of immortality called *prakṛti-laya* or merging into *prakṛti* in a kind of unconscious sleep. The "a" of the *asambhūti* earlier in the verse is deleted.

Progression and destruction,
One who knows both together
Crossing death by destruction
Gains immortality by progression. (14)

Śaṅkara's Commentary

sambhūtiṃ ca vināśaṃ ca yas tad veda ubhayaṃ saha *vināśo dharmo yasya kāryasya sa tena dharmiṇā abhedena ucyate vināśa iti, tena tad upāsanena anaiśvaryam adharma-kāmādidoṣajātaṃ ca mṛtyuṃ tīrtvā hiraṇyagarbhopāsanena āpti hy aṇimādi-prāptiḥ phalam, tena anaiśvaryādimṛtyum atītya asambhūtyā avyākṛtopāsanayā* **amṛtaṃ** *prakṛtilayalakṣaṇam* **aśnute|** **sambhūtiṃ ca vināśaṃ ca** *ity atra avarṇalopena nirdeśo draṣṭavyaḥ prakṛtilayaphalaśrutyanurodhāt|| 14||*

Progression and destruction, one who knows both together: destruction means the characteristic state of an effect when it becomes one with its substratum [or cause] [unmanifest matter], thus destruction; **this** [destruction], by this, by meditation on this; **death**, i.e. lack of supernormal power produced by weaknesses such as vice, desire, etc.; **crossing death** by meditation on the Golden Embryo (Hiraṇya-garbha) whose result is indeed the advent of the supernormal powers of minification, etc.; going beyond death [understood as] lack of supernormal power, etc. by meditation on the unmanifest, that is, by meditation on the undeveloped [materiality]; **Gains immortality**, meaning the state of being dissolved into unmanifest materiality. **Progression and destruction** (*[a]sambhūtiṃ ca vināśaṃ ca*); here, because of compliance with the scriptural result of merging into unmanifest matter, one is to understand the dropping of the letter "a" [in the first *asambhūti*] as an indication of that.[5] (14)

[5]Śaṅkara wants us to understand that the word *sambhūti* which occurs twice in the verse is really *a-sambhūti*. In the second occurrence it is possible that the "a" at its beginning has been joined with the final "ā" in the preceding word *tīrthvā* in external *sandhi*. In the first occurrence of *sambhūti*, however, it comes at the very beginning of the verse and clearly has no "a" at its beginning. If the word is really *asambhūti* Śaṅkara has to explain why the "a" is missing in the first occurrence of the word. He argues that, in order to reinforce the teachings which he sees as given by this verse, "immortality" here really means the merging of the living being into primordial matter (*prakṛti-laya*). Thus one should see the elision of the letter "a" in the first *sambhūti* as a lingusitic illustration or indication of the merging of the living being into *prakṛti*. As the "a" has disappeared from *sambhūti* so has the living being disappeared into primordial matter. Śaṅkara, thus, claims here that destruction (*vināśa*) is equivalent to the progression (*sambhūti* and *sambhava*) of the previous two mantras because meditation on the progression brings the supernormal powers whereas through *asambhūti* one gains the result of merging into primordial matter. This interpetation is forced on Śaṅkara because he refuses to accept the Upaniṣad's plain and simple claim that death can really be transcended by *asambhūti* and immortality can really be gained by *sambhūti*. While it is not clear what these two terms meant to the author of the text or the original audience of the text, it seems clear that real transcendence of death and real immortality were intended. Why would one write about the non-real versions of them? If, for example, we were to take *asambhūti* as disengagement or detachment from impermanent, unchangeable things and *sambhūti* as engagement with or attachment to the unchanging Self, then we find a meaning for the mantra that resonates with thousands of later Indic texts (Hindu, Buddhist, and Jaina) and that can be connected with a pan-Indic belief about how liberation can be achieved.

Discussion

Here Śaṅkara interprets the meaning of the word *vināśa* which we have translated in the verse, "[physical] destruction." He takes it to mean "effect" (*kārya*) because effects are said to be non-different from their causes and thus they do not truly exist separately from their causes, the substratum of unmanifest materiality. They thus represent what all material forms dissolve back into. By meditation on destruction one overcomes death which Śaṅkara regards as impotence produced by vice (*adharma*), lust (*kāma*) and so forth. The result of this meditation on destruction which Śaṅkara equates with "meditating on the Golden Embryo (*hiraṇya-garbha*)" is the acquisition of the eight supernormal powers or *siddhis*. In Sāṃkha-Yoga these eight *siddhis* or supernormal powers are called mastery of the elements (earth, fire, water, air, and space)

The undeveloped (*avyākṛta*) here refers to *prakṛti*, or untransformed, material nature (*prakṛtir avikṛtiḥ*, *Sāṅkhya-kārikā*, 3). It is regarded as the material cause (*upādāna*) of the universe. It is different from the spiritual principle, *puruṣa*, which is not material and is not subject to transformation (*na prakṛtir na vikṛtiḥ puruṣaḥ*, *Sāṅkhya-kārikā*, 3).

Study Questions

1. The crux of what the ĪU is saying comes down to a reconciliation of the opposites by transcending and/or combining both. This is again one of the most puzzling passages (like Mantra 11K) of the whole ĪU. What do you make of it—this secret cryptic formula for liberation?
2. Again compare the Śaṅkara and Madhva interpretations of the two verses.
3. If one understands the description of the true Self, the Lord, given in *mantra*-s 4-8, why is verse 14 not a surprise?
4. Ježić argues that this verse in the ĪUM is originally the last verse, the last thought of the whole ĪU. Why might the ĪU end in this way? What effect would this *mantra* have as the final thought?

Mantra Fifteen

Śaṅkara's Introduction to Mantra Fifteen

mānuṣadaivavittasādhyaṃ phalaṃ śāstralakṣaṇaṃ prakṛti-laya-antam| etāvatī saṃsāra-gatiḥ| ataḥ paraṃ pūrvoktam **ātmā eva abhūd vijānata** *iti sarva-ātma-bhāva eva sarva-eṣaṇāsaṃnyāsajñānaniṣṭhāphalam| evaṃ dviprakāraḥ pravṛttinivṛttilakṣaṇo vedārtho 'tra prakāśitaḥ| tatra pravṛttilakṣaṇasya vedārthasya vidhipratiṣedhalakṣaṇasya kṛtsnasya prakāśane pravargya-antaṃ brāhmaṇam upayuktam| nivṛttilakṣaṇasya vedārthasya prakāśane 'ta ūrdhvaṃ bṛhad-āraṇyakam upayuktam|*

The goal of [finally] becoming one with primordial matter (*prakṛti-laya-anta*) according to the scriptures is the result acquired by human and divine attainments. The cycle of birth and death extends up to that. Beyond that, as it was said earlier [in mantra 7]: **realizing "the self has become all beings,"** becoming the Self of all, is indeed the result of the path of knowledge by renunciation of all desires. Indeed, the goal of the Veda here is elucidated as having two modes called activity and quiescence. With respect to this the *Brāhmaṇas* ending with the "ceremony of the earthenware pot" (*pravargya*)[6] are useful for the whole elucidation of the goal of the Veda called activity (*pravṛtti*), i.e. injunctions and prohibitions. With respect to elucidating the goal of the Veda characterized as quiescence (*nivṛtti*), the later Great Forest [Upaniṣad, *Bṛhad-āraṇyaka*] is useful.

tatra niṣeka-ādi-śmaśāna-antaṃ karma kurvan jijīviṣed yo vidyayā saha apara-brahma-viṣayayā tad-uktaṃ **vidyāṃ ca avidyāṃ ca yas tad veda ubhayaṃ saha| avidyayā mṛtyuṃ tīrtvā vidyayā amṛtam asnute** *iti|*

In this matter, beginning with insemination and ending with the cremation ground, one who wishes to live doing rituals through knowledge of the lower Brahman is described [in Mantra 11]: **Knowledge and ignorance, one who knows both together, crossing death by ignorance, gains immortality by knowledge.**

tatra kena mārgeṇa amṛtatvam aśnuta ity ucyate| tad yat tat satyam asau sa āditỵo ya eṣa etasmin maṇḍale puruṣo yaś ca ayaṃ dakṣiṇe 'kṣan puruṣa etad ubhayaṃ satyam| brahma-upāsīno yathā ukta-karma-kṛc ca yaḥ so 'nta-kāle prāpte satya-ātmānam ātmanaḥ prāpti-dvāraṃ yācate hiraṇ-mayena pātreṇa iti|

[Question:] By what path will he attain immortality?

[Answer:] With reference to this matter it is stated: that which is Truth, he is the Infinite Sun who is the

[6]The *Īśā Upaniṣad* forms the fortieth or final chapter of the *Vājasaneyī Saṃhitā* or the *White Yajur Veda.* The three chapters before it in the *saṃhitā* text contain the *mantras* for the performance of the *pravargya* rite. Similarly, the *brāhmaṇa* text for the *saṃhitā*, which is the *Śatapatha-brāhmaṇa*, discusses the *pravargya* rite just before the beginning of the *Bṛhad-āraṇyaka Upaniṣad*, which forms the final chapters of that *brāhmaṇa*. Thus, the *Īśā* and the *Bṛhad-āraṇyaka* are in parallel positions, the first belonging to the *mantra* or hymn part of the Veda and the latter to *brāhmaṇa* or commentary part. The BU is meant to be considered the *brāhmaṇa* commentary on the ĪU. The *pravargya* rite was a ceremony that preceded the *agniṣṭoma* or *soma* sacrifice. Fresh milk is poured into a heated earthenware vessel called a *mahavīra* or a *gharma* and is offered to the twin gods, the Aśvins or "horsemen." The transition from *pravargya* rite to Upaniṣad signals the end of the activity path and the beginning of the quiescence path of the Veda.

Person (spirit) in this orb and the Person (spirit) in the right eye—both are the Truth. He who worships [this lower] Brahman and does rituals as stated, having come to his final moment, prays to the true Self for the gateway to the Self, with the words "By a golden disc ... ."

हिरण्मयेन पात्रेण
सत्यस्यापिहितं मुखम्।
तत्त्वं पूषन्नपावृणु
सत्यधर्माय दृष्टये॥ १५ ॥

By a golden disc
The door of truth is hid.
Do thou uncover it, Oh Nourishing Sun,
Reveal it for one firm in the Truth. (15)

hiraṇmayena pātreṇa
satyasyāpihitaṃ mukham|
tattvaṃ pūṣannapāvṛṇu
satyadharmāya dṛṣṭaye|| 15||

हिरण्मयेन पात्रेण
सत्यस्यापिहितं मुखम्।
तत्त्वं पूषन्नपावृणु
सत्यधर्माय दृष्टये॥ १५॥

हिरण्मयेन पात्रेण
hiraṇ-mayena pātreṇa
Made of gold, by a disc

सत्यस्यापिहितं मुखम्।
satyasya apihitaṃ mukham|
Of the truth, covered, the door [face]

तत्त्वं पूषन्नपावृणु
tat tvaṃ pūṣann apāvṛṇu
It thou, oh Nourishing Sun, uncover

सत्य-धर्माय दृष्टये॥
satya-dharmāya dṛṣṭaye||
For one in Truth firm to see.

hiraṇ-mayena (neut. sing. instr.) adj. formed with the *mayaṭ* ending, which when added to the end of *hiraṇya* (gold) means "made of gold, golden." Here: "golden."

pātreṇa (neut. sing. instr.) *pātra*: "a drinking-vessel, goblet, bowl, cup, dish, pot, plate, utensil." Here: "by a disc."

satyasya (neut. sing. gen.) *satya*: "truth, reality." Here: "of the truth."

apihitam (neut. sing. nom.) *apihita* p.p. of the root $\sqrt{\textit{apidhā}}$ (Vedic verb, no cl. id.): "to place upon or into, put to, give; to shut, close, cover, conceal." Here: "covered."

mukham (neut. sing. nom.) *mukha*: "the mouth, face, countenance."

tat (neut. sing. acc.) demonstrative pronoun *tad*: "he, she, it, that, this." Here: "it."

tvam (2nd pers. sing. nom.) Second pers. personal pronoun *tva*: "you."

pūṣan (masc. sing. voc.) *pūṣan*: "name of a Vedic deity originally connected with the sun." Here: "Oh Nourishing Sun."

apāvṛṇu (2nd. pers. sing. imper.) *apa* + *ā* + $\sqrt{\textit{vṛ}}$ (cl. 5, U): "to open, uncover, reveal." Here: "reveal."

satya-dharmāya (masc. sing. dat.) comp. *satya* (truth, reality) + *dharma* (virtue, morality, practice, conduct, merit). Here: "for one firm in the truth."

dṛṣṭaye (fem. sing. dat.) *dṛṣṭi*: " sight, the faculty of seeing; the mind's eye, wisdom, intelligence." Here: "to reveal."

By a golden disc
The door of truth is hid
Do thou uncover it, Oh Nourishing Sun,
Reveal it for one firm in the Truth. (15)

Śaṅkara's Commentary

hiraṇ-mayam *iva hiraṇ-mayaṃ jyotir-mayam ity etat| tena* **pātreṇa** *iva apidhāna-bhūtena* **satyasya** *eva āditya-maṇḍala-sthasya brahmaṇo* **'pihitam** *ācchāditaṃ* **mukhaṃ** *dvāram|* **tat tvaṃ he pūṣann apāvṛṇv** *apasāraya satya-sya upāsanāt* **satyaṃ dharmo** *yasya mama so 'haṃ satya-dharmā tasmai mahyamathavā yathābhūtasya dharmasyā-nuṣṭhātre* **dṛṣṭaye** *tava satya-ātmana upalabdhaye|| 15||*

Golden, as it were, resplendent. **By a golden plate**, by an object which covers; **of Truth**, abiding in the orb of the Infinite Sun, i.e., of Brahman; **concealed**, i.e., covered; **the mouth**, i.e., the gateway. **Do thou uncover [it] Oh Nourishing Sun**, remove [it], on account of [my] meditating on the Truth, **the one firm in the Truth** for whom Truth is characteristic, i.e., for me: "I am that one whose reality is Truth, for that one or for me or for the one undertaking duties of such nature; **to reveal [it]**, for the perception of your true Self." (15)

Discussion

The word *dharma* used here in the compound word *satya-dharmāya*, which we have translated "to one firm in the truth," is an extremely important term in Indian philosophy and culture. One might say that it is in one form or another the central theme. *Dharma* has a number of meanings which are interrelated. Its essential facets are captured nicely in an introductory text on logic with the definition: "that which is upheld, endures, exists is *dharma*."[1] All things that exist somewhere, with the exception of space and a few other things are *dharmas*. Thus our choice of the word "truth" (in the sense of a really existing thing or a reality) to translate this is justified by this part of the definition. But, *dharma* is more than this. All things that stand in or reside in other things are also *dharmas*. Thus, qualities or characteristics that exist in substances are *dharmas* as well. Qualities like color, shape, type, action and other types of things are the *dharmas* of a thing. A table is a table because it has the *dharma* of table-ness. It is a brown table because it has the *dharma* brown. Thus a thing is what it is because of its *dharma*. The same applies to human beings. They are what they are because of their *dharmas*. Here *dharma* takes on a social meaning. As long as human beings uphold their *dharmas* understood as laws, customs, rules, righteous modes of behavior, proper occupations, and such, human society will be peaceful, fruitful, and well ordered. In this final sense *dharma* has much in common with the Chinese notion of the Dao, the Way, nature sustaining everything.

The reference here could be to the brilliant solar disc, arguably the chief symbol of the manifest Divine in the Vedas. Referring to it as a *pātra* or drinking vessel, dish, plate, disc, etc, implies it both contains something and blocks our vision. Usually opaque things block our vision, block the light, metaphorically block the Ultimate Truth or Ultimate Being. The dying person implores the Ultimate Being to reveal now, at the last moment, its True Nature. An advaitic interpretation works well such that the glorious brilliant disc of the sun as Īś, the Lord, dazzling and visible at this juncture, is understood to reveal that which is transcendent to the outward brightness, the ultimate, *nirguṇa* brahman, the Ultimate Being without qualities, who we find is exactly the same as the True Self of the righteous dying person.

The door, or opening, *mukha*, also means face, so also the Ultimate has a brilliant personal face, but beyond that splendor is a transcendent reality beyond form. The Vedic trope is that the Sun itself is an opening into the higther spheres, the heavenly worlds one wishes to reach after death. The earth sphere opens into the *antarikṣa*, the middle world of the atmosphere and stars, and beyond that *svar* (*svarga*) the heavenly world of Brahmā (*brahma-loka*). So taken literally the fire within the eye of the human and the fire within the sun, are not two things but one. The spirit of the dying man wishes to exit through the right eye and ascend the beam of life energy (*prāṇa*) that extends from the eye to the sun, meeting its gaze, joining in essence with its ray, and penetrating the solar disk (door) into the higher worlds of immortality.

Perhaps a qualified non-dual reading of this would be that the solar disk, with its effugence, conceived either as the non-dual aspect of pure consciousness or as the material sun, can, upon righteous entreaty, spread its rays and reveal the personal Lord who allows entry into his heavenly world. In either viewpoint the visible sun is a transitional gateway blocking true knowledge and the highest spiritual destination. What is beyond the physical brilliance, is, like in meditation with closed eyes, a darkness, glittering with transcendent spiritual brightness. The dying person in the next verse (16K) identifies with the essence of what is revealed, the *puruṣa*, pure consciousness, the cosmic person, behind the mask of solar brilliance.

Śaṅkara identifies this solar disc as Hiraṇya-garbha, the Golden Embryo, which he sees as both differentiated and undiffentiated, or in other words as lower and higher Brahman. See his commentary on BUK 1.4.1-10.

This *mantra* and the following *mantra* surely refer to BUK 5.5.2. There it is said:

> The one that is there is the truth; he is the sun. The person who is in the circle of the sun and the person who is in the right eye, those two are situated in each other. That one (the sun) by its rays is situated in this one (the one in the eye). By its life forces this one (in the eye) is situated in that one (the sun). When he is passing on [dying] he sees that pure circle [of the sun]. These rays do not return to him.[2]

---

[1]Maheśacandra Nyāyaratna, *A Lamp on the Terminology of Neo-logic* (*Navya-nyāya-bhāṣā-pradīpaḥ*), p. 1: *dhriyate tiṣṭhati vartate iti yaḥ, sa dharmaḥ*. (Calcutta: Sanskrit College, 1973) The *Amara-kośa* (p. 52) has *dharati viśvam*, "it supports the world." (Dillī: Caukhambā Saṃskṛta Pratisthāna, [repr. of 1915 edition] 1987)

[2]BUK, 5.5.2: *tad yat tat satyam asau sa ādityaḥ ya eṣa etasmin maṇḍale puruṣaḥ, yaś cāyaṃ dakṣiṇe'kṣan puruṣaḥ; tāv etāv anyonyasmin pratiṣṭitau; raśmibhir eṣo'smin pratiṣṭitaḥ, prāṇair ayam amuṣmin; sa yadotkramiṣyan bhavati śuddham evaitan maṇḍalaṃ paśyati; nainam ete raśmayaḥ pratyāyanti || 2 ||*

Study Questions

1. The last verses are largely taken from earlier texts, the BUK (and BUM). Consult the context for verse 15 in the BUK. Generally these verses are used in the Vedic cremation ritual for the dead—how does that impact your understanding? Where, according to Vedic thinking, do the dead possibly go at the end of life? What does this have to do with the sun?
2. Why are we suddenly addressing the sun? What role does the sun play in early Vedic ritual and thought? What might the sun symbolize? How did Vedic thinking understand the sun in terms of the structure of the universe and its parts and functioning? What happens in this view when the sun rises and sets? Why is the rising of the sun such an important time for religious ritual? (See Olivelle, *Vedic Cosmologies*, xlx-xlix,).
3. What is the golden disc which covers the Truth? Why?
4. In Vedic literature the deity of the sun has a multitude of names (see *mantra* 16); why do you think it is addressed now as *pūṣan*, the Nourisher?
5. Again compare Śaṅkara and Madhva interpretations and commentaries.

Mantra Sixteen

पूषन्नेकर्षे यम सूर्य प्राजापत्य
व्यूह रश्मीन् समूह तेजः।
यत्ते रूपं कल्याणतमं तत्ते पश्यामि
यो ऽसावसौ पुरुषः सो ऽहमस्मि॥ १६॥

Oh Nourishing Sun, the One Seer, Psychopomp,
Solar Orb, Scion of the Lord of Progeny,
Disperse your rays, gather up your brilliance:
So that I take in that most auspicious form of yours—
That very Person, that am I! (16)

pūṣannekarṣe yama sūrya prājāpatya
vyūha raśmīn samūha tejaḥ|
yatte rūpaṃ kalyāṇatamaṃ tatte paśyāmi
yo 'sāvasau puruṣaḥ so 'hamasmi|| 16||

पूषन्नेकर्षे यम सूर्य प्राजापत्य
व्यूह रश्मीन् समूह तेजः।
यत्ते रूपं कल्याणतमं तत्ते पश्यामि
यो ऽसावसौ पुरुषः सो ऽहमस्मि॥ १६॥

पूषन् एकर्षे यम सूर्य प्राजापत्य
pūṣann ekarṣe yama sūrya prājāpatya
Oh Nourishing Sun, One Seer, Psychopomp, Solar Orb, Scion of the Lord of Progeny,

pūṣan (masc. sing. voc.) *pūṣan*: "N. of a Vedic deity (originally connected with the sun, and therefore the surveyor of all things and the conductor on journeys and on the way to the next world."
eka-ṛṣe (masc. sing. voc.) *eka* ("one") + *ṛṣi* ("sage or seer"): "the only or chief sage or seer "
yama (masc. sing. voc.) *yama*: "N. of the god who presides over the forefathers and rules the spirits of the dead." Here: "psychopomp."
sūrya (masc. sing. voc.) *sūrya*: "the sun or its deity (in the Veda the name Sūrya is generally distinguished from Savitṛ, and denotes the most concrete of the solar gods."
prājāpatya (masc. sing. voc.) *prājāpatya*: "related to or born from *prajāpati* (the lord of creatures)."

व्यूह रश्मीन् समूह तेजः।
vyūha raśmīn samūha tejaḥ|
Disperse rays, gather up brilliance:

vyūha (2nd pers. sing. imp.) *vi* + $\sqrt{\bar{u}h}$ (cl 1, U): "to push or move apart, place asunder, divide, distribute."
raśmīn (masc. plu. acc.) *raśmi*: "a ray of light, beam, splendour."
samūha (2nd pers. sing. imp.) *sam* + $\sqrt{\bar{u}h}$ (cl 1, U): "to sweep together, bring or gather together, collect, unite."
tejaḥ (neut. sing. acc.) *tejas*: "point or top of a flame or ray, glow, glare, splendor, brilliance, light, fire."

यत्ते रूपं कल्याणतमं तत्ते पश्यामि
yat te rūpaṃ kalyāṇatamaṃ tat te paśyāmi
That which is your form most auspicious that I see—

yat (neut. sing. acc.) relative pron. *yad*: "who, which." Here: "which."
te (masc. sing. gen.) personal pron. *yuṣmad*: "you." Here: "your."
rūpam (neut. sing. acc.) *rūpa*: "any outward appearance or phenomenon or colour (often pl.), form, shape, figure."
kalyāṇatamam (neut. sing. acc.) *kalyāṇa-tama*: "most beautiful, agreeable; illustrious, noble, generous; excellent, virtuous, good." *Tama* is a superlative affix.
tat (neut. sing. acc.) demonstrative pron. *tad*: "that, he, she."
te See above.
paśyāmi (1st pers. sing. pres.) $\sqrt{paś}$ (only in pres. P.): "behold, look at, envision, observe, perceive, notice."

योऽसावसौ पुरुषः सोऽहमस्मि
yo 'sāv asau puruṣaḥ so 'ham asmi
Who is that person, he I am!

yaḥ (masc. sing. nom.) relative pron. *yad*: "who, which." Here: "who."
asau (masc. sing. nom.) demonstrative pron. *adas*: "that, he, she." Here: "he."
puruṣaḥ (masc. sing. nom.) *puruṣa*: "a man, male, human being; the primeval man as the soul and original source of the universe; the Supreme Being or Soul of the universe."
saḥ (masc. sing. nom.) demonstrative pron. *tad*: "that, he, she." Here: "he."
aham (masc./fem. sing. nom) personal pron. *asmad*: "I, we." Here: "I."
asmi (1st pers. sing. pres.) $\sqrt{as}$ (cl 2, P.): "to be, live, exist, be present; to take place, happen; to abide, dwell, stay; to belong to." Here: "am."

Oh Nourishing Sun, the One Seer, Psychopomp,
Solar Orb, Scion of the Lord of Progeny,
Disperse your rays, gather up your brilliance:
So that I take in that most auspicious form of yours—
That very Person, that am I! (16)

Śaṅkara's Commentary

he **pūṣan** *jagataḥ poṣaṇāt pūṣā ravis tathā eka eva ṛṣati gacchati ity* **ekarṣiḥ**—*he ekarṣe tathā sarvasya saṃyamanād* **yamaḥ**—*he yama tathā raśmīnāṃ prāṇānāṃ rasānāñca svīkaraṇāt sūryaḥ—he sūrya prajāpaterapatyaṃ* **prājāpatyaḥ**—*he prājāpatya* **vyūha** *vigamaya* **raśmīn** *svān*| **samūha** *ekīkuru upasaṃharate tejas tāpakaṃ jyotiḥ*|

Oh Nourishing Sun, *pūṣan*, "nourisher," [from] he nourishes the world, i.e., the Sun (*ravi*), similarly, **the One Seer [Traveler]**,[7] (*ekarṣe*), from he rushes on alone, he goes; likewise, **oh Psychopomp** (*yama*), from "guiding" (*sam* + *yam*) everything; likewise, **oh Solar Orb**, (*sūrya*), from appropriating the essences, the rays, the life energies; **oh Scion of the Lord of Progeny** (*prajāpati*), meaning offspring of Prajāpati; **spread out your rays**, spread out, separate your rays; **focus**, unite; collect; **brilliance**, burning light.

yat te *tava* **rūpaṃ kalyāṇatamam** *atyanta-śobhanaṃ* **tat te** *tava ātmanaḥ prasādāt* **paśyāmi**| *kiñca ahaṃ na tu tvāṃ bhṛtyavad yāce yo* **'sāv** *ādityamaṇḍalastho vyāhṛtyavayavaḥ puruṣaḥ puruṣākāratvātpūrṇaṃ vānena prāṇa-buddhyā ātmanā jagat samastam iti puruṣaḥ puri śayanād vā puruṣaḥ* **so 'ham asmi** *bhavāmi*|| *16*||

That most auspicious form of yours, i.e. exceedingly glorious, **I take in that form of yours**, by the grace of the Self; but in no way do I implore you as a subordinate. He who resides in the circle of the sun, with the *vyāhṛti*-s[8] as his limbs, a "person" because of having the form of a person, or because the whole world is filled (*pūrṇam*) by his nature as intelligence (*buddhi*) and life energy (*prāṇa*); or because he dwells in the "city" (*pur*) [of the body or heart]. Thus is he a "person" (*puruṣa*). **That (Person) am I**, I become. (16)

[7] The word *ṛṣi* generally means "seer, sage, singer of hymns." Śaṅkara also connects the word with the verbal root $\sqrt{ṛṣ}$ "to go or to move," which one could translate "traveler." Together with *eka* "one" it means the "one or only traveler or mover."

[8] The utterances *bhūḥ, bhuvaḥ, svaḥ* denoting the three worlds: earth, sky, and heaven.

Study Questions

1. Again we have verses quoted from earlier sources. Explain the original contexts: BUK 5.15.2 (BUM 5.3), RS 1.189.1->18b, AS 4.39.10b)
2. The sun here is being asked to diminish its light, "Disperse your rays, gather up your brilliance." Why?
3. The key phrase at the end of the verse needs explanation—"That very Person, that am I!" Use the first half of the ĪU to explain this mysterious statement. Why is it particularly important at the time of death?
4. Again compare the Śaṅkara and Madhva interpretations and commentaries. How do they differ? Why?
5. Notice that most of 16K is not in the M version, which does not include 16K abc! What more does the addition of these lines add to the ĪU? Would it be incomplete without them as in M?

Mantra Seventeen

वायुरनिलममृतम्
अथेदं भस्मान्तं शरीरम्।
ओं क्रतो स्मर कृतं स्मर
क्रतो स्मर कृतं स्मर॥ १७॥

[May my] vital breath [repair] to immortal air,
And this body now to its end in ashes;
Oṃ, oh Mental Fire, remember what has been done,
Remember, oh Mental Fire, remember what has been done!

vāyuranilamamṛtam
athedaṃ bhasmāntaṃ śarīram|
oṃ krato smara kṛtaṃ smara
krato smara kṛtaṃ smara|| 17||

वायुरनिलममृतम्
अथेदं भस्मान्तं शरीरम्।
ओं क्रतो स्मर कृतं स्मर
क्रतो स्मर कृतं स्मर॥ १७॥

वायुरनिलममृतम्
vāyur anilam amṛtam
Vital breath to air immortal

अथ इदं भस्मान्तं शरीरम्
atha idaṃ bhasmāntaṃ śarīram
And this end in ashes body;

ओं क्रतो स्मर कृतं स्मर
oṃ krato smara kṛtaṃ smara
Oṁ, oh Mental Fire, remember what has been done, remember!

क्रतो स्मर कृतं स्मर
krato smara kṛtaṃ smara
Oh Mental Fire, remember what has been done, remember!

vāyuḥ (masc. nom. sing.) *vāyu*:"wind, air; the god of the wind."
anilam (masc. acc. sing.) *anila*: "air or wind; the god of wind;"
amṛtam (masc. acc. sing.) mfn. *amṛta*: "immortal; imperishable."
atha ind.: "now; then; moreover; rather; certainly; but; else; what? how else?"
idam (neut. nom. sing.) dem. pron. (*idam*): "this."
bhasma-antam (neut. nom. sing.) mfn. *bhasman* ("ashes") + *anta* ("end"); "that which ends in ashes."
śarīram (neut. nom. sing.) *śarīra*: "the body, bodily frame, solid parts of the body."
om ind.: "a word of solemn affirmation and respectful assent, sometimes translated by 'yes, verily, so be it;' appears first in the Upaniṣads as a mystic monosyllable, and is there set forth as the object of profound religious meditation, the highest spiritual efficacy being attributed not only to the whole word but also to the three sounds: a, u, m."
krato (masc. voc. sing.) *kratu*: "plan, design, intention, resolution, determination, purpose; sacrificial rite or ceremony, sacrifice, offering, worship." Here: "mental fire."
smara (2nd pers. impv.) $\sqrt{smṛ}$ (cl. 1, P.): "to remember, recollect, bear in mind, call to mind, think of, be mindful of."
kṛtam (neut. acc. sing.) *kṛta*: "deed, work, action; service done, kind action, benefit."
smara Same as above.
krato Same as above.
smara Same as above.
kṛtam Same as above.
smara Same as above.

[May my] vital breath [repair] to immortal air,
And this body now to its end in ashes;
Oṃ, oh Mental Fire,[1] remember what has been done,
Remember, oh Mental Fire, remember what has been done! (17)

[1]It is difficult to determine how to translate this word *krato*. It is clearly *kratu* in the vocative case. So, *kratu* is being addressed, but who or what is *kratu*? *Kratu* does not seem to refer to some deity or external power here. It seems instead to refer to some aspect of oneself: one's wisdom, intelligence, good judgement, good intention, or will. One is reminded of the teaching in the *Bhagavad-gītā* (8.6) to the effect that whatever one remembers at the time of death, to that state or condition one goes. One's awareness, therefore, should be directed to one's best achievements at the time of death.

Śaṅkara's Commentary

atha *idānīṃ mama mariṣyato* **vāyuḥ** *prāṇo 'dhyātma-paricchedaṃ hitvā adhidaivatā-ātmānaṃ sarva-ātmakam* **anilam amṛtaṃ** *sūtra-ātmānaṃ pratipadyatām iti vākya-śeṣaḥ| liṅgaṃ ca idaṃ jñāna-karma-saṃskṛtam utkrāmatv iti draṣṭavyaṃ mārga-yācana-sāmarthyāt| atha* **idaṃ śarī-**

Now, at this very moment may my dying **breath**, my vital energy, becoming separated from its own limitation, attain the **immortal**, universal [expanse of] divine **air**, the Thread-Self [pervading all, like a thread links the beads of a necklace]. "May it attain" is the unstated

ram *agnau hutaṃ* **bhasmāntaṃ** *bhūyāt| om iti yathā upāsanam oṃ-pratīka-ātmakatvāt satyātmakam agnyākhyaṃ brahma-abhedena ucyate|* **he krato** *saṅkalpātmaka* **smara** *yanmama smartavyaṃ tasya kālo 'yaṃ pratyupasthito 'taḥ smara| etāvantaṃ kālaṃ bhāvitaṃ kṛtam agne smara yan mayā bālya-prabhṛty-anuṣṭhitaṃ karma tacca smara|* **krato smara kṛtaṃ smara** *iti punar vacanam ādara-artham|| 17||*

remainder of the expression. Moreover, "may this subtle body, perfected by both rituals and knowledge, ascend," is to be seen in this passage because of the sense of entreating the [best] path [beyond death]. And [may] **this body now to its end in ashes**; i.e., be offered as oblation to the sacred fire. **Om**, due to its nature as a symbol, is said to be identical with Brahman, whose nature is truth, called fire, according to this prayerful invocation [by the dying person]. **Oh Mental Fire**, whose nature is focused intention, **remember** that which is to be remembered by me at this time which has arrived—thus **remember. Remember** what I have dwelled upon up to this time; **oh Mental Fire, remember** that which was accomplished from my youth forward. **Remember, oh Mental Fire, remember what has been done**. The repetition of the expression is to show deep concern. (17)

Study Questions

1. This verse makes the context of death and cremation explicit. Research Hindu cremation practices—what do they have to do with sacrifice? What is the role of the deity Agni? Is there any possible connection with the sun?
2. Why do you think the injunction to remember repeatedly is so important? Who is to remember what? Why?
3. Why is the breath (the life energy) enjoined to return to the air and the body to the ashes? What remains—where will the remaider go?
4. Again compare the Śaṅkara and Madhva interpretations and commentaries. How do they differ? Why?
5. Notice that the possibly older M version of the ĪU begins the last section with this 16K verse as 15M. Why might this verse be moved forward?

Mantra Eighteen

Śaṅkara's Introduction to Mantra Eighteen

punar anyena mantreṇa mārgaṃ yācate—

Once again, with another *mantra* he asks for the path:

अग्ने नय सुपथा राये अस्मान्
विश्वानि देव वयुनानि विद्वान्।
युयोध्यस्मज्जुहुराणमेनो
भूयिष्ठां ते नम उक्तिं विधेम॥ १८॥

Oh Sacred Fire, lead us for glory on the path of light!
Oh God, knowing all [our] ways,
Overcome our crooked misdeeds.
We offer to you the greatest praise! (18)

agne naya supathā rāye asmān
viśvāni deva vayunāni vidvān|
yuyodhyasmajjuhurāṇam eno
bhūyiṣṭhāṃ te nama uktiṃ vidhema|| 18||

अग्ने नय सुपथा राये अस्मान्
विश्वानि देव वयुनानि विद्वान्।
युयोध्यस्मज्जुहुराणम् एनो
भूयिष्ठां ते नम उक्तिं विधेम॥ १८॥

अग्ने नय सुपथा राये अस्मान्
agne naya supathā rāye asmān
Oh Sacred Fire, lead by virtuous path for glory us!

विश्वानि देव वयुनानि विद्वान्।
viśvāni deva vayunāni vidvān|
All, oh God, ways knowing,

युयोध्यस्मज्जुहुराणम् एनो
yuyodhy asmaj juhurāṇam eno
Overcome our crooked misdeeds.

भूयिष्ठां ते नम उक्तिं विधेम
bhūyiṣṭhāṃ te nama uktiṃ vidhema
Greatest to you reverence-statement we offer!

agne (masc. voc. sing.) *agni*: "fire, sacrificial fire; the god of fire."
naya (2nd pers. impv. sing.) $\sqrt{}$*nī* (cl. 1, U.): "to lead, guide, conduct, direct, govern."
supathā (masc. instr. sing.) *su* ("good") + *pathin* ("a way, path, road, course"): "a good road; virtuous course, good conduct."
rāye (fem. dat. sing.) *rai*: "property, possessions, goods, wealth , riches."
asmān (masc. acc. pl.) 1st. pers. pron. *asmad*: "I, we (du.), we (pl.)." Here: "us."
viśvāni (neut. acc. pl.) mfn. *viśva*: "all, every, every one; whole, entire, universal."
deva (masc. voc. sing.) *deva*: "a deity, god."
vayunāni (neut. acc. pl.) *vayuna*: "a path, way; mark, aim; knowledge, wisdom."
vidvān (masc. nom. sing.) mfn. *vidvas*: "one who knows, knowing, understanding, learned, intelligent, wise, mindful of, familiar with, skilled in."
yuyodhi (2nd pers. pf. impv. sing.) $\sqrt{}$*yudh* (cl. 4, Ā.): "to fight, wage war, oppose or (rarely) overcome in battle; to fight with."
asmat (masc. gen. pl.) 1st. pers. pron. *asmad*: "I, we (du., pl.)." Here: "our."
juhurāṇam (neut. acc. sing.) mfn. *juhurāṇa* from the root $\sqrt{}$*jvṛ* (cl. 1, P.) : "to deviate or diverge from the right line, be crooked or curved, bend, go crookedly or wrongly or deviously, stumble, fall down." This form appears to be a perfect participle in the *Ātmanepada*.
enaḥ (neut. acc. sing.) *enas*: "mischief, crime, sin, offence, fault."
bhūyiṣṭhām (fem. acc. sing.) mfn. *bhūyiṣṭha*: "most numerous or abundant or great or important, chief, principal."
te (masc. dat. sing.) pers. pron. *yuṣmad*: "you." Here: "unto you."
namaḥ-uktim (fem. acc. sing.) *namas* ("bow, obeisance, reverential salutation, adoration") + *ukti* ("sentence, proclamation, speech, expression, word"): "words of adoration."
vidhema (1st pers. opt. pl.) $\sqrt{}$*vidh* (cl. 6, P.): "to present reverentially, offer, dedicate."

Oh Sacred Fire, lead us for glory on the path of light!
Oh God, knowing all [our] ways,
Overcome our crooked misdeeds.
We offer to you the greatest praise! (18)

Śaṅkara's Commentary

he agne naya *gamaya* **supathā** *śobhanena mārgeṇa| supathā iti viśeṣaṇaṃ dakṣiṇa-mārga-nivṛtty-artham | nirviṇ-ṇo'haṃ dakṣiṇena mārgeṇa gata-āgata-lakṣaṇena ato yāce tvāṃ punaḥ punar gamanāgamanavarjitena śobhanena pathā naya|* **rāye** *dhanāya karma-phala-bhogāya ityarthaḥ*

Oh Sacred Fire, **lead us on**, cause [us] to go [along], **the path of light**, the auspicious path. **Path of light** specifically negates the [less auspicious] southern path [to the world of the ancestors and reincarnation]. I am disgusted by the southern path, characterized by coming

asmān *yathā-ukta-dharma-phala-viśiṣṭān* **viśvāni** *sarvāṇi* **he deva vayunāni** *karmāṇi prajñānāni vā* **vidvāñ** *jānan*|

and going. Thus "I implore you again and again to lead [me] onto the auspicious path without [such] repetitive reincarnation." **For glory** means for wealth, for the enjoyment of the fruits of action. **Us** means us who are qualified by the results of *dharma* previously described; **all**, every one; **oh god**, [our] **ways**, [our] actions or understandings, **knowing**, discerning.

kiñca **yuyodhi** *viyojaya vināśaya* **asmad** *asmatto* **juhurāṇaṃ** *kuṭilaṃ vañcanā-ātmakam* **enaḥ** *pāpam*| *tato vayaṃ viśuddhāḥ santa iṣṭaṃ prāpsyāma ity abhiprāyaḥ*| *kintu vayam idānīṃ te na śaknumaḥ paricaryāṃ kartum*| **bhūyiṣṭhāṃ** *bahutarāṃ te tubhyaṃ* **nama uktiṃ** *namaskāravacanaṃ* **vidhema** *namas-kāreṇa paricarema ity arthaḥ*|

Moreover, **overcome**, destroy, unshackle us from, **our crooked**, characterized by delusion, dishonest, **misdeeds**, evil. Thus, we, being pure, will attain what is desired; this is the intended meaning. But we now are not [even] capable of doing your worship. The **greatest**, the most, **to you, praise**, expressions of homage, **we offer**; "we worship [you] by praising" is meant.

> *avidyayā mṛtyuṃ tīrtvā*
> *vidyayā amṛtam aśnute*| *(ī.u. 11)*
>
> *vināśena mṛtyuṃ tīrtvā*
> *(a)sambhūtyā amṛtam aśnute*| *(ī.u. 14)*

> Crossing death by ignorance,
> Gains immortality by knowledge. (Mantra 11)
>
> Crossing death by destruction,
> Gains immortality by progression. (Mantra 14)

iti śrutvā kecit saṃśayaṃ kurvanti| *atas tannirākaraṇa-arthaṃ saṃkṣepato vicāraṇāṃ kariṣyāmaḥ*|

tatra tāvat kiṃ nimittaḥ saṃśaya ity ucyate|

vidyā-śabdena mukhyā parama-ātma-vidyā eva kasmān na gṛhyate 'mṛtatvaṃ ca|

Hearing those *mantras*, some begin to doubt. Thus, for dispelling those [doubts] we will briefly discuss them.

In this matter firstly, what is the cause of this doubt?

[Objection:] By the word "knowledge" primarily knowledge of the supreme Self is meant; why should we not take it that way here and the same [also for the term] immortality?

nanu uktāyāḥ paramātmavidyāyāḥ karmaṇaś ca virodhāt samuccaya-anupapattiḥ|

[Answer:] Has not the gross insufficiency (*anupapattiḥ*) of their combination due to the antithesis of ritual action and the knowledge of the supreme self already been mentioned?

satyam| *virodhas tu na avagamyate virodha-avirodhayoḥ śāstra-pramāṇakatvāt*| *yathā avidyānuṣṭhānaṃ vidyopāsanañca śāstra-pramāṇakaṃ tathā tad virodha-avirodhāv api*| *yathā ca na hiṃsyāt sarvā bhūtāni iti śāstrād avagataṃ punaḥ śāstreṇa eva bādhyate 'dhvare paśuṃ hiṃsyād iti*| *evaṃ vidyā-avidyayor api syāt*| *vidyā-karmaṇoś ca samuccayaḥ*|

[Objection:] Truly it has! But the incompatibility is not intelligible due to the scriptural proof of both compatibility and incompatibility! Just as the performance of (ritual) (*avidyā*) and the devotion to knowledge [of the gods] is based in scripture, likewise their compatibility and incompatibility is also. Just as: "Do not harm any creature" is taught in scripture and yet again is contradicted by the scripture: "an animal is to be killed in sacrifice," so this should be true of knowledge and ignorance, too, as well as the combination of knowledge and ritual action.

na:

> *dūram ete viparīte viṣūcī*
> *avidyā yā ca vidyā (ka.u. 1.2.4) iti śruteḥ*|

[Answer:] Not at all! For the Veda says:

> These two—knowledge and ignorance—
> Are contrary and divergent.[1]

vidyāṃ ca avidyāṃ ca iti vacanād avirodha iti cen

[Objection:] [But] from the [scriptural] expression [conjoining them] "both knowledge and ignorance," there is no incompatibility.

[1]KaU 1.2.4.

na hetu-svarūpa-phala-virodhāt|

[Reply:] It is not so because of the incompatibility of their results, character, and motivations!

vidyāvidyāvirodhāvirodhayor vikalpāsambhavātsamuccayavidhānādavirodha eva iti cen

[Objection:] Due to the illogical alternative of both the consistency and inconsistency of knowledge and ignorance, [and] because of the explicit (*eva*) placement [here] of them in combination, there is no inconsistency.

na saha-sambhavānupapatteḥ|

[Answer:] This is not so because their co-existence is unintelligible.

krameṇa eka-āśraye syātāṃ vidyā-avidye iti cen

[Objection:] What if knowledge and ignorance occur to one person in succession?

na vidyā-utpattau avidyāyā hy āstatvāt tad-āśraye 'vidyā-anupapatteḥ| na hy agnir uṣṇaḥ prakāśaś ca iti vijñāna-utpattau yasminn āśraye tad-utpannaṃ tasminn eva āśraye śīto 'gnir aprakāśo vā ity avidyāyā utpattir na api saṃśayo 'jñānaṃ vā:

[Reply:] No. Because on the rising of knowledge ignorance sets, therefore the existence of ignorance in the same person is absurd. For indeed with the rising of the certain knowledge that "fire is hot and bright" within someone, then in that same person, of course, the ignorant notion, doubt, or error that "fire is cold or dark" does not occur.

yasmin sarvāṇi bhūtāny
ātmā eva abhūd vijānataḥ|
tatra ko mohaḥ kaḥ śoka
ekatvam anupaśyataḥ|| (ī.u. 7)

When one realizes "the self
Has become all beings,"
Then for the seer of oneness
What delusion and sorrow can there be? (Mantra 7)

iti śokamohādyasambhava-śruteḥ| avidyāsambhavāt tadupādānasya karmaṇo 'py anupapattimavocāma|

From scripture thus [we have the declaration of] the impossibility of sorrow and delusion, etc. [for the self-realized wise]. Since ignorance is non-existant, ritual action resulting from that [*avidyā*] is also logically inconsistent, as we have said.

amṛtam aśnuta ity āpekṣikam amṛtam| vidyā-śabdena parama-ātma-vidyā-grahaṇe hiraṇ-mayena ity ādinā dvāra-mārga-ādi-yācanam anupapannaṃ syāt| tasmād upāsanayā samuccayo na parama-ātma-vijñānena iti yathā asmābhir vyākhyāta eva mantrāṇām artha ity uparamyate|| 18||

[The mantra stating he] "attains immortality" (14) indicates a relative immortality. [If] by the word "knowledge," knowledge of the supreme Self be understood, imploring the [opening] of the gate, etc. by [Mantra 15]: "By a golden disc [the door of the truth is covered]" is logically inconsistent. For this reason the combination [of karma] is with the practice of meditation not with the knowledge of the supreme Self—thus as we have said this is the meaning of the mantras. The matter is concluded. (18)

iti śrīmatparamahaṃsaparivrājakācāryasya śrīśaṅkarabhagavataḥ kṛtāv īśāvāsya-upaniṣad-bhāṣyaṃ sampūrṇam|

Thus, complete is the commentary on the *Īśāvāsya Upaniṣad*, in the work of the blessed Lord Śaṅkara, exemplary teacher, *parama-haṃsa* (supreme swan) among renunciates.

Discussion

As the dying person dissolves, his vital energies and elements (*prāṇas*) dissipating into their spheres, breath to air, body to ashes and earth, mental fire (or willpower or desire), is asked to remember the *karma*, the actions, accumulated over a lifetime, or over many lifetimes, which apparently guide the exiting self to its proper destination. Wrong deeds, it is implored, are to be consumed by the last religious action, the cremation sacrifice. The hope for immortality ends with hopeful praise for the grace of the divine at this last moment.

The BU parallels belong to a different section of the BU than the other triplets, according to Ježić. BUK 5.15.1-4, which gives them a later date than the others; ĪUM 15-16 likewise correspond to BUM 5.3 (except for ĪUM 17 which is a possibly earlier version of ĪUK 15). Ježić believes this means that BUM 5.3 is the oldest.

The ĪUM, possibly the older form of the ĪU, begins this last section with the dissolution of the energetic and physical. It skips ĪUK 16 altogether, with its more explicit non-dualist equasion, "I am He" (*so'ham asmi*),[1] and simply ends with a prayer to the solar disc to uncover higher reality. The verse is striking and makes for a more forceful ending.

Study Questions

1. This verse seems concerned with paths using two different words—*patha* and *vayuna*—why the concern? What other translations of the word *supatha* might be offered?
2. Why is Agni, the deity (*deva*) of fire, being addressed?
3. Compare the Śaṅkara and Madhva interpretations and commentaries. How do they differ? Why?
4. The M version of the ĪU ends with a slightly different version of ĪUK 15. Which ending do you prefer? Why?
5. What new thought does 17Md "*Oṃ*! Space is Brahman" add? What does the sacred sound of Brahman *oṃ*, have to do with space? Why would this version wish to end with that thought? Does that change the meaning fo the ĪU in any way?

[1] Very close to "That you are," *tat tvam asi* (CU, 6.8.7).

Part V

Īśopaniṣad with Another Commentary

Madhva on the *Īśāvāsya Upaniṣad*

Madhvācārya, or simply Madhva (1199-1278 CE) was a great South Indian spiritual leader and commentator on important religious texts, particularly the three source texts of Vedānta (*prasthāna-traya*).[1] He founded or promoted a pre-existing Vaiṣṇava tradition that is still active in South India today. He is known within his tradition by two other names: Pūrṇaprajña ("full wisdom") and Ānandatīrtha ("crossing of bliss"). He advocated the philosophical/religious tradition known as *dvaita*, or [theistic] dualism. Thus, his interpretation of the *Īśā Upaniṣad* differs dramatically from Śaṅkara's non-dualistic approach which is one of the reasons we have included it here. The Upaniṣads have been interpreted differently by different schools of Vedānta, often, it seems, in dialog, either directly or indirectly, with Śaṅkara's interpretation, which is the earliest surviving commentary. The major schools of Vedānta are Śaṅkara's (7th cent. CE.) Non-dualism (Advaita) school, Rāmānuja's (11-12th cents. CE.) Qualified Non-dualism (Viśiṣṭādvaita) school, Nimbārka's (12-13th cents. CE.) Dualism-Non-dualism (Dvaitādvaita) school, Madhva's (12th cent. CE.) Dualism (Dvaita) school, and Caitanya's (16th cent. CE.) Inconceivable Difference-Non-difference (Acintya-bhedābheda) school.

Madhva's commentary is short and relies heavily on Purāṇic quotes, none of which have we been able to trace in any of the currently available editions of those Purāṇas. Madhva was well known for citing verses either from texts that are now lost or from works in which those verses cannot be found. Naturally, the suggestion has been made by his sectarian opponents that he himself has written those verses and ascribed them fictitiously to their sources. Nevertheless, Madhva's view is clear and valuable whether it is authenticated by any of the Purāṇic texts or not. Citing scripture in support of a position does not prove that position true. But in India, it was customary to appeal to authority in support of one's arguments and the authorities were naturally the scriptures or the authors of those scriptures. In Madhva's interpretation the *īś* (Lord, Owner) of the first verse means Viṣṇu, one of the major personal gods of the time. By contrast Śaṅkara and the Upaniṣad itself take Īś to mean the Self or Ātman. Moreover, he explains "killers of the self" (*ātma-hanaḥ*) in the third verse as those who are hostile or inimical towards Viṣṇu. Madhva's is clearly a theistic reading of the Upaniṣad. There are a number of other places in which Madhva's interpretation is quite different from Śaṅkara's. We have changed some of our earlier translations of the *mantras* to reflect Madhva's understanding of them.

Select Bibliography on Madhva

Sarma, Deepak, *An Introduction to Madhva Vedanta.* (Ashgate Pub. Ltd., 2003)

Sharma, B. N. Krishnamurti, *History of the Dvaita school of Vedānta and its literature : from the earliest beginnings to our own time.* 2nd rev. ed. (Delhi: Motilal Banarsidass, 1981.)

Sharma, B. N. Krishnamurti, *Philosophy of Śrī Madhvācārya.* Revised ed. (Delhi: Motilal Banarsidass, 1991, [1986].)

[1] I.e., the Upaniṣads, the *Brahma-sūtras*, and the *Bhagavad-gītā*. A school of Vedānta should have commentaries on these three texts, preferably by the founder of the school.

Īśopaniṣad-bhāṣya—Madhva's commentary on the Īśopaniṣad

nityānitya-jagad-dhātre
nityāya jñāna-mūrtaye|
pūrṇānandāya haraye
sarva-yajña-bhuje namaḥ||

Of worlds eternal and temporary the architect,
Knowledge's eternal form,
The fullness of bliss,
Enjoyer of all sacrifices,
To Hari (Viṣṇu) I bow.

yasmād brahmendrarudrādi-
devatānāṃ śriyo'pi ca|
jñāna-sphūrtiḥ sadā tasmai
haraye gurave namaḥ||

From whom come flashes of wisdom
To gods like Brahmā, Indra, Rudra, and Śrī.
Unto him, Hari, the Guru, I bow.

svāyambhuvo manur etair mantrair bhagavantam ākūti-sūnuṃ yajña-nāmānaṃ viṣṇuṃ tuṣṭāva

Svāyambhuva Manu[2] praised Lord Viṣṇu, [who appeared as] his daughter Ākūti's son [in other words, as his grandson], named Yajña, with these *mantras.*

oṃ īśāvāsyam idaṃ sarvaṃ
yat kiṃ ca jagatyāṃ jagat|
tena tyaktena bhuñjīthā
mā gṛdhaḥ kasya svid dhanam|| 1||

By the Lord indwelt
Is all this, whatever moves
In the world of motion.
Enjoy [only] what is bestowed by him.
Do not steal anyone's property. (1)

svāyambhuvaḥ sva-dauhitraṃ
viṣṇuṃ yajñābhidhaṃ manuḥ|
īśāvāsyādibhir mantrais-
tuṣṭāvāvahitātmanā||

rakṣobhir ugraiḥ samprāptaḥ
khāditum mocitas tadā|
stotraṃ śrutvaiva yajñena
tān hatvā 'vadhyatāṃ gatān||

prādād dhi bhagavāṃs teṣām
avadhyatvaṃ haraḥ prabhuḥ|
tair vadhyatvaṃ tathā'nyeṣām
ataḥ ko 'nyo hareḥ prabhuḥ||
iti brahmāṇḍe|

Svāyambhuva Manu eulogized
Yajña, his daughter's son, who was Viṣṇu
With the *mantras* of the Īśā Upaniṣad,
With concentrated mind.
Captured by fierce goblins
Who wanted to devour him,
He was freed from them then
By Yajña who heard his eulogy,
Killing them who were made invincible.
Lord Hara (Śiva) the mighty
Had made them invulnerable
And made others vulnerable to them.
Thus, who other than Hari is the Almighty?
(Brahmāṇḍa Purāṇa)[3]

bhāgavate cāyam evārtha uktaḥ| īśasyāvāsayogyam īśāvāsyam| jagatyāṃ prakṛtau| teneśena tyaktena dattena bhuñjīthāḥ|

And this is the interpretation presented in the *Bhāga-*

[2]Svāyamabhuva Manu is first of the fourteen Manus who are considered in traditional Hinduism to be the progenitors of mankind in different periods. Svāyambhuva means that he himself came from the "self-born" Brahmā who is according to Hindu cosmology a periodic creator of the universe. Manu's wife was Śatarūpā (hundred-formed) and he had two daughters, Ākūti, and Devahūti.

[3]The verses cited here cannot be found in standard editions of the *Brahmāṇḍa Purāṇa* such as that published by Motilal Banarsidass (Delhi: Motilal Banarsidass, 1973).

vata Purāṇa.[4] Suitable for indwelling by the Lord (Owner) is the meaning of *īśāvāsya*. In the world (*jagatyām*) means in matter (*prakṛti*). You should enjoy what is provided by the Owner.

svataḥ pravṛtty-aśaktatvād
īśāvāsyam idaṃ jagat|
pravṛttaye prakṛtigaṃ
yasmāt sa prakṛtīśvaraḥ||

Since it's unable to function on its own
This world's indwelt by the Owner.
Since he indwells Matter (*prakṛti*)
To make it function,
He is the Lord of Matter.

tad-adhīna-pravṛttitvāt
tadīyaṃ sarvam eva yat|
tad dattenaiva bhuñjīthā
ato nānyaṃ prayācayet||
iti brahmāṇḍe|| 1||

Because its function depends on him
And because everything is his.
You may enjoy whatever he provides.
And one should not ask more.
(Brahmāṇḍa Purāṇa) (1)

kurvann eveha karmāṇi
jijīviṣec chataṁ samāḥ|
evaṃ tvayi nānyatheto 'sti
na karma lipyate nare|| 2||

In this way, by performing actions here
One should live a hundred years.
So there is no other way for you;
No *karma* thus adheres to one. (2)

akurvataḥ karma na lipyate iti nāsti|

[Objection:] Isn't it true that actions do not stick to one who does not act? [Reply:] Not at all!

ajñasya karma lipyeta
kṛṣṇopāstim akurvataḥ|
jñānino'pi yato hrāsa
ānandasya bhaved dhruvam|
ato'lepe'pi lepaḥ syād
ataḥ kāryaiva sā sadā||
iti nāradīye|| 2||

The actions of a fool
Who does not worship Kṛṣṇa
Would definitely stick to him.
For even a wise person's
Joy would surely diminish.
Therefore, even one untouched
Would be soiled. Thus,
It [worship] is always to be done.
(*Nārada Purāṇa*) (2)

asuryā nāma te lokā
andhena tamasāvṛtāḥ|
tāṃs te pretyābhigacchanti
ye ke cātma-hano janāḥ|| 3||

Demonic indeed are those worlds
Covered by blind ignorance,
To which they go after dying
Those people who smother the Self. (3)

suṣṭhu ramaṇa-viruddhatvād asurāṇāṃ prāpyatvāc cāsuryāḥ| na ca ramanty aho asad-upāsanayātma-hana ity uktatvāt|

They [the worlds] are demonic because they are suitably contrary to happiness and attained by demons. And because it is not said that "those who smother the Self, who worship the unreal, are happy."

[4]*Bhāgavata Purāṇa*, Eighth Skandha, Chapter One. The *Bhāgavata Purāṇa* is one of the major sources of modern Hindu belief and practice, especially for those who are worshippers of Viṣṇu or Kṛṣṇa. It is also highly respected among followers of the non-dualistic (Advaita) school of Vedānta. It contains strong strains of non-dualism and theism blended together in its vast corpus.

mahā-duḥkhaika-hetutvāt
prāpyatvād asurais tathā|
asuryā nāma te lokās
tān yānti vimukhā harau||
iti vāmane||

Because they are the one cause
Of extreme misery and by demons won
They are called the demonic worlds.
To them those hostile to Hari go.
(*Vāmana Purāṇa*)

ye ke cety anena niyama uktaḥ| niyamena tamo yānti sarve 'pi vimukhā harau iti ca|| 3||

"Whosoever," by this expression a principle is being stated. By principle all those hostile to Hari go into darkness. (3)

anejad ekaṃ manaso javīyo
nainad devā āpnuvan pūrvam arṣat|
tad dhāvato'nyān atyeti tiṣṭhat
tasminn apo mātariśvā dadhāti|| 4||

One, unshaking, faster than mind,
He knows all before the gods,
Who are unable to know Him.[5]
Though unmoving, He[6] passes up the other runners.
Since He is present Life-energy generates activity. (4)

anejan nirbhayatvāt tad
ekaṃ prādhānyatas tathā|
samyag-jñātum aśakyatvād
agamyaṃ tat-surair api||
svayaṃ tu sarvān agamat
pūrvam eva svabhāvataḥ|
acintya-śaktitaś caiva
sarva-gatvāc ca tat-param||
dravato'tyeti santiṣṭat
tasmin karmāṇy adhān marut|
māruty eva yataś ceṣṭā
sarvā tāṃ haraye 'rpayet||
iti brahmāṇḍe

He does not move because He is fearless.
He is one because He's supreme.
Since they cannot fully understand Him,
He's unknowable even to the gods.
But He himself inherently knew all first.
By His unthinkable power
And all-pervasiveness, He is supreme.
Standing still, He catches those running.
In His presence, the Wind (*marut*) becomes active.
Since movement comes from the Wind,[7]
One should offer all action to Hari.[8]
(Brahmāṇḍa Purāṇa)

ṛṣa jñāne|| 4||

Ṛṣa [in the verb *arṣat*] means to know [as opposed to "to move quickly"]. (4)

tad ejati tan naijati
tad dūre tad v antike|
tad antar asya sarvasya
tad u sarvasyāsya bāhyataḥ|| 5||

Because of Him others shake; He shakes not.
He is far away, but He is near,
He is within everything,
But outside all of this, too.[9] (5)

tadejati tata eva ejatyanyat| tat svayaṃ naijati|

Because of Him things other than Him shake. He himself

[5]This according to Madhva. Compare with our earlier translation:

One, unmoving, faster than the mind,
It rushes ahead of the gods, [who are] unable to overtake It.

[6]The text uses the pronoun *tat* which means "it." Our use of "He" reflects Madhva's theistic interpretation of this Upaniṣad.

[7]*Māruti*, born of or related to the wind or breath (*marut*).

[8]This verse is suggestive of the idea that the wind blows out of fear of Him as found at Taittirīya U., 2.8.1, and Kaṭha U., 2.3.3.

[9]Madhva's interpretation requires a change in the first quarter verse. The rest remains the same.

does not shake.

tato bibheti sarvo'pi
na bibheti hariḥ svayam|
sarva-gatvāt sa dūre ca
bāhye'ntaś ca samīpa-gaḥ||
iti tattva-saṃhitāyām|| 5||

Because of Him all things are afraid.
Hari himself does not fear anything.
He is far because he pervades everything
He comes near, being inside and outside.
(*Tattva-saṃhitā*[10]) (5)

yas tu sarvāṇi bhūtāni
ātmany evānupaśyati|
sarva-bhūteṣu cātmānaṃ
tato na vijugupsate|| 6||

But one who sees
All beings in this very Self
And this Self in all beings
Thenceforth does not wish to hide himself.[11] **(6)**

sarvagaṃ paramātmānaṃ
sarvaṃ ca paramātmani|
yaḥ paśyet sa bhayābhāvān
nātmānaṃ goptum icchati||
iti saukarāyaṇaśrutiḥ|| 6||

That the supreme Self is all-pervading
And all are in the supreme Self,
One who can see that, free from fear,
Does does not wish to hide.
(*Saukarāyaṇa-śruti*) (6)

yasmin sarvāṇi bhūtāny
ātmaivābhūd vijānataḥ|
tatra ko mohaḥ kaḥ śoka
ekatvam anupaśyataḥ|| 7||

When one realizes "the self
Has become all beings,"
Then for the seer of oneness
What delusion, what sorrow can there be? (7)

yasmin paramātmani sarva-bhūtāni sa paramātmaiva tatra sarvabhūteṣv abhūt| evaṃ sarvabhūteṣv ekatvena paramātmānaṃ vijānataḥ ko mohaḥ?

That supreme Self in which all beings exist is itself in all beings. What delusion is there for one who thus knows the supreme Self through its uniformity in all beings?

yasmin sarvāṇi bhūtāni
sa ātmā sarva-bhūtagaḥ|
evaṃ sarvatra yo viṣṇuṃ
paśyet tasya vijānataḥ||
ko mohaḥ ko'thavā śokaḥ
sa viṣṇuṃ paryagād yataḥ||
iti pippalāda-śākhāyām|

He in whom all beings exist
Is the Self exisitng in all beings.
Whoever should thus see Viṣṇu
Everywhere, for such a knower
What delusion, what sorrow can there be,
Since he has completely realized Viṣṇu?
(In the Pippalāda branch)[12]

pūrvoktānuvādena śoka-mohābhāvo'pi vijānataś cātrocyate| abhyāsaś ca sarva-gatvasya tātparya-dyotanārthaḥ|| 7||

Along with the reiteration of things previously stated,[13] the absence of the knower's delusion and sorrow is pre-

[10]This is an unknown text like many that Madhva quotes.

[11]The first three quarter verses are the same as our translation. The fourth, however, differs due to Madhva's interpretation. Ours is: Because of this does not recoil. (6)

[12]Pippalāda, or more properly, Paippalāda is a branch of the Atharva Veda, the other being the Śaunaka branch. Moreover the sage Pippalāda from whom the branch gets its name is said to be the author of the *Praśna Upaniṣad*.

[13]That is, this verse seems to repeat the concept of the omniscience of the Self.

sented here.[14] And the repetition is simply to illuminate the meaning of the concept all-pervading (*sarva-gatatva*). (7)

sa paryagāc chukram akāyam avraṇam
asnāviraṃ śuddham apāpa-viddham|
kavir manīṣī paribhūḥ svayam-bhūr
yāthātathyato 'rthān vyadadhāc chāśvatībhyaḥ samābhyaḥ|| 8||

He[15] attains him[16] who is without sorrow,
Without body or any lack,
Who is without nerves and always pure,
And impervious to evil.
The seer, owner of all minds,
The best of all, self-sufficient,
Who allots things as they should be
For aeons eternal. (8)

śukraṃ tac chokarāhityād
avraṇaṃ nitya-pūrṇataḥ|
pāvanatvād sadā śuddham
akāyaṃ liṅga-varjanāt|
sthūla-dehasya rāhityād
asnāviram udāhṛtam||
evambhūto'pi sārvajñāt
kavir ity eva śabdyate|
brahmādi-sarva-manasāṃ
prakṛter manaso'pi ca||
īśitṛtvān manīṣī sa
paribhūs sarvato varaḥ|
sadā'nyāśrayatvāc ca
svaymabhūḥ parikīrtitaḥ||
sa satyaṃ jagad etādṛṅ
nityam eva pravāhataḥ|
anādy-ananta-kāleṣu
pravāhaika-prakārataḥ||
niyamenaiva sasṛje
bhagavān puruṣottamaḥ|
saj-jñānānanda-śīrṣo'sau
saj-jñānānanda-bāhukaḥ|
saj-jñānānanda-dehaś ca
saj-jñānānanda-pādavān||
evambhūto mahā-viṣṇu-
ryathārthaṃ jagad īdṛśam|
anādy-ananta-kālīnaṃ
sasarjātmecchayā prabhuḥ||
iti vārāhe|| 8||

Because that is without sorrow,
He is called sorrowless (*śukra*).
He is woundless (*avraṇa*)
Since he is always full.
Because he is always purifying,
He is known as pure (*śuddha*).
Since he has no subtle body,
He is without body (*akāya*).
Because he has no gross body,
Being without sinews (*asnāvira*),
Is given as an example.
Even so [without a body], due to his omniscience
He is called the seer (*kavi*).
And because he is owner of the minds
Of Brahmā and the rest and Prakṛti,
He is called wise (*manīṣī*).
He is the best of all (*paribhū*).
Being always without dependence on any other thing,
He is celebrated as self-sufficient.
Bhagavān Puruṣottama truly fashioned,
According to his laws, this eternal world
From one unbroken stream of emanation,
In beginningless and endless time.
His head is being, consciousness, and bliss;
His arms are being, consciousness, and bliss;
His body is being, consciousness, and bliss;
His feet are being, consciousness, and bliss.
Great Viṣṇu, whose nature is such,
Created, this very universe out of his own will
From beginningless and endless time.
(*Varāha Purāṇa*) (8)

[14] This absence of delusion and sorrow is not stated in the previous verse.
[15] The knower of the previous verses.
[16] I.e., Viṣṇu.

andhaṃ tamaḥ praviśanti
ye'vidyām upāsate|
tato bhūya iva te tamo
ya u vidyāyāṃ ratāḥ|| 9||

They enter into blind darkness
Who devote themselves to ignorance
To greater gloom than that go they,
Who desire knowledge. (9)

anyad evāhur vidyayā-
nyad āhur avidyayā|
iti śuśruma dhīrāṇāṃ
ye nas tad vicacakṣire|| 10||

They say one thing indeed
Results from knowledge.
Another from ignorance they say.
Thus have we heard from the wise,
Those who have perceived it for us. (10)

anyathopāsakā ye tu
tamo'ndhaṃ yānty asaṃśayam|
tato'dhikam iva vyaktaṃ
yānti teṣām anindakāḥ||
tasmād yathā-svarūpaṃ tu
nārāyaṇam anāmayam|
ayathārthasya nindāṃ ca ... || 9|| 10||

But those who worship in other ways
Doubtless go to blind darkness.
Clearly into greater gloom
Go those who do not condemn them.
Thus, [those good people who correctly understand]
Both Nārāyaṇa as he really is
And the censure of the unreal ... . (9-10)

vidyāṃ cāvidyāṃ ca yas
tad vedobhayaṃ saha|
avidyayā mṛtyuṃ tīrtvā
vidyayāmṛtam aśnute|| 11||

Knowledge and ignorance,
One who knows both together
Crossing death by ignorance,
Gains immortality by knowledge. (11)

... ye viduḥ saha saj-janāḥ|
te nindayā'yathārthasya
duḥkhājñānādi-rūpiṇaḥ|
duḥkhājñānādi-santīrṇāḥ
sukha-jñānādi-rūpiṇaḥ||
yathārthasya parijñānāt
sukha-jñānādi-rūpatām|
yānty evaṃ ... || 11||

The righteous, who know them both,
By censure of the unreal,
Namely suffering, ignorance, and the rest,
Transcend suffering and ignorance.
By completely knowing the real,
Namely, happiness, knowledge, and so forth
They thus achieve them all. (11)

andhaṃ tamaḥ praviśanti
ye'sambhūtim upāsate|
tato bhūya iva te tamo
ya u sambhūtyāṃ ratāḥ|| 12||

They enter into blind darkness
Who do not worship [Hari as] creator.
To even greater gloom than that go they
Who delight in [Hari as] merely the creator. (12)

anyad evāhuḥ saṃbhavād
anyad āhur asaṃbhavāt|
iti śuśruma dhīrāṇāṃ
ye nas tad vicacakṣire|| 13||

They say one thing indeed results
From worship of [Hari as] only creator,
Another from not worshiping [Hari as] creator.
Thus have we heard from the wise.
Those who have perceived it for us. (13)

... sṛṣṭikartṛtvaṃ
nāṅgīkurvanti ye hareḥ||
te'pi yānti tamo ghoraṃ
tathā saṃhāra-kartṛtām|
nāṅgīkurvanti te'py evaṃ
tasmāt sarva-guṇātmakam||
sarva-kartāram īśeśaṃ
sarva-saṃhāra-kārakam|| 12, 13||

Those who do not accept Hari
As the creator of the world
Go into terrible darkness.
So also go those who do not accept Hari
As the destroyer of the world.
To greater gloom than that go they
Who do not accept Hari as
Possessing all good qualities,
Doer of all, lord of lords,

Destroyer of all. (12-13)

saṃbhūtiṃ ca vināśaṃ ca
yas tad vedobhayaṃ saha|
vināśena mṛtyuṃ tīrtvā
saṃbhūtyāmṛtam aśnute|| 14||

Creation and Destruction, He who knows both together,
Crossing death by destruction,
Gains immortality by creation. (14)

yo veda saṃhṛti-jñānād
deha-bandhād vimucyate|
sukha-jñānādi-kartṛtva-
jñānāt tad-vyaktim āvrajet||
sarva-doṣa-vinirmuktaṃ
guṇa-rūpaṃ janārdanam|
jānīyān na guṇānāṃ ca
bhāga-hāniṃ prakalpayet||
na muktānām api hareḥ
sāmyaṃ viṣṇor abhinnatām|
naiva pracintayet tasmād
brahmādeḥ sāmyam eva vā||
mānuṣādi-viriñcāntaṃ
tāratamyaṃ vimukti-gam|
tato viṣṇoḥ parotkarṣaṃ
samyag jñātvā vimucyate||
iti kaurme|| 14||

One who knows [Hari's role in] destruction,
Is freed from bondage to the body
And, by knowing [Hari's role in] creating
Happiness, knowledge, and such,
Obtains those things for himself.
One should know that the Destroyer of Evil Ones[17]
Is free from all faults, embodies only good traits,
And one should not imagine that
Qualities are inconsistent with blessedness
Nor should one even begin to think
That the liberated are either the same as Hari,
Or are indistinguishable from Viṣṇu.
Nor, therefore, should Brahmā and the rest
Be equated [with him] either.
From humans to Viriñci (Brahmā) there are
Gradations in the attainment of liberation.
Therefore, completely recognizing the
Ultimate supremacy of Viṣṇu, one is liberated.
(*Kūrma Purāṇa*) (14)

hiraṇmayena pātreṇa
satyasyāpihitaṃ mukham|
tattvaṃ pūṣann apāvṛṇu
satyadharmāya dṛṣṭaye|| 15||

By a golden disc
The face of Truth is hid
Do thou uncover it, Oh Nourishing Sun,
Reveal [it] for the one firm in Truth. (15)

pātraṃ hiraṇmayaṃ sūrya-
maṇḍalaṃ samudāhṛtaṃ|
viṣṇoḥ satyasya tenaiva
sarvadā'pihitaṃ mukhaṃ||
tat tu pūrṇatvataḥ pūṣā
viṣṇur darśayati svayam|
satya-dharmāya bhaktāya ... || 15||

The golden plate exemplifies
The disc of the sun. Viṣṇu, or Truth's
Face is always concealed by that.
That, however, because of being full,
Pūṣan or Viṣṇu himself reveals
To his devotee who has the true *Dharma*. (15)

pūṣann ekarṣe yama sūrya
prājāpatya vyūha raśmīn|
samūha tejaḥ yat te rūpaṃ
kalyāṇatamaṃ tat te paśyāmi|| 16||

Oh Nourishing Sun, the One Seer [or Traveler], Psychopomp,
Solar Orb, Scion of the Lord of Progeny,
Disperse your rays, gather up your brilliance:
So that I may see that most auspicious form of yours. (16)

... pradhāna-jñāna-rūpataḥ|
viṣṇur ekarṣir jñeyo
yamo niyamanād dhariḥ|
sūryaḥ sa sūri-gamyatvāt

Because of having primordial knowledge,
Viṣṇu is to be known as the First Seer (*ekarṣi*).

[17] Janārdana, another name for Viṣṇu.

prājāpatya prajāpateḥ|
viśeṣeṇaiva gamyatvāt ... || 16||

And Yama, because of ruling, is Hari.
He's Sūrya because he is
Attained by learned sages (*sūri*).
He is described as Prājāpatya
Because of being known as
The Lord of Progeny. (16)

yo 'sāv asau puruṣaḥ so 'ham asmi|| 17||

That very Person is inescapable, existing eternally! (17)

... ahaṃ cāsāv aheyataḥ|
asmi nityāstitāmānāt
sarva-jīveṣu saṃsthitaḥ|
svayaṃ tu sarva-jīvebhyo
vyatiriktaḥ paro hariḥ|
sa kratur jñāna-rūpatvād
agnir aṅga-praṇetṛtaḥ||
iti brahmāṇḍe|| 17||

And he is inescapable (*a-ham*) because
He cannot be avoided.
And, because his form (*mi*) is eternal being (*as*)
Present in all living beings,
But he himself is separate from
All living beings, the supreme Hari.
He is Mental Fire (*kratuḥ*) because his
Very nature is knowledge and *Agni*.
Because he is creator (*ni*) of lesser beings (*ag*).[18]
(*Brahmāṇḍa Purāṇa*) (17)

vāyur anilam amṛtam
athedaṃ bhasmāntaṃ śarīram|| 18||

[May my] vital breath [repair] to immortal air,
And this body now to its end in ashes. (18)

yasminn ayaṃ sthitaḥ so'py amṛtaṃ, kim u paraḥ? aḥ brahmaiva nilayanaṃ yasya vāyoḥ so'nilam|

That in which this one is situated is also immortal. What indeed is superior to that? "*A*" is Brahman itself and that which is the dwelling place (*nilayana*) of the wind or breath (*vāyu*) is Brahman (*a-nila*).

atirohita-vijñānād
vāyur apy amṛtaḥ smṛtaḥ|
mukhyāmṛtaḥ svayaṃ rāmaḥ
paramātmā sanātanaḥ||
iti rāmasaṃhitāyām|| 18||

Because consciousness does not disappear,
Wind, too, is traditionally known as immortal.
The chief immortal is Rāma himself,
The supreme Self everlasting.
(*Rāma-saṃhitā*) (18)

oṃ krato smara kṛtaṃ smara
krato smara kṛtaṃ smara|| 19||

Oṃ, o Mental Fire, remember what has been done,
Remember, o Mental Fire, remember what has been done! (19)

bhaktānāṃ smaraṇaṃ viṣṇor-
nitya-jñapti-svarūpataḥ|
anugrahonmukhatvaṃ tu
naivānyat kvacid iṣyate||
iti brahmatarke|| 19||

The bhaktas' remembering of Viṣṇu,
Being in essence eternal consciousness,
Is in anticipation of divine favor;

[18]The text Madhva cites from the *Brahmāṇḍa Purāṇa* dramatically reinterprets, some would even say misinterprets, the Sanskrit phrase "*aham asmi*" ("I am") because the Upaniṣadic text establishes a relationship of identity or non-duality between the speaker, a *jīva* or living being, and the supreme being or person (*puruṣa*). This contradicts Madhva's theology and his view of the meaning of the Upaniṣads. Therefore, he cites a text attributed to the *Brahmāṇḍa*, but probably written by him, that takes the words *aham* and *asmi* as names of Viṣṇu, his chosen deity. Hari is thus "inescapable" (*a-ham*, i.e., *a-heya*) and measured by or formed of eternal being (*asmi*, i.e. *nityāstitāmāna*). Similary, the words *kratu* and *agni* are taken as names of Viṣṇu and supplied with novel interpretations.

Nothing else is ever desired.
(*Brahma-tarka*) (19)

agne naya supathā rāye asmān
viśvāni deva vayunāni vidvān|
yuyodhy asmaj-juhurāṇam eno
bhūyiṣṭhāṃ te nama-uktiṃ vidhema||
20||

O Sacred Fire, lead us for glory on the path of light!
O God, knowing all our understandings,[19]
Overcome our crooked misdeeds.
We offer to you the greatest praise! (20)

vayunaṃ jñānam| tvad-dattayā vayunayedam acaṣṭa viśvam iti vacanād| juhurāṇaṃ asmān alpīkurvat| yuyodhi viyojaya|

Vayuna means understanding, because of the statement: "through knowledge (*vayunā*) given by you he sees[20] this world." Crooked (*juhurāṇa*) means "making us small." Overcome (*yuyodhi*) means "unlink them from us."

yad asmān kurute 'tyalpāṃs-
tad eno 'smad viyojaya|
naya no mokṣa-vittāye-
tyastaud yajñaṃ manuḥ svarāḍ||
iti skānde||

That which makes us very tiny,
Our misdeeds; unlink them from us!
Lead us to liberation's door!
So prayed self-ruling Manu to Yajña.
(*Skanda Purāṇa*)

yuyu viyoge iti dhātuḥ| bhakti-jñānābhyāṃ bhūyiṣṭhāṃ nama-uktiṃ vidhema|| 20||

The verb root *yuyu* has the sense of "disconnect." With *bhakti* and knowledge we offer the greatest expression of reverential adoration. (20)

pūrṇa-śakti-cid-ānanda-
śrī-tejaḥ-spaṣṭa-mūrtaye|
mamābhyadhika-mitrāya
namo nārāyaṇāya te||

To you whose clear form
Has complete power, consciousness,
Bliss, beauty, and splendor,
To my greatest friend,
To you Nārāyaṇa I bow.

iti śrīmad-ānandatīrtha-bhagavat-pādācārya-viracitam īśāvāsyopaniṣad-bhāṣyaṃ sampūrṇam||

The commentary on the *Īśāvāsyopaniṣad*, written by that teacher at the feet of the Lord, Śrīmad Ānandatīrtha, is thus complete.

[19] *Vayuna*. We translated it "ways" previously. Here Madhva wants us to take it as knowledge or understanding.
[20] This verb *cakṣ* also means "leaves."

Appendices

The Flow of the Iśopaniṣad

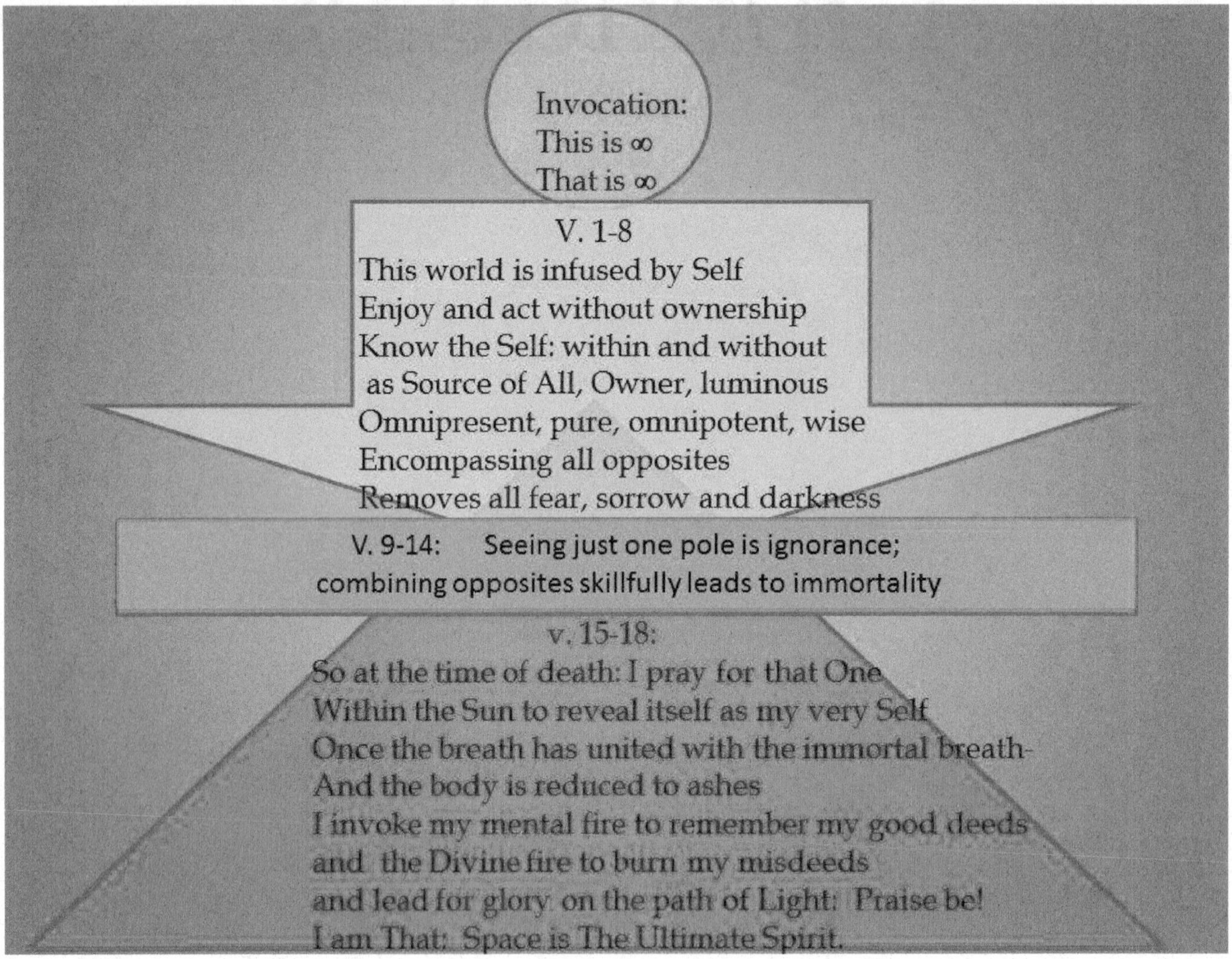

Invocation:
This is ∞
That is ∞
V. 1-8
This world is infused by Self
Enjoy and act without ownership
Know the Self: within and without
as Source of All, Owner, luminous
Omnipresent, pure, omnipotent, wise
Encompassing all opposites
Removes all fear, sorrow and darkness
V. 9-14: Seeing just one pole is ignorance;
combining opposites skillfully leads to immortality
v. 15-18:
So at the time of death: I pray for that One
Within the Sun to reveal itself as my very Self
Once the breath has united with the immortal breath-
And the body is reduced to ashes
I invoke my mental fire to remember my good deeds
and the Divine fire to burn my misdeeds
and lead for glory on the path of Light: Praise be!
I am That: Space is The Ultimate Spirit.

Īśā-upaniṣad: History of the Text in the Light of the Upaniṣadic Parallels by Mislav Ježić

Summary

The Īśā-upaniṣad (IU)[1] is a very short text preserved in two traditions: the Kāṇva (K) and the Mādhyaṃdina (M). The former consists of 18 stanzas, the latter of 17. The stanzas 9-11 of the K appear as stanzas 12-14 of the M, the stanzas 12-14 of the K as 9-11 of the M. On the other hand, stanza 9 of each recension appears in the Bṛhadāraṇyaka-upaniṣad (BĀU 4, 4) of the same recension, while stanza 12 (and the rest) of each recension does not appear there. There are other parallels between the IU of both recensions and the BĀU of the respective recensions, and even the Kaṭha-upaniṣad, that can help us to complete the survey of Upaniṣadic variants related to the IU. The last 3 stanzas in the IU M, or 4 in the IU K, equally have parallels in BĀU 5, which enable us to reconstruct the probable history of the text(s) of the IU. That is very instructive in several respects: it illustrates the oral composition technique and its repertory of varying formulas, it presents us with a good example of the intertextual relations among the upaniṣadic texts, and it permits us to reconstruct the history of the text in several consecutive phases; this historical reconstruction, on the other hand, helps us in more precisely understanding the messages and contents of the text itself.[2]

History of the Text

In his masterly analysis of the IU, with precious linguistic, metrical and philological notes, Paul Thieme (1965) conjectures that the whole IU — "exclusive of the concluding prayers: verses IU K 15-18 / IU M 15-17 — can be explained as consisting of little discussions."[3] Only in the concluding prayers, he says, "bold metaphysical speculation finally is exchanged for modest, but confidential, religious attitude, as it is in the Bhagavad Gītā."[4]

While his claim that we have here four groups of *pūrvapakṣas* (1, 7-8), *uttarapakṣas* (2, 4-5, 9-10, 12-13) and *siddhāntas* (3, 6, 11, 14)[5] looks ingenious, but rather forced, and certainly non-historical, the idea of little groups of stanzas may prove fruitful. Namely, if we apply a structural and comparative philological analysis to the text, an original composition consisting of regular groups of stanzas will emerge as a result of it.

---

[1]This essay is by Dr. Mislav Ježić, Zagreb University, Department of Indology and Far Eastern Studies.

[2]This analysis has been worked out in the framework of the scholarly project *The Upaniṣads in Comparative Perspective: Text history, reception, parallels* sponsored by the Ministry of Science, Education and Sports of the Republic of Croatia.

[3]Thieme 1965, 93.

[4]Thieme 1965, 99.

[5]The *pūrva-pakṣa* is the first assertion in a discussion; the *uttara-pakṣa* is the reply to that assertion; and the *siddhānta* is the conclusion or final finding in a discussion or debate. [Ed.]

1. Triplets IU K 9-11, 12-14 / IU M 12-14, 9-11

We can take as a starting point the variation of formulae in stanzas 9-11 and 12-14 of the Mādhyaṃdina and Kāṇva recensions.
IU K 9 / IU M 12 = BĀU K 4.4.10; cf. BĀU M 4.4.13
IU K 9-11 / IU M 12-14

andháṃ támaḥ prá viśanti yé (á)vidyām upā́sate /
táto bhū́ya iva té támo yá u vidyā́yāṃ ratā́ḥ //9//

anyád evā́húr vidyáyā (a)nyád āhur ávidyayā /[6]
íti śuśruma dhī́rāṇāṃ yé nas tád vicacakṣiré //10//

vidyā́ṃ cā́vidyāṃ ca yás tád védobháyaṁ sahá //
ávidyayā mṛtyúṃ tīrtvā́ vidyáyāmṛ́tam aśnute //11//[7]

These stanzas appear in the IU K as st. 9-11, but in the IU M as st. 12 - 14. The first of them, IU K 9 / IU M 12, however, figures in the BĀU K as the passage 4.4.10 (in the context of the dialogue between Yājñavalkya and Janaka on the knowledge of ātman, as an illustration in ślokas: *tad ete ślokā bhavanti / tadapy ete ślokāḥ* (BĀU K 8-21 / cf. M 11-23)). In this variant, it is absent from the BĀU M. On the other hand, in another variant, which appears in the BĀU M 4.4.13, it is the first stanza of the triplet that follows in the IU K, but in the IU M precedes the above cited triplet:
IU K 12 / IU M 9 = BĀU M 4.4.13; cf. BĀU K 4.4.10
IU K 12-14 / IU M 9-11

andháṃ támaḥ prá viśanti yé 'sàṃbhūtim upā́sate /
táto bhū́ya iva té támo yá u sáṃbhūt(i)yāṁ ratā́ḥ //12//

anyád evā́húḥ saṃbhavā́d (a)nyád āhur ásaṃbhavāt /
íti śuśruma dhī́rāṇāṃ yé nas tád vicacakṣiré //13//

sáṃbhūtiṃ ca vināśáṃ ca yás tád védobháyaṁ sahá //
vināśéna mṛtyúṃ tīrtvā́ sáṃbhūtyāmṛ́tam aśnute //14//[8]

These stanzas appear in the IU M as st. 9-11, and in the IU K as 12-14. The first stanza in this group figures in the BĀU M as the passage 4.4.13. Of course, it is a variant of the formula occuring in the BĀU K as 4.4.10, but it is not identical to it. The BĀU M variant uses the opposition of *saṃbhūti* and *asaṃbhūti*, while the BĀU K introduces the opposition of *vidyā* and *avidyā*. It is a good example of the formulaic nature of the cited *ślokas* and of the typical variation in their composition.

Naturally, it is not only a variation in expression, but also in content. However, the fundamental structure of stanzas IU 9 and 12 is the same, and the opposition of the two terms in each of them serves an analogous purpose: to relativize them, to make them complementary.

However, it is not easy to interpret them. What do *vidyā* and *avidyā*, or *saṃbhūti* and *asaṃbhūti* mean in this context? Śaṅkara in his commentary to the IU interprets *avidyā* as *karman* in the sense of the ritual activity (he cites the *agnihotra* as an instance) which is opposed to the *vidyā* in the sense of knowledge, or as he puts it, of *devatājñāna*, the knowledge of deities. The *karman* leads to the world of the fathers, *pitṛloka*, and the knowledge leads to the world of gods, *devaloka*, he says, according to BĀU K 1.5.16, which he cites. His interpretation of *saṃbhūti* and *asaṃbhūti* is still more complex: *asaṃbhūti* "non-becoming" is *prakṛti* "the unmanifested nature," *kāraṇa* "the cause (of manifestation)" (he identifies it here with *avidyā*), and *saṃbhūti* "becoming" is *kārya-brahman* "the brahman

[6] IU M 12 v. l. anyád evā́húr vidyā́yā (a)nyád āhur ávidyāyāḥ / It is in Thieme's opinion lectio facilior.

[7] Olivelle (1998) translates: *9. Into blind darkness they enter, people who worship ignorance; And into still blinder darkness, people who delight in learning. 10. It's far different from knowledge, they say, Different also from ignorance, we're told—so have we heard from wise men, who have explained it to us. 11. Knowledge and ignorance—a man who knows them both together, Passes beyond death by ignorance, and by knowledge attains immortality.*

[8] Olivelle (1998) : *12. Into blind darkness they enter, people who worship nonbecoming; And into still blinder darkness, people who delight in becoming. 13. It's far different from coming-into-being, they say, Different also from not coming-into-being, we're told—so have we heard from wise men, who have explained it to us. 14. The becoming and the destruction—a man who knows them both together, Passes beyond death by the destruction, and by the becoming attains immortality.*

as effect;" in his terminology the *kārya-brahman* is Hiraṇyagarbha "the golden germ" (Sun) as the manifested (or lower) *brahman*. Worshipping the non-becoming, one attains the absorption into *prakṛti* ("as the *paurāṇikas* call it"), and worshipping the becoming one achieves (supernormal) powers (*aiśvarya*: like becoming subtle, aṇu, etc.). The ritual activity (*pravṛtti*), he says, as explained in the *(Śatapatha-)brāhmaṇa* ending with *pravargya*,[9] serves the satisfaction of desires, and the inactivity (*nivṛtti*), the way of knowledge, as explained in the *Bṛhadāraṇyaka (-upaniṣad)*, serves the renouncing of the desires. Worshipping the lower *brahman*, Hiraṇyagarbha, one will achieve immortality on the way to the Sun (cf. IU K 15 / M 17ab).

The intricacies of Śankara's interpretation need not convince everybody, but they exemplify the difficulties in understanding the two cited groups of stanzas which are so paradoxically formulated. In the case of *saṃbhūti*, the substitution of *asaṃbhūti* with *vināśa* "destruction" helps understand it. Olivelle (1998, p. 613) therefore concludes that "nonbecoming" refers to the belief in non-existence after death, and "becoming" to the belief in the continued existence, probably rebirth.[10]

Otto Schrader (1933)[11] interprets *vidyā* as consciousness, and *avidyā* as unconsciousness, *saṃbhūti* as existence, and *asaṃbhūti* as non-existence. Gambhīrānanda (1957/1989)[12] in his translation of Śaṅkara's commentary, interprets the former two as rites and meditation (as different from the knowledge of the supreme Self), and translates the latter two as the manifested and the unmanifested (i. e. *prakṛti*). Thieme (1965) translates the former two as knowledge and ignorance, and the latter two as becoming and non-becoming. Olivelle (1998) follows him.

However, although we have to deal with two triplets of stanzas in the text(s) of the IU, in the corresponding redactions of the BĀU, we find in both cases only the first stanza of the respective first triplet. It implies that this first stanza shows two oral variants, one in each recension, and that the respective variant was incorporated into the IU and elaborated into a triplet. We may ask which variant could be the older one. It cannot be decided from the text(s) of the IU, it can be inferred only from the BĀU passage.

The *śloka* passage in the BĀU describes the knowledge of *ātman*, and the consequences of the ignorance. The consequence of knowledge is attaining immortality (BĀU K 4.4.14c, 17d / M 4.4.15c, 19), and that of ignorance is destruction (BĀU K 11, 14bd / M 14bd, 15bd), or rebirth (repeated death) and renewed union with the body (BĀU K 12cd, 19cd / M 16cd, 22ab). Therefore, if we take *asaṃbhūti* as "destruction" (*vināśa*, st. BĀU K 14 / M 11) and *saṃbhūti* as becoming again and again through rebirth (*mṛtyóḥ sa mṛtyúm āpnoti*, st. BĀU K 19cd / M 22ab), it will fit the BĀU context very well.

How does it fit the IU context? The stanzas follow the group of stanzas (IU 4-8, see below) expressing the paradoxical nature of the *ātmavidyā*. They refer to the IU 3, which threatens that the *ātmahanaḥ* "the people who kill the self" will go to the "demonic" or "sunless" worlds cloaked in "blind darkness," and elaborate the threatening in the sense that those who worship non-becoming will enter into "blind darkness," and that those who delight in becoming will enter into "a still blinder darkness." It may mean that those who believe in destruction, the people who kill the self, the materialists, enter into blind darkness, but those who delight in becoming, in the (good) rebirths, in the *saṃsāra* or *prapañca*, enter into a still blinder darkness,[13] because the liberation (or the liberating knowledge of the self, leading to)—the immortality, the *amṛta*, is different from the reincarnation, as it is different from the destruction. Only those who know both (IU M 11 / K 14), according to the paradoxes of the *ātmavidyā*, cross death by destruction of the body (cf. BĀU M 4.4.16 / K 4.4.12), and attain immortality by (knowing the limitations of) reincarnation, (of) the *saṃsāra* or *prapañca*, but also (by knowing) the immanence of the Lord or *ātman* in it, by whom one can reach immortality.[14]

On the other hand, *vidyā* and *avidyā* will confront us with the problem how to interpret *vidyā* in IU K 9 / M 12 if those who delight in it enter into still blinder darkness, which occurs equally in BĀU K 4.4.10, but does not occur in the BĀU M (which has the variant with *saṃbhūti*). It is still more puzzling because the next *śloka* BĀU K 4.4.11 / BĀU M 4.4.14 reads:

asuryà nā́ma té lokā́ andhéna támasāvṛtāḥ /

---

[9] I. e. including the BĀ, but excluding the BĀU.

[10] Olivelle 1998, 613, fn 12.

[11] Otto Schrader 1933, 4, 5.

[12] Gambhīrānanda 1957/1989, 19 ff, 22ff.

[13] Cf. Schrader 1933, 4ff.

[14] Śaṅkara's explanation that by worshipping the lower *brahman*, Hiraṇyagarbha, one will achieve immortality on the way to the Sun (cf. IU K 15 / M 17ab), is in the end not at all far from the target.

tā́ṃs té prétyā́pigacchanti ávidvāṃso 'budhā́ jánāḥ //14// (M)[15]

K v. l.: anandā nāma

From the above, it would look as if both kinds of those entering into blind darkness are *ávidvāṃso 'budhā́ jánāḥ* "men who are not knowers nor wise," including those "who delight in knowledge / learning." That does not make the task of interpreting the concept *vidyā* easier because even *yá u vidyā́yāṃ ratā́ḥ* should be categorized as *ávidvāṃso 'budhā́ jánāḥ*.

On the other hand, the reading of BĀU M corresponds even more than that of K to IU 3, which reads equally except for using the formula in the *pāda* d *yé ké cātmaháno jánāḥ* instead of *ávidvāṃso 'budhā́ jánāḥ*. The expression *yé ké cātmaháno jánāḥ* in IU 3 "has caused much controversy" (Olivelle 1998),[16] and was interpreted as 1. those who kill themselves, as 2. those who kill living beings (Thieme) or as 3. those who do not know the self. The BĀU M 4.4.14 / K 4.4.11 favours the third option.

Anyway, obviously the stanzas in BĀU M 4.4 are very close to the IU.

Moreover, formally, the IU M 13 text *anyád evā́húr vidyā́yā anyád āhur ávidyāyā / íti śuśruma dhī́rāṇāṃ yé nas tád vicacakṣiré*[17] is a semantically easier reading, but metrically irregular, while the IU K 10 has a metrically correct form, but semantically and syntactically it is *lectio difficilior*: *anyád evā́húr vidyáyānyád āhur ávidyayā / íti śuśruma dhī́rāṇāṃ yé nas tád vicacakṣiré*.[18] That is why it was given preference by Thieme.[19] However, each variant of the *vidyā* stanza has its difficulties.

The passage is closely paralleled by Kena 4 *anyad eva tad viditād atho aviditād adhi / iti śuśruma pūrveṣām ye nas tad vyācacakṣire*.[20] Two stanzas before it, Kena 2 reads: *śrotrasya śrotram manaso mano yad vāco ha vācaṃ sa u ha prāṇasya prāṇaḥ*[21] */ cakṣuṣaś cakṣur atimucya dhīrāḥ pretyāsmāl lokād amṛtā bhavanti.* That is very close to BĀU K 4.4.18 (corresponding to M 4.4.21): *prāṇasya prāṇam uta cakṣuṣaś cakṣur uta śrotrasya śrotram (M: annasyānnam) / manaso ye mano viduḥ te nicikyur brahma purāṇam agryam*,[22] while the formula *amṛtās te bhavanti*[23] appears in K 4.4.14c / M 4.4.15c.

The close affinity of the Kena and BĀU K passages is striking, but while Kena 4 is fittingly formulated, the akin BĀU K and IU stanzas are opaque, probably because of the mechanical combination of 1. the *saṃbhūti* formula, with *vidyā* substituted for *saṃbhūti*, and 2. the *anyad eva tad viditād* formula, with *vidyayā / vidyāyāḥ* in the place of *viditād* (which is metrically and semantically better).

Therefore, we may infer from parallel Upaniṣadic passages that the *saṃbhūti* formula, as preserved in the M tradition, is probably the original one, and that the *vidyā* formula in the K recension is derived from it under the influence of akin formulas. In the BĀU 4.4 the starting point was st. BĀU M 4.4.13. From it, the variant in K 4.4.10 derived. The former was transferred to IU M 9, the latter to the IU K 9.

This initial stanza (in the original and in the derived variant) was then elaborated to a triplet under the influence of adjacent stanzas. In which recension it happened first, and which thereby influenced the other, cannot be readily determined. Both variant triplets are completely parallel. Maybe the original Mādhyaṃdina variant developed in the IU into the triplet, before the probably later Kāṇva variant appeared in the BĀU K 4.4, and, after appearing there, was transferred to the IU K changing in it not only stanza 9, but the whole already developed triplet.

---

[15] Olivelle 1998, 123 & 612 translates: *'Demonic' (M) / 'Joyless' (K) are those regions called, in blind darkness they are cloaked; Into them after death they go, men who are not learned or wise.*

[16] Olivelle 1998, 612, fn 3.

[17] Olivelle 1998, 409: *It's far different from knowledge, they say, Different also from ignorance, we're told—so have we heard from wise men, who have explained it to us.*

[18] Translation same as above.

[19] Thieme 1965, 95: Metrically most satisfying would be *vidyāyās* in a (/—), *avidyayā* in b (/⏑--). Perhaps both K and M have harmonized in a different sense.

[20] Olivelle 1998, 365: *It is far different from what is known. And is farther than the unknown—so have we heard from men of old, who have explained it all to us.*

[21] This *pāda* has a redundant syllable and an anakoluthon. It is possible to emend *vācam* (transposed from Kena 1) to *vāk*. That is how Olivelle 1998, 365, translates: *That which is the hearing behind hearing, the thinking behind thinking, the speech behind speech, the sight behind sight— It is also the breathing behind breathing— Freed completely from these, the wise become immortal, when they depart from this world.* Radhakrishnan 1953, 581, understands *atimucya* differently: *the wise, giving up (wrong notions of their self-sufficiency) and departing from the world, become immortal.*

[22] Olivelle 1998, 125: *The breathing behind breathing, the sight behind sight, the hearing behind hearing, the thinking behind thinking — Those who know this perceive brahman, the first, the ancient.* The greatest difference from Kena 2 occurs in the final formula.

[23] I. e. they become immortal.

In the end the triplet from the Kāṇva recension was added to the Mādhyaṃdina IU after its own triplet 9-11 as stanzas 12-14, and vice-versa.

A provisory scheme of these relationships could look like this:

BĀU M 4.4.13	→	BĀU K 4.4.10	←	(Kena 4 or similar?)
↓		↓		
IU M 9		(IU K 9 ?)		
↓		↓		
IU M 9-11	→	IU K 9-11		
	↘ ↙			
IU M 12-14	↙ ↘	IU K 12-14		

An implication of these textual relationships is that Kena 4 could be older than the variant reading of BĀU K 4.4.10, and, consequently, older than IU K 9 (but not older than BĀU M 4.4.13 nor IU M 9). Even if some other similar stanza could have influenced the reading in BĀU K 4.4.10, the probability that it was Kena 2 is not negligible because it looks metrically and semantically more authentic, and seems to fit its own context closer than BĀU K 4.4.10 does.

2. Triplet IU 1-3

The IU begins with three stanzas, the last of which corresponds to the BĀU (M) 4.4.14abc / BĀU (K) 4.4.11abc:

IU K 1-2 / IU M 1-2

> īśā́vāsyàm[24] idáṁ sárvaṃ yát kíṃ ca jágatyāṃ jágat /
> téna tyakténa bhuñjīthā mā́ gṛdhaḥ kásya svid dhánam //1//[25]
>
> kurvánn evéhá kármāṇi jijīviṣéc[26] chatáṁ sámāḥ /
> eváṃ tváyi[27] nā́nyáthetó [(a)sti][28] ná kárma lipyate nā́re //2//[29]

---

[24]*Īś* = (Śaṅkara:) *paramātmā sarvasya.*

[25]It is possible to understand st. 1 with Morton Smith (ABORI 1967/1968, pp. 123-136) as addressing the heir of a dying proprietor of a household (*īśa*). This is a reasonable guess if we assume that this stanza could have belonged to some pre-Upaniṣadic text, possibly concerning some rules of inheritance or rituals connected with death. However, in this case "*téna tyakténa bhuñjīthāḥ*" would not imply either "renunciation" or "this renounced," as quoted by Smith, but "Enjoy what was left by him! And do not covet the wealth of anyone (else)!" However, when "*idaṁ sarvam*" "all this" was understood as "this whole world," "*īśa*" must have been understood as "Lord" and no more as "proprietor." Even if Smith's assumption about the previous secular use and meaning of stanza 1 is correct, such a shift of meaning must have occurred as soon as the stanza was (re-)used in an Upaniṣadic context, i. e. the stanza must have had this meaning from the moment of the composition of the Īśā-upaniṣad.

[26]*jijīviṣa ít* (Thieme)—impv. not opt.

[27]Emend. *evaṃvídi*? I. e. náre. Cf. ChU 4.14.3: *yathā puṣkalapalāśa āpo na śliṣyanta evam evaṃvidi pāpaṃ karma na lipyate.* Olivelle 1998, 225: *When someone knows it, bad actions do not stick to him, just as water does not stick to a lotus leaf.* A similar statement, without the comparison occurs in the cognate passage BĀU K 4.4.23 / BĀU M 4.4.28: *taṃ viditvā na karmaṇā lipyate pāpakena.* Thieme compares the passage from the IU with the well-known passage in BhG 5.10. Cf. Horsch 1966, 173.

[28]Skt. *nā́nyáthétó* or emendation *nā́nyáthéti*? The *pāda* is hypermetrical (10 syllables instead of 8). Thieme discusses the possible omission of *asti* or *náre* (he inclines to the latter.). It seems more advisable to omit *asti* for metrical and syntactical reasons because *pādas* c and d are in that case syntactically complete; if *náre* is omitted, the phrase makes an enjambement and continues in d, ends there, and a new short sentence completes the *pāda* (Thieme does not take it that way, but understands *asti* adverbially: actually). If we emend, according to ChU 4.14.3, *eváṃ tváyi* to *evaṃvídi*, the omission of *asti* and retaining of *náre* becomes even more probable. Moreover, the occurence of *tváyi* can be explained away as an adaptation to the 2nd person in 1cd and in 2ab. Finally, hypermetrical *nā́nyáthétó (a)sti* can be emended by omitting two syllables to *nā́nyáthéti*; in that case the text would indicate what is the content of the knowledge of the one who knows thus (by referring to the content of 1cd, and indirectly of 1ab). It maybe explains why the conjectured expression could have been expanded to an understandable phrase *nā́nyáthet(ó ast)i* after the possible introduction of *tváyi* which eliminated the reference to the content of knowledge by decomposing the expression *evaṃvídi.*

Therefore the double emendation of 2cd would make a lot of sense:

> evaṃvídi nā́nyáthéti ná kárma lipyate náre //2//

The work does not smear off on the man who knows thus "it is not otherwise."

[29]Olivelle 1998, 407: 1. *This whole world is to be dwelt in by the Lord, whatever living being there is in the world. So you should eat what has been*

IU K 3 / IU M 3 = BĀU (K) 4. 4.11, (M) 4.4.14 (v. l.); cf. Kaṭha 1.1.3

> asuryà[30] nā́ma té lokā́ andhéna támasā́vṛtāḥ/
> tā́ṃs té prétyābhígacchanti[31] yé ké cātmaháno jánāḥ //3//[32]

The first two stanzas expound a theistic (or panentheistic) world view, "the whole world is to be dwelt in by the Lord," and give moral injunctions:

- (1) enjoy only what has been left (by the Lord? or by others?),
- (1) do not covet anybody's wealth,
- (2) perform works in this way (and live one hundred years)
- (2) so that the work cannot smear off on a person who does so / or: knows thus.

Thieme 1965, 89, is right in stressing that the beginning of the IU "is a prescription—not a philosophically founded theoretical attitude, as it is taken by Śaṅkara, but—of a religiously founded practical behavior, as emerges most clearly from d." Stanza 2 enjoins activity and promises therefore a long life of one hundred years.[33]

The third stanza warns that all those people "who kill the self" go after their death to the "demonic" worlds (?) or to the "sunless" worlds "cloaked in blind darkness."

It was already discussed, in connection with the concepts of *vidyā* and *avidyā* in IU K 9 / M 12, where *andhaṃ tamas* and *bhūyaḥ tamas* are also mentioned, that IU 3 has a clear parallel in BĀU K 4.4.11abc / BĀU M 4.4.14abc.[34] However, here both IU M and IU K start with the same reading as the BĀU M *asuryā lokāḥ* "demonic worlds," while only BĀU K reads *anandā lokāḥ* "joyless worlds," as if later a gloss interpreting the less current expression crept into the text and supplanted that expression (which could have been much more intelligible earlier if it had read *asūryā lokāḥ*). Of course, it could equally be just another oral variant, but it is still significant that the BĀU M preserves the text that most probably influenced the IU of both recensions, i. e. the older text. In this case, the BĀU K did not produce the change in IU K, as it did in the case of IU K 9. On the other hand, *anandā lokāḥ* occurs in KaU 1.3: could it have influenced BĀU K 4.4.11 at some later point when it had no more repercussions on the IU?[35]

It was also mentioned above that the controversial expression *ātmaháno jánāḥ* in IU 3 appears in BĀU K 4.4.11 / BĀU M 4.4.14 as *ávidvāṃso 'budhā́ jánāḥ* "men who are not knowers nor wise."[36]

The mentioned relations can be brought together in the following scheme:

---

abandoned; and do not covet anyone's wealth. O translates *tena* with "so." Already Th understands it adverbially and translates it "therefore." Two Indian commentators Anantācārya and Bālakṛṣṇadāsa explain *tena* by *īśā* (abandoned by him, i.e. the Lord). Cf. Schrader 1933, 1. Although Th 1965, 89, rejects that *tena* could refer to the Lord, and suggests that "The agent of 'abandoned' is most likely he whose 'property' is not to be coveted," and although Schrader doubts whether *tyaktena* can be interpreted as *dattena*, as the commentators suggest, I still believe that it is worth considering that 1c might mean: *You should enjoy what he (the Lord) has left (for you).* If Th refers to *uñchaśila* and *bhaikṣa* in the ŚGS, one could think of a gift or donation (*tyāga*) as in the KŚS. Olivelle: 2. *Just performing works in this world, you should desire to live your hundred years. Thus, and not otherwise, in fact, does work not smear off on you.* However, see conjectural emendations in fn 25.

[30] V. l. *asūryā́ nā́ma*, H, (LV), Horsch 1966, 166. Cf. RS 5.32.6 *asūryé támasi vāvṛdhānám*. Cf. speculations on *asura* and *asūrya* already in ŚB 3.2.1.24 (LV 1958, 2).

[31] M v. l. *prétyā́pi gacchanti*

[32] Olivelle 1998, 407: *"Demonic" are those worlds called, in blind darkness they are cloaked; into them after death they go, all those people who kill the self.* With v. l.: *"Sunless" are those worlds called ... .*

[33] Thieme 1965, 92, interprets it: *Īśop.2 obviously is in contradiction to 1. The first verse says: You should not rob or kill a living being, for every living being is a dwelling place of the LORD, that is the 'Self.' The second verse says: You may do anything (even rob or kill a living being), provided you are acting without 'attachment' (passion, fear, hope, desire): for thus the sin will not soil you. It amounts to what Kṛṣṇa tells Arjuna in BhG 5.* It is an ingenious interpretation, and faithful to many Upaniṣadic passages. However, if we understand *evaṃ tvayi*, or even *evaṃvidi nare*, in the context of the IU, it will be not only non-attachment but also the knowledge of the Lord or of the Self that is required in order not to be smeared off by the deeds, and that is the main content of stanzas 4-8. In that sense st. 2 in a way does contrast 1, but does not contradict it.

[34] BĀU K 4.4.11d and M 4.4.14d have the reading: *ávidvāṃso 'budhā́ jánāḥ*.

[35] Thieme 1965, 93, knows well all the text passages, but argues that *anandāḥ* is the original reading in the BĀU, that *asuryāḥ* is the original reading of the IU, and that it influenced the BĀU M. His speculative arguments are attractive, but the textual evidence seems to me to point to different conclusions regarding the text history. The BĀU M reading seems to be the original and to have influenced the IU, and the BĀU K reading seems secondary. The literal, non-metaphorical, meaning of *ātmahan* (Th: killer of souls), that would connect IU 3 with 1, need not be excluded, but does not seem to me primary in the context, and would hardly connect IU 3 with 4-8. Besides this, it opposes the IU 3 and the BĀU passage, which must be closely connected. It does so on grounds that are rather speculative than textual (Can we be sure that *asuryāḥ lokāḥ* means hell, and *anandāḥ lokāḥ* something very different like Hades? For the latter cf. KaU 1.3).

[36] Cf. *ātmaháno jánāḥ* and BhG 13.28: *na hinasty ātmanātmānaṃ tato yāty parāṃ gatim* (LV 1958, 2).

IU M & K 1
IU M & K 2 ⇐ BĀU K 4.4.23 & M 4.4.28 ⇐ ChU 4.14.3
IU M & K 3 ← BĀU M 4.4.14 → BĀU K 4.4.11 ← KaU 1.3

Stanza 3, at the same time, by mentioning the self, introduces the topic of the next group of stanzas: 4-8. It lies at hand to see that the self is what connects every person addressed in the first two stanzas and the Lord. Thieme 1965, 89, cites the passages like BĀU K 4.4.22 / M 4.4.24 to show that the Lord himself in IU 1 should be understood as the Self, or vice versa that the Self is the Lord: *sa vā eṣa mahān aja ātmā ... sarvasya vaśī sarvasyeśānaḥ sarvasyādhipatiḥ. sarvam idaṃ praśāsti yad idaṃ kiṃ ca ... eṣa sarveśvaraḥ, eṣa bhūtādhipatiḥ, eṣa bhūtapālaḥ, "Verily, this great unborn Self is the master of everything, the lord of everything, the overlord of everything: it commends all this that is here (=in this earthly world) ... he is lord of everything, the overlord of the beings, the protector of the beings ... ."*

3. Triplet IU 5-7 & triṣṭubhs 4 and 8

The following five stanzas make a coherent unity treating of the nature of *ātman*, and precede the two triplets that have been discussed at the outset.

IU K 4-5 / IU M 4-5

ánejad ékaṃ mánaso jávīyo
naínad devā́ āpnuvan pū́rvam árṣat[37] /
tád dhā́vato 'nyā́n áti eti tíṣṭhat
tásminn apó mātaríśvā dadhāti //4//[38]

tád ejati tán naíjati tád dūré tád u antiké
tád antár asya sárvasya tád u sárvasyāsya bāhyatáḥ[39] //5//[40]

IU K 6 / IU M 6, cf BĀU K 4.4.15 / M 4.4.18 (*pāda* d different)

yás tú sárvāṇi bhūtā́ni ātmánn evā́nu páśyati /
sarvabhūtéṣu cātmā́naṃ táto ná ví jugupsate[41] //6//

IU K 7-8 / IU M 7-8

yásmint sárvāṇi bhūtā́ny ātmaívā́bhūd vijānatáḥ /
tátra kó móhaḥ káḥ śóka ekatvám anupáśyataḥ //7//[42]

sá páryagāc chukrám akāyám avraṇám
asnāvirám̐ śuddhám ápāpaviddham /
kavír manīṣī́ paribhū́ḥ svayaṃbhū́r

---

[37]M v. l. árśat

[38]Cf. KaU 2.21 *asīno dūraṃ vrajati śayāno yāti sarvataḥ aśarīraṃ śarīreṣv anavastheṣv avasthitam*; MuU 3.1.7; BhG 13.14-16, etc. Paradoxical expressions for the inexpressible.

[39]5d is hypermetrical. Th. proposes to omit *u* or *asya*. The latter seems easier to argue: it omits unnecessarily repeated syllables. It looks like a scribal error, not like an oral variant. The emended text reads: *tád antár asya sárvasya tád u sárvasya bāhyatáḥ*

[40]Olivelle 1998, 407: *4. Although not moving, the one is swifter than the mind; the gods cannot catch it, as it speeds on in front. Standing, it outpaces others who run; within it Mātariśvan places the waters. 5. It moves—yet it does not move! It's far away—yet it is near at hand! It is within this whole world—yet it's also outside this whole world.*

[41]BĀU K 4.4.15 and IU K 6 have corresponding readings: *na tato / tato na vi jugupsate*, just as BĀU M 4.4.18 and IU M 6 have: *na tadā / tato na vi cikitsati*. Thieme 1965, 94, assumed that the former reading was original in the IU, and the latter in the BĀU, that the BĀU influenced IU M, and the IU K influenced the BĀU K. The combination of pronouns *yaḥ ... tato* in the IU, and *yadā ... tadā* in the BĀU M, along with *yadā ... tato* in the BĀU K, corroborates the conclusion that BĀU K has a changed text, that BĀU M has the original text, and that *yaḥ ... tato na vi jugupsate* could be the original reading of the IU. Anyway, it is another example of harmonization of formulae in the tradition of each school in these two texts. (The formula *na tato vi jugupsate* occurs in KaU 4.5 too. Thieme assumes that it was modeled upon the BĀU K 4.4.15 reading.)

[42]Cf. ŚB 13.7.1.1 *hantāhaṃ bhūteṣv ātmānaṃ juhavāni bhūtāni cātmanīti*; BhG 6.29-30, etc.

[yāthātathyató] (á)rthān vyàdadhāc chā́śvatī́bhyaḥ sámābhyaḥ[43] //8//[44]

In this group stanzas 5-7 in the *śloka* meter are framed by stanzas 4 and 8 in the *triṣṭubh* meter.[45]

In st. 6 again we find a formula in *pāda* d from the BĀU M 4.4.18d / K 4.4.15d varying in the recensions of the IU, now in conformity with the the form of the formula in the recensions of the BĀU.[46]

It is probable that the IU was at some time composed of a triplet of *ślokas*, framed by two *triṣṭubhs*, all of it framed once more within the preceding triplet IU 1-3 and the following one IU 9-11.

4. The conclusion of the original IU M and IU K with the third triplet

The third triplet IU 9-11 was again composed on the basis of the stanza IU 9 taken from the BĀU: it is M 4.4.13 / K 4.4.10 , just as the stanza IU 3, speaking of the dark worlds, was taken from the BĀU, occurring there as M 4.4.14abc / BĀU K 4.4.11abc (which again has a parallel in KaU 1.3).

Stanza 9 was elaborated, according to the structure of the IU (the first two triplets), into a triplet as well.

The result could have been that, after the creation of the triplet IU 9-11, the harmonious composition of the IU in numbers of stanzas looked like this:

3 *ślokas* - 1 *triṣṭubh* - 3 *ślokas* - 1 *triṣṭubh* - 3 *ślokas*

That is the form in which it seems to be preserved in the actual IU M 1-11.

The triplet IU 9-11 underwent the modification discussed above in the IU K.[47] An important motive for the creation of the *avidyā-vidyā* variant of the triplet from the *asaṃbhūti-saṃbhūti* triplet may have been the description of *ātman* in IU 4-8 as a being that cannot be comprehended, and that can be described in paradoxical expressions which show our knowledge and ignorance at the same time.

The modifications in the BĀU K 4.4.13 and IU K 9 have produced two parallel variants M and K of the IU 1-11 of the same compositional structure.

Moreover, the relationships with BĀU 4.4 were also structurally clear, proceeding from the same text framing method, based on the same principles of ring composition:

---

[43] 8d is hypermetrical. What can most easily be omitted is *yāthātathyató*. Thieme stresses that cancelling it, we obtain a flawless *triṣṭubh* line (?); otherwise a *triṣṭubh* with two precaesura parts (98).

[44] Olivelle 1998, 407: *6. When a man sees all beings within his very self, and his self within all beings, It will not seek to hide from him. 7. When in the self of a discerning man, his very self has become all beings, What bewilderment, what sorrow can there be, regarding that self of him who sees this oneness. 8. He has reached the seed—without body or wound, without sinews, pure, not riddled by evil. Self-existent and all-encompassing, the wise sage has dispensed objects through endless years.* Cf. KaU 5.13, ŚvU 6.13: *eko bhūtvā yo vidadhāti kāmān.*

[45] Belvalkar and Ranade 1927, 2: 1974, 90: *Stanzas 4 and 8 seem to be quotations, not introduced as such, from some unindentifiable source.*

Or, alternatively, stanzas 6 and 7 which are very closely interconnected and different from the rest could be a later development of the subject. Whatever be the case, either there were five stanzas in the second group, consisting of two *triṣṭubhs* enclosing the group of three *ślokas* from the outset (which is most probable), or there was initially a triplet—a group of only three stanzas—again, either simply three *ślokas* or two *triṣṭubhs* enclosing one *śloka* (possibly st. 5 which seems connected with st. 4, maybe even partly modeled upon it).

[46] See fn 39

[47] In doing so, corresponding passages in the wider corpus, like Kena 4, could have helped in transforming the IU M triplet 9-11 into the Kāṇva triplet 9-11.

	IU M 1	IU K 1	
	IU M 2	IU K 2	
BĀU M4.4.14abc → *andhéna támasā́vṛtāḥ*	IU M 3	IU K 3	← BĀU K 4.4.11abc *andhéna támasā́vṛtāḥ*
	IU M 4 *triṣṭubh*	IU K 4 *triṣṭubh*	
	IU M 5	IU K 5	
(BĀU M 4.4.18d →)	IU M 6	IU K 6	(← BĀU K 4.4.15d)
	IU M 7	IU K 7	
	IU M 8 *triṣṭubh*	IU K 8 *triṣṭubh*	
BĀU M 4.4.13 → *andhám̐ támaḥ prá viśanti (saṃbhūti)*	IU M 9	IU K 9	← BĀU K 4.4.10 *andhám̐ támaḥ prá viśanti (vidyā)*
	IU M 10	IU K 10	
	IU M 11	IU K 11	

This was the harmonious composition of the original IU, in the framework of the tradition of each school, Mādhyaṃdina and Kāṇva, in a probably older (M) and a probably younger (K) variant. The two variants were subsequently contaminated, and the text in both variants expanded.

5. The first extension of the IU M and the IU K, stanzas 12-14, two contaminated versions

Thereafter, the harmonious composition of the three triplets separated by the two *triṣṭubhs*, has been enlarged by the next triplet borrowed in each recension of the IU from the other recension, as has already been clearly stated by Belvalkar and Ranade 1927.[48]

6. The last triplet IU M 15-17 and its extension in IU K 15-18

It now remains to look at the last 3 (M) or 4 (K) stanzas of the IU. They have been borrowed from a still later part of the BĀU, from *adhyāya* 5.

IU K 15-18 = BĀU K 5.15.1-4
IU K 15ab = IU M 17ab

> hiraṇmáyena pā́treṇa satyásyā́pihitaṃ múkham /
> tát tváṃ pūṣann ápā́vṛṇu satyádharmāya dṛṣṭáye //15//

IU K 16c(e) - M 17c

> pū́ṣann eka ṛṣe yama sūrya prā́jāpatya vyū̀ha raśmī́nt sámūha téjo
> yát te rūpáṃ kályāṇatamaṃ tát te paśyāmi /
> yo 'sā́v asaú púruṣaḥ[49] só 'hám asmi //16//[50]

IU K 17 = IU M 15
IU M 15-16 = BĀU M 5.3

> vāyúr ánilam amṛ́tam áthedáṃ bhásmāntaṁ śárīram /
> aúṁ3 kráto smára kṛtáṁ smara kráto[51] smára kṛtáṁ smara //17//[52]

[48]Belvalkar and Ranade 1927, 2: 1974, 90: we find that the extra triplet taken over in each case occupies a secondary position.

[49]IU M 17 v. l. M 17c *yo 'sā́v ādityé púruṣaḥ só 'sā́v ahám*

[50]Olivelle 1998, 409: *15. The face of truth is covered with a golden dish. Open it, O Pūṣan, for me, a man faithful to the truth. Open it, O Pūṣan, for me to see. 16. O Pūṣan, sole seer! Yama! Sun! Son of Prajāpati! Spread out your rays! I see your fairest form. That person up there, I am he!*

[51]IU M 15 v. l. *ó3m kráto smára klibé smara*

[52]Olivelle 1998, 409: *17. The never-resting is the wind, the immortal! Ashes are this body's lot. Oṃ! Mind, remember the deed! Remember! Mind, remember the deed! Remember!*

IU K 18 = RS 1.189.1; 18b = AS 4.39.10b
IU K 18 = IU M 16

> ágne náya supáthā rāyé asmā́n
> víśvāni deva vayū́nāni vidvā́n /
> yuyodhi àsmáj juhurāṇám éno
> bhū́yiṣṭhāṃ te námauktíṃ vidhema //18//[53]

Renou 1943, 3, considers them evidently different from the rest, and sees them as an appendix representing, according to tradition, a prayer for a dying person, not connected with the preceeding text. Thieme simply omits them from his analysis, as mentioned at the beginning. It can be shown that the last stanzas form a separate passage by the fact that their parallels, which can again be found in the BĀU, belong to a different section of the BĀU.

All the four stanzas of the Kāṇva recension appear in the BĀU K as 5.15.1-4, in the Khilakāṇḍa, which could point to their later date in comparison with the rest. On the other hand, IU M 15-16 corresponds to the BĀU M 5.3, but IU M 17 is not to be found there.

The IU K recension contains the verses 15cd and 16ab, which are missing in the IU M. The IU M contains only 17ab = K 15ab and 17c = K 16c (e). This longer text in the K recension refers to Pūṣan whom the dying person prays to uncover the face of truth.

From all of the above, one could infer that BĀU M 5.3 may contain the oldest text, that IU M 17 could have been the first extension, forming the conclusion after stanzas 15-16.

On the other hand, the BĀU K 3.15 and the IU K accepted additional extensions (IU K 15cd and 16ab), and placed them in the middle of IU M 17, between ab and c, but before IU M 15 and 16, making the extensions nos. 15cd and 16ab, and shifting the previous stanzas 15 and 16 to positions 17 and 18.

Moreover, the most appropriate place for the formula M 17c *yo'sā́v ādityé púruṣaḥ só 'sā́v ahám / K yo'sā́v asaú púruṣaḥ só 'hám asmi* — is at the very end. This formula connects the last triplet with the preceding ones, concerned with the paradoxes of the *ātma-vidyā*, showing that the prayer is a prayer for and of an *ātma-vid*. Especially in the Mādhyaṃdina version, this new conclusion shows that the Lord whose dwelling is all beings (st. 1), i. e. the *ātman*, the ignorance about whom leads to sunless worlds cloaked in blind darkness (st. 3), is the Person in the Sun, with whom an *ātma-vid* knows himself to be one.

These can be sufficient reasons—in addition to the fact that the Mādhyaṃdina recension again created a triplet at the end of the text—to give preference to the sequence of the concluding stanzas in the Mādhyaṃdina recension, and to consider the composition of the Kāṇva recension again as younger,[54] more innovating and more deviating.[55]

Appendix 1

A short recapitulation of the history of the text of the IU and of the Upaniṣadic parallels can be given in the following table:

[53] Olivelle 1998, 411: *18. O Fire, you know all coverings; O god, lead us to riches, along an easy path. Keep the sin that angers, far away from us; And the highest song of praise, we shall offer to you!*

[54] It does not mean that K does not offer several better readings, as was stressed by Thieme and Horsch:

- IU K 4b: *árṣat* vs. IU M 4b: *árśat*, which is a corruption.
- IU K 6d: BĀU K 4.4.15 and IU K 6: *na tato / tato na vi jugupsate.* BĀU M 4.4.18 and IU M 6: *na tadā / tato na vi cikitsati.* Cf. Thieme 1965, 94. BĀU M has the original text of the BĀU, and *yaḥ ... tato na vi jugupsate* could be the original reading of the IU.
- IU K 9ab: anyád evā́húr vidyáyā (a)nyád āhur ávidyayā vs. IU M 13ab v. l. anyád evā́húr vidyā́yā (a)nyád āhur ávidyāyāḥ / Thieme: lectio facilior.

(There is also a difference in IU K 3c: *prétyābhígacchanti,* vs. IU M 3c: *prétyā́pi gacchanti*)

[55] Thieme 1965, 99, after his metrical analysis of the IU concludes: *This conclusion is vague enough: it puts the Upaniṣad in the vicinity of the BĀU, which presupposes the existence of ChU, and before the Kaṭha (above p. 97) and Kena (above note 12).* I would add: the analysis in this article puts: (1) IU (M) 1-11 in the vicinity of the *anuṣṭubhs* in BĀU M 4.4 (Horsch 1966, 173 states that the bad textual tradition of these *ślokas* implies their relatively late age, i.e. with respect to the BĀU); (2) IU K 9-11, just as BĀU K 4.4.10, after Kena 1.4 (even the reading of BĀU K 4.4.11 possibly after KaU 1.3); (3) IU M 12-14 follows IU K 9-11; (4) IU M 15-16 is close to BĀU M 5.3 (a *khila* of the BĀU!); while (5) IU K 15-18 is close to BĀU K 5.15.1-4 (which is younger than BĀU M 5.3). Such an analysis implies a more detailed relative chronology which refers not only to whole texts, but to their layers, and, moreover, to their interactions during the whole period of their interconnected (intertextual) tradition. It is difficult to say what it means in absolute chronology: most probably the period of the younger layers of the BĀU: 5-4th cents. BCE.?

A. The final text

Triplet 1

IU M & K 1
IU M & K 2 ⇐ BĀU K 4.4.23 & M 4.4.28 ⇐ ChU 4.14.3
IU M & K 3 ← BĀU M 4.4.14 → BĀU K 4.4.11 ← KaU 1.3

Triplet 2 + 2 triṣṭubhs (4 & 8)

IU M & K 4-5
IU K 6 / IU M 6, cf BĀU K 4.4.15 / M 4.4.18 (*pāda* d different)
IU M & K 7-8

Triplet 3 & 4

BĀU M 4.4.13	→	BĀU K 4.4.10	←	(Kena 4 or similar?)
↓		↓		
IU M 9		(IU K 9 ?)		
↓		↓		
IU M 9-11	→	IU K 9-11		
	↘ ↙			
Original		conclusion of the IU		
IU M 12-14	↙ ↘	IU K 12-14		

Triplet 5

IU M 15-16 = BĀU M 5.3 / IU K 15-18 = BĀU K 5.15.1-4
IU K 15ab = IU M 17ab
(IU K 15cd-16ab)
IU K 16c(e) - M 17c
IU K 17 = IU M 15
IU K 18 = IU M 16 = RS 1.189.1; 18b = AS 4.39.10b

B. The reconstruction of the original text in both variants:

With structural relationships with BĀU 4.4:

	IU M 1	IU K 1	
	IU M 2	IU K 2	
BĀU M4.4.14abc → *andhéna támasā́vṛtāḥ*	IU M 3	IU K 3	← BĀU K 4.4.11abc *andhéna támasā́vṛtāḥ*
	IU M 4 *triṣṭubh*	IU K 4 *triṣṭubh*	
	IU M 5	IU K 5	
(BĀU M 4.4.18d →)	IU M 6	IU K 6	(← BĀU K 4.4.15d)
	IU M 7	IU K 7	
	IU M 8 *triṣṭubh*	IU K 8 *triṣṭubh*	
BĀU M 4.4.13 → *andhám támaḥ prá viśanti (saṃbhūti)*	IU M 9	IU K 9	← BĀU K 4.4.10 *andhám támaḥ prá viśanti (vidyā)*
	IU M 10	IU K 10	
	IU M 11	IU K 11	

This was the harmonious composition of the original IU, in the framework of the tradition of each school, Mādhyaṃdina and Kāṇva, in a probably older (M) and a probably younger (K) variant.

Appendix 2

Recapitulation: The final text (A), and a tentative reconstruction of the original text and its extensions (B)

A. The final Kāṇva recension:

The omnipresence of the Lord / ātman, moral injunctions, punishment

īśā́vāsyàm[56] idáṁ sárvaṃ yát kíṃ ca jágatyāṃ jágat /
téna tyakténa bhuñjīthā mā́ gṛdhaḥ kásya svid dhánam //1//

kurvánn evéhá kármāṇi jijīviṣéc[57] chatáṁ sámāḥ /
evám tváyi[58] nā́nyáthetó [(a)sti][59] ná kárma lipyate náre //2//

asuryā̀[60] nā́ma té lokā́ andhéna támasā́vṛtāḥ/
tā́ṃs té prétyābhígacchanti yé ké cātmaháno jánāḥ //3//

The paradoxes of the ātma-vidyā

ánejad ékaṃ mánaso jávīyo
naínad devā́ āpnuvan pū́rvam árṣat[61] /
tád dhā́vato 'nyā́n áti eti tíṣṭhat
tásminn apó mātaríśvā dadhāti //4//[62]

tád ejati tán naíjati tád dūré tád u antiké
tád antár asya sárvasya tád u sárvasyāsya bāhyatáḥ[63]35 //5//

yás tú sárvāṇi bhūtā́ni ātmánn evā́nu páśyati /
sarvabhūtéṣu cātmā́naṃ táto ná ví jugupsate[64] //6//

yásmint sárvāṇi bhūtā́ny ātmaívā́bhūd vijānatáḥ /
tátra kó móhaḥ káḥ śóka ekatvám anupáśyataḥ //7//

sá páryagāc chukrám akāyám avraṇám
asnāviráṁ śuddhám ápāpaviddham /
kavír manīṣī́ paribhū́ḥ svayaṃbhū́r
[yāthātathyató] (á)rthān vyàdadhāc chāśvatī́bhyaḥ sámābhyaḥ[65] //8//

---

[56]*Īś* = (Śaṅkara:) *paramātmā sarvasya.*

[57]*jijīviṣa ít* (Thieme)—impv. not opt.

[58]Emend. *evaṃvídi?* I. e. náre.

[59]The *pāda* is hypermetrical (10 syllables instead of 8). Conjecture 1: *nā́nyáthét(ó ast)i.* Conjecture 2: instead of *evā́ṃ tváyi: evaṃvídi.* Therefore the double emendation of 2cd would make a lot of sense:

evaṃvídi nā́nyáthéti ná kárma lipyate náre //2//

[60]V. l. *asūryā́ nā́ma*, H, (LV), Horsch 1966, 166. Cf. RS 5.32.6.

[61]M v. l. árśat

[62]Cf. KaU 2.21 *asīno dūraṃ vrajati śayāno yāti sarvataḥ aśarīraṃ śarīreṣv anavastheṣv avasthitam*; MuU 3.1.7; BhG 13.14-16, etc. Paradoxical expressions for the inexpressible.

[63]5d is hypermetrical. Thieme proposes to omit *u* or *asya*. The latter seems easier to argue: it omits unnecessarily repeated syllables. It looks like a scribal error, not like an oral variant. The emended text reads: *tád antár asya sárvasya tád u sárvasya bāhyatáḥ*

[64]BĀU K 4.4.15 and IU K 6 have corresponding readings: *na tato / tato na vi jugupsate*, just as BĀU M 4.4.18 and IU M 6 have: *na tadā / tato na vi cikitsati*. Thieme 1965, 94, assumed that the former reading was original in the IU, and the latter in the BĀU, that the BĀU influenced IU M, and the IU K influenced the BĀU K. The combination of pronouns *yaḥ ... tato* in the IU, and *yadā ... tadā* in the BĀU M, along with *yadā ... tato* in the BĀU K, corroborates the conclusion that BĀU K has a changed text, that BĀU M has the original text, and that *yaḥ ... tato na vi jugupsate* could be the original reading of the IU.

[65]8d is hypermetrical. What can most easily be omitted is *yāthātathyató*. Thieme stresses that cancelling it, we obtain *a flawless triṣṭubh line (?); otherwise a triṣṭubh with two precaesura parts* (98).

The paradoxes of the vidyā *and of the* saṃbhūti *(the reverse order of the triplets in the IU M)*

andháṃ támaḥ prá viśanti yé (á)vidyām upā́sate /
táto bhū́ya iva té, támo yá u vidyā́yāṃ ratā́ḥ //9//

anyád evā́húr vidyáyā (a)nyád āhur ávidyayā /[66]
íti śuśruma dhī́rāṇāṃ yé, nas tád vicacakṣiré //10//

vidyā́ṃ cā́vidyāṃ ca yás tád védobháyaṁ sahá //
ávidyayā mṛtyúṃ tīrtvā́ vidyáyāmṛ́tam aśnute //11//

andháṃ támaḥ prá viśanti yé 'sàṃbhūtim upā́sate /
táto bhū́ya iva té támo yá u sáṃbhūt(i)yāṁ ratā́ḥ //12//

anyád evā́húḥ saṃbhavā́d (a)nyád āhur ásaṃbhavāt /
íti śuśruma dhī́rāṇāṃ yé nas tád vicacakṣiré //13//

sáṃbhūtiṃ ca vināśáṃ ca yás tád védobháyaṁ sahá //
vināśéna mṛtyúṃ tīrtvā́ sáṃbhūtyāmṛ́tam aśnute //14//

The prayer at the death of an ātmavid (the reverse order of 15ab-16c(e) and 17-18 than in the IU M; addition of 15cd and 16ab(cd) in IU K)

hiraṇmáyena pā́treṇa satyásyā́pihitaṃ múkham /
tát tváṃ pūṣann ápā́vṛṇu satyádharmāya dṛṣṭáye //15//

pū́ṣann eka ṛṣe yama sūrya prā́jāpatya vyū̀ha raśmī́nt sámūha téjo
yát te rūpáṃ kályāṇatamaṃ tát te paśyāmi /
yo 'sā́v asaú púruṣaḥ[67] só 'hám asmi //16//

vāyúr ánilam amṛ́tam áthedáṃ bhásmāntaṁ śárīram /
aúṁ3 kráto smára kṛtáṁ smara kráto[68] smára kṛtáṁ smara //17//

ágne náya supáthā rāyé asmā́n
víśvāni deva vayū́nāni vidvā́n /
yuyodhi àsmáj juhurāṇám éno
bhū́yiṣṭhāṃ te námauktíṃ vidhema //18//

B. The tentative reconstruction of the original Mādhyaṃdina recension and its extensions:

The first triplet (IU M 3abc = BĀU M 4.4.14abc)

īśā́vāsyàm idaṁ sárvaṃ yát kiṃca jágatyāṃ jágat|
téna tyakténa bhuñjīthā mā́ gṛdhaḥ kásya svid dhánam|| 1||

kurvánn evéhá kármāṇi jijīviṣéc[69] chatáṁ sámāḥ|
evámvidi[70] nā́nyátheti[71] ná kárma lipyate náre|| 2||

asūryā́[72] nā́ma te lokā́ andhéna tamasā́vṛtāḥ|
tā́ṁs te prétyā́pi gacchanti[73] yé ké cātmaháno jánāḥ|| 3||

Triṣṭubh 1

[66] IU M 12 v. l. *anyád evā́húr vidyā́yā (a)nyád āhur ávidyāyāḥ* / It is in Thieme's opinion lectio facilior.

[67] IU M 17 v. l. M 17c *yo 'sā́v ādityé púruṣaḥ só 'sā́v ahám*

[68] IU M 15 v. l. *63m kráto smára klibé smara*

[69] *jijīviṣa īt* (Thieme) = impv. If we accept Ježić's emendation of the third line to *evámvídi*, Thieme's suggestion is unnecessary since the verse is not a construction in the second person.

[70] In place of *evaṃ tvayi.* Goes better with *nare* later in the verse.

[71] In place of *nā́nyáthetó'sti* which makes the verse hypermetrical.

[72] Alt. reading: *asuryà nā́ma*: demonic.

[73] ĪUM 3abc = BUM 4.4.1.

ánejad ékaṃ mánaso jávīyo naínad devā́ āpnuvan pū́rvam árśat|[74]
tád dhā́vato'nyā́n átyeti tíṣṭhat tásminn apó mātaríśvā dadhāti|| 4||

The second triplet (IU M 6d emended = IU K 6d, BĀU K 4.4.15d = BĀU M 4.4.18d)

tád ejati tán naíjati tád dūré tád u antiké|
tád antár asya sárvasya tád u sárvasya bāhyatáḥ[75]|| 5||

yás tú sárvāṇi bhūtā́ni ātmánn evā́nu paśyati|
sarvabhūtéṣu cātmā́nam táto ná vi cikitsati|| 6||[76]

yásmint sárvāṇi bhūtā́ny ātmaivā́bhūd vijānatáḥ|
tátra kó móhaḥ káḥ śóka ekatvám anupáśyataḥ|| 7||

Triṣṭubh 2

sá páryagāc chukrám akāyám avraṇám
asnāvirám̐ śuddhám ápāpaviddham|
kavir manīṣī́ paribhū́ḥ svayaṃbhū́r
árthān vyàdadhāc chā́śvatī́bhyaḥ sámābhyaḥ[77]|| 8||

The third triplet (IU M 9 = BĀU M 4.4.13)

andhám̐ támaḥ prá viśanti yé 'sàṃbhūtim upā́sate|
táto bhū́ya iva té támo yá u sáṃbhūt(i)yām̐ ratā́ḥ|| 9||[78]

anyád evā́húḥ saṃbhavā́d (a)nyád āhur ásaṃbhavāt|
íti śuśruma dhī́rāṇāṃ yé nas tád vicacakṣiré|| 10||

sáṃbhūtiṃ ca vināśáṃ ca yás tád védobháyam̐ sahá|
vināśéna mṛtyúṃ tīrtvā́ sáṃbhūtyāmṛ́tam aśnute|| 11||

Here ended the original IU.
First extension: the fourth triplet (IU M 12-14 = IU K 9-11; IU K 9 = BĀU K 4.4.10)

andhám̐ támaḥ prá viśanti yé (á)vidyām upā́sate|
táto bhū́ya iva té támo yá u vidyā́yām̐ ratā́ḥ|| 12||[79]

anyád evā́húr vidyáyā (a)nyád āhur ávidyayā|[80]
íti śuśruma dhī́rāṇāṃ yé nas tád vicacakṣiré|| 13||

vidyā́ṃ cā́vidyāṃ ca yás tád védobháyam̐ sahá|
ávidyayā mṛtyúṃ tīrtvā́ vidyáyāmṛ́tam aśnute|| 14||

Second extension: the fifth triplet (IU M 15-16 = BĀU M 5.3; addition of IU M 17)

[74] K v. l. árṣat

[75] 5d is hypermetrical. Th. proposes to omit *u* or *asya*. The latter seems easier to argue for: it omits unnecessarily repeated syllables.

[76] BĀU K 4.4.15 and IU K 6 have corresponding readings: *na tato / tato na vi jugupsate*. BĀU M 4.4.18 and IU M 6 have: *na tadā / tato na vi cikitsati*. Cf. Thieme 1965, 94. The combination of pronouns *yaḥ ... tato* in the IU, and *yadā ... tadā* in the BĀU M, along with *yadā ... tato* in the BĀU K, corroborates the conclusion that BĀU K has a changed text, that BĀU M has the original text, and that *yaḥ ... tato na vi jugupsate* could be the original reading of the IU.

[77] 8d is hypermetrical. Omit *yāthātathyató*. Thieme: *a flawless triṣṭubh line (?); otherwise a triṣṭubh with two precaesura parts (98)*.

[78] ĪUM 9 = BUM 4.4.13.

[79] ĪUM 12-14 = ĪUK 9-11; ĪUK 9 = BUK 4.4.10.

[80] IU M 13 v. l. *anyád evā́húr vidyā́yā (a)nyád āhur ávidyāyāḥ* / Thieme: *lectio facilior*. Therefore the K reading was introduced in this reconstruction; the stanza was anyway taken over from the K recension.

vayúr ánilam amŕ̥tam áthedáṃ bhásmāntaṁ śarīram|
óṃ kráto smára klibé smara kráto smára kr̥táṁ smara|| 15||

ágne náya supáthā rāyé asmā́n
víśvāni deva vayǘnāni vidvā́n|
yuyodhi àsmáj juhurāṇám éno
bhū́yiṣṭhāṃ te námauktiṃ vidhema|| 16||[81]

hiraṇmáyena pā́treṇa satyásyā́pihitaṃ múkham|
yo 'sā́v ādityé púruṣaḥ só 'sā́v ahám|
ó3m khám̐ bráhma|| 17||

Abbreviations

AS	Atharva-saṃhitā
BĀU	Br̥had-āraṇyaka-upaniṣad
BĀU K	Br̥had-āraṇyaka-upaniṣad (Kāṇva)
BĀU M	Br̥had-āraṇyaka-upaniṣad (Mādhyaṃdina)
BhG	Bhagavadgītā
ChU	Chāndogya-upaniṣad
IU / Īśā	Īśā-upaniṣad
K	Kāṇva
KaU, Kaṭha	Kaṭha-upaniṣad
KeU / Kena	Kena-upaniṣad
KŚS	Kātyāyana-śrautasūtra
M	Mādhyaṃdina
MuU	Muṇḍaka-upaniṣad
RS	R̥ksaṃhitā
ŚB	Śatapatha-brāhmaṇa
ŚB (K)	Śatapatha-brāhmaṇa (Kāṇva)
ŚB (M)	Śatapatha-brāhmaṇa (Mādhyaṃdina)
ŚvU	Śvetāsvatara-upaniṣad
ŚGS	Śāṅkhāyana-gr̥hyasūtra
VS	Vājasaneyi-saṃhitā
VS (K)	Vājasaneyi-saṃhitā (Kāṇva)
VS (M)	Vājasaneyi-saṃhitā (Mādhyaṃdina)
YV	Yajurveda

D	Deussen, Paul
H	Hume, Robert Ernest
LV	Limaye, V. P. - Vadekar, R. D.
O	Olivelle, Patrick
R	Renou, Louis
Th	Thieme, Paul

[81] This verse is from the *R̥g-saṃhitā*, 1.189.1. And 16b occurs also in *Atharva-saṃhitā*, 4.39.10b.

Select Bibliography

1. Editions of Upaniṣads

Böhtlingk, Otto (ed. & transl.) (1889a), *Bṛhadāraṇjakopanishad in der Mādhjaṃdina-Recension*, Sankt Petersburg, Kaiserliche Akademie der Wissenschaften.

Limaye, V. P., and Vadekar, R. D. (ed.) (1958.), *Eighteen Principal Upaniṣads*, Poona, Vaidika Saṃśodhana Maṇóala. (LV)

Olivelle, Patrick (annotated text & transl.) (1998.), *The Early Upaniṣads*, Oxford - New York, Oxford University Press / Delhi, Munshiram Manoharlal Publishers. (O)

Radhakrishnan, S. (transl. & text) (1953.), *The Principal Upaniṣads*, London, George Allen & Unwin.

Renou, Louis (ed. & transl.) (1943.), *Isa Upanishad, Les Upanishad I*, Paris, Adrien Maisonneuve. (R)

Sātvalekar, Śrīpād Dāmodar (ed.) (1983.), *Śuklayajurvedīya Kāṇvasaṃhitā*, Pārḍī, Svādhyāya-maṇḍala.

Sātvalekar, Śrīpād Dāmodar (ed.) (1983.?), *Vājasaneyi-mādhyandina-śukla Yajurvedasaṃhitā*, Pārḍī, Svādhyāya-maṇḍala.

Śankarācārya (1964.), *Īśādidaśopaniṣadaḥ Śāṃkarabhāṣyasametāḥ / Ten Principal Upanishads with Śānkarabhāṣya, u: Śrīśaṃkarācāryagranthāvalī / Works of Sankarācārya in Original Sanskrit*, 3 Vols. (Vol. I), Motilal Banarsidass.

Swami Gambhīrānanda (1957, 2nd ed. 1989), *Eight Upaniṣads. Vol. One (Īśā, Kena, Kaṭha and Taittirīya). With the Commentary of Śaṅkarācārya*, Calcutta, Advaita Ashrama.

Varadachari, K. C. - Thathacharya, D. T. (1975), *Isavasyopanishad Bhashya by Sri Vedanta Desika Critically Edited with Introduction, Translation and Notes*, Madras, Vedanta Desika Research Society.

2. Translations without the original text

Della Casa, Carlo (transl.) (1986.), *Upaniṣad*, Classici UTET, Torino, Unione tipografico-editrice Torinese.

Deussen, Paul (transl.) (1897., 1921.), *Sechzig Upaniṣad's des Veda*, Leipzig, F. A. Brockhaus. (D)

Hume, Robert Ernest (transl.) (1931.), *The Thirteen Principal Upanishads*, Oxford, Oxford University Press. (H)

Müller, Max (transl.) (1879., 1884.), *The Upanishads*, 2 vols., SBE 1, 15; repr. 1981., Delhi, Motilal Banarsidass. (MM)

3. Other Vedic texts

Caland, W. - Raghu Vira (1926.) (ed.), *The Śatapatha Brāhmaṇa in the Kaṇvīya Recension*, Lahore; repr. Motilal Banarsidass 1983.

Eggeling, Julius (transl.) (1882. (I), 1885. (II), 1894. (III), 1895. (?IV), 1900. (V)), *The Śatapatha-Brāhmaṇa, According to the Text of the Mādhyandina School*, SBE 12, 26, 41, 43, 44; Oxford, Clarendon Press.

Weber, Albrecht (ed.) (1855.), *The Śatapatha-Brāhmaṇa in the Mādhyandina-śākhā with extracts from the commentaries of Sāyaṇa, Harisvāmin and Dvivedaganga*, Berlin-London. (SB)

4. Selected secondary literature

Belvalkar S. K. & R. D. Ranade (1927.), *History of Indian Philosophy, vol. 2: The Creative Period. Brāhmaṇa and Upanishadic philosophy and post-upanishadic thought-ferment*, Poona, Bilvakuṭja Publishing House.

Deussen, Paul (T. & T. Clark 1906., repr. 1996.), *The Philosophy of the Upanishads*, New York, Dover Publications.

Gonda, Jan (1975.), *Vedic Literature (Saṃhitās and Brāhmaṇas)*, HIL, vol. I, fasc. 1, Wiesbaden, Otto Harrassowitz.

Horsch, Paul (1966), *Die vedische Gāthā- und Śloka-Literatur*, Bern, Francke Verlag.

Jacob, Colonel G. A. (Bombay, 1891., repr. 1971...1985.), *A Concordance to the Principal Upanishads and Bhagavadgītā*, Motilal Banarsidass.

Keith, Arthur Berriedale (1925., repr. 1976. Motilal Banarsidass), *The Religion and Philosophy of the Veda and Upanishads*, HOS, Vol. 31.

Macdonell, Arthur Antony - Keith, Arthur Berriedale (1912.), *Vedic Index of Names and Subjects*, 2 vols., London, John Murray.

Ranade, R. D. (1926., 1986.), *A Constructive Survey of Upanishadic Philosophy*, Chowpatti : Bombay, Bharatiya Vidya Bhavan.

Schrader, Otto (1933), *A Critical Study of Īśopaniṣad, The Indian Antiquary 82*, p. 205-212 (1-8). Kleine Schriften (1983), ed. J. F. Sprockhoff, Wiesbaden, F. Steiner Verlag, pp. 156-163.

Thieme, Paul (1965.), *Īśopaniṣad (= Vājasaneyi-saṃhitā 40)* 1-14, JAOS 85, pp. 89-99; repr. P. T., Kleine Schriften II, pp. 228-238.

Thieme, Paul (1966.), *Upanischaden* (Ausgewählte Stücke), Stuttgart, Reclam, Universal Bibliothek 8723.

Visva Bandhu, *A Vedic Word Concordance* (I / Saṃhitās 1-6: 1942, (1976.)-1963.; II / Brāhmaṇas 1-2: 1973.; III / Upaniṣads 1-4: 1958.-1961.; V / Indices 1-2: 1964.-1965. Lahore - Hoshiarpur, Vishveshvaranand Vedic Research Institute.

Witzel, Michael (1987.), "On the Localisation of Vedic Texts and Schools," in G. Pollet (ed.), *India and the Ancient World: History, Trade and Culture before AD. 650* (Orientalia Lovaniensia Analecta, 25; Leuven: Department Oriëntalistiek), pp. 174-213.

Witzel, Michael (1997), "The Vedic Canon and its Political Milieu," in *Inside the Texts, Beyond the Texts. New Approaches to the Study of the Vedas*, ed. M. Witzel, HOS, Opera Minora Vol. 2, Cambridge MA, Harvard University, pp. 257-345.

Introduction to the Sanskrit Language (Delmonico)

Sanskrit is one of the ancient, classical, and hieratic languages of India.[1] In that sense it occupies a position in Indian civilization similar to those of classical Greek (the Greek of Homer [800 BCE-701 BCE ?], for instance) and Latin (the Latin of Ciceronian period [80-43 BCE], for instance) in Western civilization and classical Chinese (the Chinese of the Five Classics [11th to 7th cents. BCE], for instance) in the civilization of China. The Sanskrit language dates back two and a half millennia to the time of the great grammarian Pāṇini (4th cent. BCE ?). Before the grammatical codification of Sanskrit the language is referred to as Vedic and is represented in a literature that extends back another thousand years earlier (Vedas, Brāhmaṇas, Āraṇyakas, and Upaniṣads). The name Sanskrit is an Anglicized version of the Sanskrit word *saṃskṛta* which means "refined, polished, purified, made whole or complete." It refers specifically to the later version of the Vedic language that was described and regulated by Pāṇini and his grammarian predecessors and successors.[2]

The term *saṃskṛta* does not appear in Pāṇini's grammar and was probably applied to the Pāṇinian language later in order to distinguish it from the language of ordinary people, called Prākṛta, once the language of the people had sufficiently diverged from the language Pāṇini described. The Prākṛtas represent the second stage in the development of Sanskrit into the modern vernacular languages of Northern India today (Hindi, Gujarati, Marathi, Bihari, Bengali, and so forth). The languages of Southern India (Telugu, Tamil, Kannada, and Malayalam) come from another language family called Dravidian, though some of them have adopted a great deal of vocabulary from Sanskrit (Telugu, for instance).

Sanskrit and the languages that developed out of it are important members of the Indo-European family of languages.[3] The discovery that Sanskrit was related to Latin and Greek and through them to most of the languages of Europe and to some of the languages of the Middle East is attributed to Sir William Jones, Chief Justice of India and founder of the Royal Asiatic Society. In 1786, in a lecture on India culture he said the following:

> The Sanskrit language, whatever may be its antiquity, is of wonderful structure; more perfect that the Greek, more copious than the Latin, and more exquisitely refined than either; yet bearing to both of them a stronger affinity, both in the roots of verbs and in the forms of grammar, than could have been produced by accident; so strong that no philologer could examine all the three without believing them to have sprung from some common source, which, perhaps, no longer exists. There is a reason, though not quite so forcible, for supposing that both the Gothic and Celtic, though blended with a different idiom, had the same origin with the Sanskrit; and the old Persian might be added to the same family.[4]

[1] The other is ancient Tamil, spoken and composed in in South India from about the 3rd cent. BCE.

[2] Pāṇini's work is called the *Book of Eight Chapters* (*Aṣṭādhyāyī*) and consists of 3,996 *sūtras* or aphorisms giving the descriptive rules for the formation of the language. Those rules were supplemented and amended by a later grammarian named Kātyāyana (3rd cent. BCE) and commented on in the *Great Commentary* (*Mahābhāṣya*) by the grammarian Patañjali (2nd cent. BCE). These three *munis* or sages together form the foundation of Sanskrit grammar.

[3] Tamil and other related languages in South India (Telugu, Kannada, Malayalam, etc.) are not Indo-European languages. They are referred to as Dravidian languages and are considered to be related to Elamite which was spoken in ancient Anatolia.

[4] Taken as cited from J. P. Mallory, *In Search of the Indo-Europeans: Language, Archaeology and Myth*, 12. (London: Thames and Hudson Ltd, 1989)

Though James Parsons had previously noticed the relationship between these languages in 1767 by comparing the terms for the numbers from one to ten in each of a number of languages,[5] Jones's formulation is considered the first modern exposition of Indo-European theory, though sadly still encumbered with Biblical pseudo-history (he traces the common source of these languages back to the Ark!). The language considered to be the source of all the members of the family is called Proto-Indo-European and Vedic/Sanskrit was once considered the oldest surviving example of that family, until Hittite (1800-1200 BCE) was discovered in central Anatolia. Nevertheless, Vedic/Sanskrit has played an important role in the reconstruction of Proto-Indo-European. The Indo-European hypothesis is relatively easy to state, though the details are still hotly contested. Mallory puts it like this:

> If the details are still a matter of controversy, the Indo-European hypothesis is most certainly not. It is the only explanation that can convincingly account for why approximately half the earth's population speaks in languages clearly related to one another. This requires the assumption that at some time and some place in Eurasia there existed a population which spoke a language directly ancestral to all of those we now recognize as Indo-European.[6]

The details over which there is still controversy are things like where the "homeland" of the original Indo-European speakers was located, when various groups separated and migrated to their new homes, how the various groups interacted with other Indo-European and non-Indo-European speaking groups and when, and so on. The earliest Indo-European texts we have in the Indian subcontinent are, of course, the Vedas, especially the Ṛg Veda which is considered the earliest of the four Vedas. Its language though ancient already shows evidence of sounds and vocabulary borrowed from non-Indo-European languages and presents no references to any places outside of Northeast India.

When the speakers of Indo-European language entered India is not certain, but the general consensus is around 1500 BCE. Some have tried to identify the Indus Valley Civilization, which produced an extraordinary city culture along the Indus river from about 3000 BCE to about 1800 BCE, with ancient Indo-Aryan speakers. The script of the language of that civilization which has survived on clay seals excavated at Indus Valley sites has not yet been deciphered, but the most likely candidate is the non-Indo-European language family called Dravidian to which the languages of present day South India all belong. The arrival of the Indo-European speakers seems to have taken place two or three centuries after the collapse of the Indus Valley Civilization, a collapse which happened probably for environmental reasons. The arrival of the Indo-European speakers is evidenced by the arrival on the scene of new kind of pottery, new kinds of burial practices, the domesticated horse, and the use of horse-drawn chariots. By around 1200 BCE the Vedas were being composed and collected into the first of four great collections in an Indo-European language containing sounds not found in the other members of the family, sounds borrowed from languages encountered in India, primarily the retroflex consonants. Eight hundred years later, Pāṇini completes his grammar and Sanskrit is born out of Vedic. Since that time, for two and a half millennia, the Sanskrit language became the pre-eminent language of learning and culture in India, and once the vernacular languages developed towards the beginning of the second millennium CE it became the *lingua franca* (common language) or the language of intellectual discourse. Over one hundred and twenty-five thousand works are written in Sanskrit on subjects ranging from mathematics, astronomy, and medicine to philosophy, mythology, religion, and literature. There are even texts on the raising and care of horses and elephants. Unlike the works in classical Greek which can be read in their entirety in a couple of years, the texts written in Sanskrit cannot be read in an entire lifetime, or, for that matter, in ten or twenty entire lifetimes. The study of Sanskrit and its literature opens up a vast, rich world populated by some of the finest thinkers and writers humankind has produced.

The presentation of the Sanskrit language that follows is merely a brief introduction. It will give only an overview of the main features of the language along with some simple examples of how each feature works. In Pāṇini's grammar the practice is, generally speaking, to present general rules for the formation and use of Sanskrit words and then dozens of exceptions. Here we will only present some of the rules and almost none of the exceptions. The main purpose of this exercise is to help

[5] This he did in his all but forgotten work, *The Remains of Japhet, being historical enquiries into the affinity and origins of the European languages.* Referred to in Mallory, ibid., 10. Edwin Bryant cites a statement made almost a century before Parsons by Andreas Jager in which he claimed almost the same thing, but without any knowledge of Sanskrit, since it had not been "discovered" yet. See Bryant, *The Quest for the Origin of Vedic Culture*, 16. (Oxford, New York: Oxford University Press, 2001)

[6] Mallory, ibid., 22-23.

students understand the meanings of the abbreviations used in our grammatic analysis of the *mantras* of the Īśā Upaniṣad. After reading this section, students hopefully will have a general sense of how Sanskrit is structured and how it creates meaning in the minds of those who hear it or read it. Suggestions will be given at the end of this for students who wish to pursue the study of the language in greater depth. There are lots of valuable and free materials and aid available on the internet and from various sources.

The components of the Sanskrit language that we will discuss here are: its alphabet and the pronunciation of the alphabet, its tendency to change letters when combined with other letters (called euphonic combination or *sandhi*), its nouns and their declension, its pronouns and their declension, its verbs and their conjugations, its adverbs and indeclinables, its compounds and nominal base formation, its syntax, and its prosody (use of meters in versification). Each of these will be discussed briefly and examples provided; because those examples are the most common ways in which Sanskrit words are formed, a great deal of Sanskrit grammar will be covered.

The Alphabet and Pronunciation

The Sanskrit alphabet is the following, organized here in one of the traditional orderings.

Vowels: Svara

	Short	Long		
gutturals	अ	आ	a	ā
palatals	इ	ई	i	ī
labials	उ	ऊ	u	ū
cerebrals	ऋ	ॠ	ṛ	ṝ
dentals	ऌ	ॡ	ḷ	ḹ
guttural-palatals	ए	ऐ	e	ai
guttural-labials	ओ	औ	o	au

Consonants: Vyañjana

gutturals	कण्ठ्य	क	ख	ग	घ	ङ	ka	kha	ga	gha	ṅa
palatals	तालव्य	च	छ	ज	झ	ञ	ca	cha	ja	jha	ña
cerebrals	मूर्धन्य	ट	ठ	ड	ढ	ण	ṭa	ṭha	ḍa	ḍha	ṇa
dentals	दन्त्य	त	थ	द	ध	न	ta	tha	da	dha	na
labials	ओष्ठ्य	प	फ	ब	भ	म	pa	pha	ba	bha	ma
semivowels	अन्तःस्थ	य	र	व	ल		ya	ra	va	la	
sibilants	ऊष्मन्	श	ष	स			śa	ṣa	sa		
aspirate	ऊष्मन्	ह					ha				

Above, in the Sanskrit script, the consonants are given with the vowel "a" (अ) following them. This is done to facilitate the pronunciation of the consonants. To write just the consonant, the sign a stroke sloping downward to the right, called *virāma* (◌्), is added at the bottom most point of the consonant sign. For example: क् = k, च् = c, ट् = ṭ, and so on.

Notice the extraordinarily well organized structure of the alphbet. All the vowels come first, the simple vowels short and long first and then the complex vowels or dipthongs. They arranged on the basis of their place of pronunciation starting at the back of the mouth. The consonants come next and are divided up into five groups or classes. Again they are organized on the basis of place of pronunciation in the mouth, starting at the back and moving to the front. Each group has five members starting with the unvoiced (k) and aspirated unvoiced (kh) members of the class followed by the voiced (g) and aspirated voiced (gh) members of the class followed by the nasal of the class (ṅ, pron. like *ng* in "sing"). The *ka*-group are all pronounced at the back of the mouth and are called gutterals. Each of the following groups is ordered in the same way. After the five groups come the semi-vowels also organized by place of pronunciation starting from the back forward. Next come the three sibilants again organized in a similar fashion.

Finally, there is "h" which stands by itself. Sanskrit dictionaries are organized in this order.

Thus, the sounds of the Sanskrit alphabet are divided among the different places of pronunciation in the mouth; taking just the vowels for example: a and ā are pronounced in the throat, i and ī at the palate, u and ū with the lips, ṛ and ṝ with the tongue curled upward at the roof of the mouth, ḷ and ḹ at the teeth, e at the palate, ai sliding from throat to palate, o at the lips, au sliding from throat to lips, and aḥ at the throat. (aṃ is a nasal sound).

Pronunciation Chart

अ — a, pronounced like "a" in "Roman,"[7]

आ — ā, pronounced like "a" in "father,"

इ — i, pronounced like "i" in "it" or "pin,"

ई — ī, pronounced like "i" in "police,"

उ — u, pronounced like "u" in "push,"

ऊ — ū, pronounced like "u" in "rude,"

ऋ — ṛ, pronounced like "er" in "fiber,"

ॠ — ṝ, pronounced like "ree" in "reel,"

ऌ — ḷ, pronounced like "le" in "angle,"

ॡ — ḹ, pronounced like "lea" in "leash,"

ए — e, pronounced like "ay" in "way,"

ऐ — ai, pronounced like "ai" in "aisle,"

ओ — o, pronounced like "o" in "note,"

औ — au, pronounced like "ow" in "now,"

आं — āṃ, pronounced like "ung" in "rung,"

आः — āḥ, pronounced like "aha,"

Consonants: Vyañjana

The ka-varga (ka-group)

These velar consonants are all pronounced in the throat.

[7]Many of these pronunciation examples have been taken from the fine introduction to Sanskrit called *Sanskrit: an easy introduction to an enchanting language* by Ashok Aklujkar. (Richmond, British Columbia: Svādhyāya Publications, 1992)

क् — k, pronounced like the "k" in "sky,"

ख् — kh, pronounced like "c" in "cat,"

ग् — g, pronounced like the "g" in "gum,"

घ् — gh, pronounced like the "gh" in "doghouse,"

ङ् — ṅ, pronounced like "ng" in "sung,"

The ca-varga (ca-group)

These palatal consonants are all pronounced at the palate.

च् — c, pronounced like the "ch" in "church,"

छ् — ch, pronounced like the "ch" in "chew,"

ज् — j, pronounced like "j" in "jump,"

झ् — jh, pronounce this like "j" with a strong outward breath,"

ञ् — ñ, pronounced like "n" in "canyon,"

The ṭa-varga (ṭa-group)

These retroflex consonants are all pronounced with the tip of the tongue curled upward touching the roof of the mouth.

ट् — ṭ, pronounced like the "t" in "art" or "stop,"

ठ् — ṭh, pronounced like the "th" in "boathouse,"

ड् — ḍ, pronounced like "d" in "ardent" or "bird,"

ढ् — ḍh, pronounce this like "dh" in "hardhat,"

ण् — ṇ, pronounced like "n" in "yarn," "land" or "tint,"

The ta-varga (ta-group)

These dental consonants are all pronounced at the teeth.

त् — t, pronounced like the "th" in "the," "them" or the French word "*tete* (head),

थ् — th, pronounced like the above letter 't', but with more aspiration,

द् — d, pronounced like in the French word "*donner*" (to give),

ध् — dh, pronounce this like "d" with a strong outward breath,

न् — n, pronounced like "n" in "no,"

The pa-varga (pa-group)

These labial consonants are all pronouced with the lips.

प् — p, pronounced like the "p" in "spin,"

फ् — pha, pronounced like the "ph" in "tophat,"

ब् — b, pronounced like "b" in "boat,"

भ् — bh, pronouned like "bh" in "abhor,"

म् — m, pronounced like "m" in "mud,"

The Semivowels

The sounds are divided thus; y is produced at the palate, r at the roof of the mouth, l at the teeth, and v at the lips.

य् — y, pronounced like the "y" in "yoga,"

र् — r, pronounced like the "r" in "relic,"

ल् — l, pronounced like "l" in "land,"

व् — v, pronounced like "v" in "vote,"

The Sibilants

The sounds are divided thus; ś is produced at the palate, ṣ at the roof of the mouth, s at the teeth, and h at the throat.

श् — ś, pronounced like the "sh" in "Swedish-chocolate,"
ष् — ṣ, pronounced with tongue curled upward touching the roof of the mouth (it nevertheless sounds much like the previous ś or the "sh" in "ship"),
स् — s, pronounced like "s" in "sun,"
ह् — h, pronounced like "h" in "house,"

The Maheśvara-sūtras

There is an older method of organizing the letters and sounds of the Sanskrit language that was probably the source of the one just presented. It goes back at least to Pāṇini and probably before. The letters of the Sanskrit language are organized into fourteen units that make it easy for Pāṇini and other grammarians to refer to groups of letters that are similar or are treated in similar ways in the rules of the grammar. These fourteen units have come to be known as the *sūtras* or aphorisms of the great god (*maheśvara*) Śiva. When pronounced properly they do conjure up the image of the great Śiva dancing wildly and playing his *ḍamaru* (a two-headed drum) at the time of the destruction of the universe. They are:

1. *a-i-u-ṇ*
2. *ṛ-ḷ-k*
3. *e-o-ṅ*
4. *ai-auc*
5. *ha-ya-va-raṭ*
6. *laṇ*

7. *ña-ma-ṅa-ṇa-nam*
8. *jha-bhañ*
9. *gha-ḍha-dhaṣ*
10. *ja-ba-ga-ḍa-daś*
11. *kha-pha-cha-ṭha-tha-ca-ṭa-tav*
12. *ka-pay*
13. *śa-ṣa-sar*
14. *hal*

The last letter in each of the aphorisms is called by the technical name "it."[8] It indicates the end of the group, but does not belong to the group. When combined with the first letter of the group the last letter, the "it," makes a convenient name for the group. For instance, *aṇ* is the name of the simple vowels, a, i, u. And *ṛk* is the name of the vocalic r (ṛ) and vocalic l (ḷ). One can combine the groups so that they refer to all the vowels, for instance, using the name *ac* (aphorisms one through four). All the consonants can be referred to by the name *hal* (aphorism five through aphorism fourteen). One does not necessarily have to begin with the first letter of one of the groups. We will see in the next section the name *ik*, which begins with the letter "i," from the middle of aphorism one, and ends with the "it" *k*, used in a grammatical rule. Pāṇini used these names in his aphorisms when he wanted to apply a particular rule to some but not all the members of the alphabet. It is an ingenious system.

The short "a-s" that come with each of the consonants are meant only for pronunciation. Without the "a" present, the consonants cannot be pronounced. Thus, the rules that Pāṇini will state for consonants apply only to the consonant and not the vowel "a." One might say, then, that these fourteen aphorisms of Maheśvara are the very foundation of Pāṇini's treatment of the Sanskrit language.

Sandhi or Euphonic Combination

One of the most vexing problems facing new students of Sanskrit is determining where one word ends and another begins. This is sometimes a problem even for experienced readers of Sanskrit. The problem arises because of what is called *sandhi* or euphonic combination. When Sanskrit words are pronounced quickly together or are written down in the native script called Devanāgarī (the city of the gods) the first letters of some words and the last letters of some words are changed depending on what precedes them or what follows them. This is called external *sandhi*. When the vowels or consonents within a word are changed because of the addition of prefixes and suffixes or because words are joined together in the formation of compound words, it is called internal *sandhi*. The changes brought by combination (*sandhi*) revolve around avoiding spaces and assimilation of the letters found in close proximity.

Here are some examples of external *sandhi* from our Upaniṣad:

In the Invocation Mantra the two words in the third line *eva* and *avaśiṣyate* are joined by *sandhi* into *evāvaśiṣyate*. The rule is that when two like simple vowels (a, i, u) follow each other they are replaced by the corresponding long vowel (ā, ī, ū). Here the final a of *eva* is followed by the first a of *avaśiṣyate* and the two are replaced by a single corresponding long vowel: *evāvaśiṣyate*.[9]

In third quarter of Mantra Two of the Upaniṣad we find the odd series *nānyatheto'sti*. When *sandhi* is removed, this turns into *na anyathā itas asti*. We have already seen the replacement of "a" (*na*) and "a" (*anyathā*) by "ā" above. In a similar way, by another set of rules the "ā" at the end of *anyathā* and the "i" at the beginning of *itas* are replaced by a single corresponding short diphthong "e."[10] The transformation of *itas* to *ito* occurs by another set of steps. First the "s" at the end of the word is changed by a *sandhi* rule to "r"[11] and then the "r" after a short "a" and before a word beginning with a short "a" (as in *asti* here) is replaced by "u."[12] By the same rule that applied to "ā" and "i" above, the "a" and the "u" are replaced by "o" (*ito*). By another rule the "a" at the beginning of *asti* is dropped.[13] Often there is a marker for the missing "a" which is indicated by an apostrophe

[8]This is established by Pāṇini's *sūtra* (1.3.3), *halantyam*, "the final consonant [is 'it']."

[9]This is one of the simplest of the *sandhi* changes and is covered by Pāṇini's aphorism-rule: *akaḥ savarṇe dīrghaḥ*, "*ak* (a, i, u, ṛ, ḷ) when followed by a homogeneous vowel (*savarṇa*) becomes long (ā, ī, ū ṝ, ḹ)." Thus, *eva* + *avaśiṣyate* = *evāvaśiṣyate*.

[10]The Pāṇinian rule covering this change is (6.1.87): *ādguṇaḥ*, "When a vowel comes after a short or long 'a,' it is replaced by the closest *guṇa* vowel (a, e, o)." Thus, ā + i = e.

[11]The aphorism/rule that applies here is (8.2.66): *sasajuṣo ruḥ*, "S at the end of a word and *sajuṣ* are replaced by 'r.'"

[12]P. (6.1.113): *ato roraplutādaplute*, "In place of 'r' after an unprolated short 'a' and before an unprolated a comes u.

[13]P. (6.1.109): *eṅaḥ padāntādati*, "When a short 'a' follows a word final 'e' or an 'o' they take the form of the prior one (e or o)." Thus, o + a = o.

in Roman transliteration. In Devanāgarī the apostrophe looks like this: ऽ.

There are only about seventy *sandhi* rules in all, but we will not give them here. Every Sanskrit grammar or learning text has a chapter devoted to them. Learning them takes a little time, but it is not too difficult. It is essential if one wants to read Sanskrit in its original script. Deciphering a text written with full *sandhi* in operation can be much like solving a puzzle in the beginning. Once one has mastered the rules, it becomes almost second nature.

The important idea to be taken from this section is that the words as they appear in the *mantras* of the text will often look different from the words listed in the word-by-word grammatical breakdown. This is because the words in the *mantras* are joined by *sandhi* combination and the words in the word-by-word sections have had their *sandhi* broken. They are listed in their original, uncombined forms. Of course, internal *sandhi* is not removed since internal *sandhi* operates within words in the formation of the verb forms and noun forms in their respective cases.

Nouns, Adjectives, Pronouns, Their Cases, and Their Declensions

The noun system constitutes a large part of the Sanskrit language. Nouns are *declined* in Sanskrit which means that nouns change their form according to their function in a sentence. Declension is the variation or change of nominal stems by means of endings. Greek and Latin are also declined languages. In English, except for the use of plural endings, the location a word has in a sentence and its prepositions tell one what role a word plays in the sentence to generate meaning. In Sanskrit it is the form of the word, produced by its endings, that tells one whether a word is the subject of the sentence or the object of the action, whether it has an instrumental role, a causative role, or a locative function in the creating the meaning of a sentence. It also tells us whether it is singular, dual, plural, masculine, feminine or neuter. Since it is the form of the word and not where it appears in a sentence, Sanskrit words can and often do appear in almost any order in a sentence and yet still convey their intended meanings. This quality of the noun system makes Sanskrit a very flexible language for poetic composition, since the words can be rearranged, without interfering with the meaning, to fit the requirements of different meters. For this reason many works in Sanskrit are written in verse. The use of verse also aids in the process of memorization of works; such memorization was, and to a degree still is, a very important way in which Sanskrit works were learned, preserved, and transmitted. Of course, there is a standard word order that is used in prose compostions. That order is usually the subject preceded by its adjectives followed by the direct object preceded by its adjectives followed finally the verb preceded by its adverbs.

A noun in Sanskrit may have as many as twenty-four different forms. There are three grammatical genders: masculine, feminine, and neuter. There are three numbers: singular, dual, and plural. And finally, there are eight cases: nominative, vocative, accusative, instrumental, dative, ablative, genitive, and locative.[14] In practice, however, several of the cases in various numbers have the same form. Later, in the section on syntax, we will discuss what the meanings of these various cases is. This will be important for users of the book, because when we analyze the mantras word by word we identify the case, gender, and number of each word. Without knowing what the various cases signify one will have difficulty understanding what functions the words play in producing the meaning of the *mantras*.

Pāṇini begins by defining the nominal stem out of which nouns in their inflected forms are created. "That which has meaning, is not a verbal root, and is not a suffix nor ends in a suffix is called a nominal stem."[15] The Sanskrit term for a nominal stem is *prātipadika*, which means the crude form or base of a noun. The suffixes refer to the endings that are added to a nominal stem to make it into a noun in one of the cases. And naturally as soon as a suffix is added to the nominal stem it is no longer a nominal stem, but a declined noun. Let's take the word *aśva*, horse, as an example of a nominal stem. It has meaning (horse), it is not a verbal root (like $\sqrt{gam}$ to go or depart), it is not a suffix (as we shall see), and it does not end in a suffix. As is often the case with Pāṇini a later aphorism adds to and gives a partial exception to the previous definition. "Words ending with primary (*kṛt*) and secondary (*taddhita*) suffixes and com-

[14] These names are not the names of the cases used by the native grammarians. These names are derived from similar cases in Latin and Greek. The Sanskrit names for this cases are, however, not very informative. They are simply First (*prathamā*), Second (*dvitīyā*), Third (*tṛtīyā*), Fourth (*caturthī*), Fifth (*pañcamī*), Sixth (*ṣaṣṭhī*), Seventh (*saptamī*). There is no special name for the vocative case since it is regarded and treated as a special instance of the First case.

[15] Pāṇini, 1.2.45: *arthavad adhātur apratyayaḥ prātipadikam*

pound words are also nominal stems."[16] We will look at compound words and primary and secondary suffixes in a later section.

All the normal case-endings or case suffixes are given in a single aphorism in Pāṇini (4.1.2) which consists of just a list of them in order from the nominative singular to the locative plural, many of which are marked or separated from the others by *it* letters.[17] In tabular form they look like this:

Case	Singular	Dual	Plural
Nominative (Voc.)	s	au	as
Accusative	am	au	as
Instrumental	ā	bhyām	bhis
Dative	e	bhyām	bhyas
Ablative	as	bhyām	bhyas
Genitive	as	os	ām
Locative	i	os	su

These are some of the suffixes referred to in Pāṇini's aphorism defining the *prātipadika* or nominal stem. The whole group is called *sup*. *Sup* (pron. "soup") is the name for all the nominal case suffixes. Similarly, we will see when we come to the verbs that the verbal endings or suffixes are called *tiṅ* (pron. "ting").

When these endings are used with the most common types of nominal stem, those ending in vowels, they take on forms that are more challenging to recognize. They, however, can be most easily and clearly recognized when used with stems that end in consonants. So, before giving a typical example of a stem ending in a vowel that has been altered by the addition of these endings, let's look at a typical stem ending in a consonant.

Let's take the stem *suhṛd* which means "friend" or literally "good heart:"

Case	Singular	Dual	Plural
Nominative (Voc.)	suhṛt	suhṛdau	suhṛdaḥ
Accusative	suhṛdam	suhṛdau	suhṛdaḥ
Instrumental	suhṛdā	suhṛdbhyām	suhṛdbhiḥ
Dative	suhṛde	suhṛdbhyām	suhṛdbhyaḥ
Ablative	suhṛdaḥ	suhṛdbhyām	suhṛdbhyaḥ
Genitive	suhṛdaḥ	suhṛdoḥ	suhṛdām
Locative	suhṛdi	suhṛdoḥ	suhṛtsu

There are only three changes made by *sandhi* in this example. The nominative singular drops the ending "s" and replaces the final "d" with a "t" giving us *suhṛt*.[18] And, the final "s" wherever it occurs in at the end of an ending is changed to "ḥ" which is called a *visarga*. Thus, *suhṛdas*, the nominative plural, becomes *suhṛdaḥ*. The same is true of all the other forms of *suhṛd* in the declension that end in "s" after the ending is added. Finally, in the the locative plural the final "d" is replaced by a "t" before the ending "su". Other than that all the case endings are recognizable.

Now compare those forms with the inflected forms of a typical nominal stem that ends in an "a." The word *rāma* is often used as an example of a word in short "a." Rāma is the name of one of the descents (*avatāras*) of the great god Viṣṇu and the subject of one of India's greatest epics, the *Rāmāyaṇa* (*The Travels of Rāma*). He is India's example of the righteous king. However, since *rāma* is a masculine word it would us give no opportunity to see how the neuter and feminine grammatical genders are declined in "a." Instead we will use an adjective, since adjectives must agree with their nouns. Take *gupta*, for instance. *Gupta* means "hidden," and as an adjective, it must agree in number, gender, and case with the noun it modifies. Therefore, it can have masculine, neuter, and feminine forms. Here is all of its forms (masc., neut., and fem.) in all numbers and cases:

[16] *ibid.*, 1.2.46: *kṛttaddhitāntau samāsāśca*

[17] *ibid.*, 4.1.2: *sv-au-jas-am-auṭ-chaṣ-ṭā-bhyām-bhis-ṅe-bhyām-bhyas-ṅasi-bhyām-bhyas-ṅas-os-ām-ṅyos-sup*

[18] The dropping of the final "s" of the nominative singular is a rule from Pāṇini (6.1.68). And the change from "d" to "t" is because words can only end in certain consonants in Sanskrit: k, ṭ, t, p, ṅ, n m and ḥ (*visarga*).

Masculine

Case	Singular	Dual	Plural
Nominative (Voc.)	guptaḥ	guptau	guptāḥ
Accusative	guptam	guptau	guptān
Instrumental	guptena	guptābhyām	guptaiḥ
Dative	guptāya	guptābhyām	guptebhyaḥ
Ablative	guptāt	guptābhyām	guptebhyaḥ
Genitive	guptasya	guptayoḥ	guptānām
Locative	gupte	guptayoḥ	gupteṣu

Neuter

Case	Singular	Dual	Plural
Nominative (Voc.)	guptam	gupte	guptāni
Accusative	guptam	gupte	guptāni
Instrumental	guptena	guptābhyām	guptaiḥ
Dative	guptāya	guptābhyām	guptebhyaḥ
Ablative	guptāt	guptābhyām	guptebhyaḥ
Genitive	guptasya	guptayoḥ	guptānām
Locative	gupte	guptayoḥ	gupteṣu

Feminine

Case	Singular	Dual	Plural
Nominative (Voc.)	guptā (gupte)	gupte	guptāḥ
Accusative	guptām	gupte	guptāḥ
Instrumental	guptayā	guptābhyām	guptābhiḥ
Dative	guptāyai	guptābhyām	guptābhyaḥ
Ablative	guptāyāḥ	guptābhyām	guptābhyaḥ
Genitive	guptāyāḥ	guptayoḥ	guptānām
Locative	guptāyām	guptayoḥ	guptāsu

One can still recognize many of the standard endings in this table, but there are several that are quite different. All the instrumental forms are different as are the dative, ablative, and genitive forms, especially in the singular. Study the tables above and look at the word by word analyses of some of the *mantras* of the Īśā. See if you can identify some of the cases.

As we can see, the neuter nouns in short "a" are declined in almost the same way as the masculine nouns. They differ only in the nominative and accusative cases. Feminine nouns, which usually end in long a (ā), are quite different, however. Many of the unusual endings found in the feminine declension came originally from the pronoun declensions.[19]

Before turning to the verbs, it might be useful to give the declension of the three main pronouns in the Sanskrit language: the personal pronouns, *aham* (I) and *tvam* (you), and the demonstrative pronouns, *saḥ/tat/sā* (he/it/she).

[19]According to MacDonell. See p. 55, fn. 3.

Aham (I)

Case	Singular	Dual	Plural
Nominative (Voc.)	aham (I)	āvām (we two)	vayam (we)
Accusative	mām (me)	āvām (us two)	asmān (us)
Instrumental	mayā (by me)	āvābhyām (by us two)	asmābhiḥ (by us)
Dative	mahyam (to me)	āvābhyām (to us two)	asmabhyam (to us)
Ablative	mad (from me)	āvābhyām (from those two)	asmad (from us)
Genitive	mama (of me)	āvayoḥ (of us two)	asmākam (of us)
Locative	mayi (in or on me)	āvayoḥ (in or on us two)	asmāsu (in or among us)

Tvam (You)

Case	Singular	Dual	Plural
Nominative (Voc.)	tvam (you)	yuvām (you two)	yūyam (you, pl.)
Accusative	tvām (you)	yuvām (you two)	yuṣmān (you)
Instrumental	tvayā (by you)	yuvābhyām (by you two)	yuṣmābhiḥ (by you, pl.)
Dative	tubhyam (to you)	yuvābhyām (to you two)	yuṣmadbhyam (to you, pl.)
Ablative	tvad (from you)	yuvābhyām (from you two)	yuṣmad (from you, pl.)
Genitive	tava (of you, your)	yuvayoḥ (of you two)	yuṣmākam (of you, pl.)
Locative	tvayi (in you)	yuvayoḥ (in you two)	yuṣmāsu (in you, pl.)

Saḥ (He)

Case	Singular	Dual	Plural
Nominative (Voc.)	saḥ (he)	tau (those two)	te (they)
Accusative	tam (him)	tau (those two)	tān (them)
Instrumental	tena (by him)	tābhyām (by those two)	taiḥ (by them)
Dative	tasmai (to him)	tābhyām (to those two)	tebhyaḥ (to them)
Ablative	tasmāt (from him)	tābhyām (from those two)	tebhyaḥ (from them)
Genitive	tasya (of him)	tayoḥ (of those two)	teṣām (of them)
Locative	tasmin (in or on him)	tayoḥ (in or on those two)	teṣu (among them)

Tad (It)

Case	Singular	Dual	Plural
Nominative (Voc.)	tad (it)	te (those two)	tāni (they)
Accusative	tad (it)	te (those two)	tāni (them)
Instrumental	tena (by it)	tābhyām (by those two)	taiḥ (by them)
Dative	tasmai (to it)	tābhyām (to those two)	tebhyaḥ (to them)
Ablative	tasmāt (from it)	tābhyām (from those two)	tebhyaḥ (from them)
Genitive	tasya (of it)	tayoḥ (of those two)	teṣām (of them)
Locative	tasmin (in it)	tayoḥ (in those two)	teṣu (among them)

Sā (She)

Case	Singular	Dual	Plural
Nominative (Voc.)	sā (she)	te (those two)	tāḥ (they)
Accusative	tām (her)	te (those two)	tāḥ (them)
Instrumental	tayā (by her)	tābhyām (by those two)	tābhiḥ (by them)
Dative	tasyai (to her)	tābhyām (to those two)	tābhyaḥ (to them)
Ablative	tasyāḥ (from her)	tābhyām (from those two)	tābhyaḥ (from them)
Genitive	tasyāḥ (of her)	tayoḥ (of those two)	tāsām (of them)
Locative	tasyām (in her)	tayoḥ (in those two)	tāsu (in or among them)

These few examples should give one a good sense of how the noun system works in Sanskrit. Noun stems end in a variety of consonants and some of two or three changeable forms, depending on where the accent falls in the word. Besides the noun stems that end in "a," there are stems that end in "i," "ī," "u," "ū," "ā," and "ṛ." There are a few stems that end in "ai," "o," and "au." By far the largest group, however, is made up of the noun stems ending in short "a." Becoming familiar with that declension brings the largest number of Sanskrit nouns into one's reach.

Verbs, Their Tenses, and Conjugations

The verb system in Sanskrit is much more complicated than the noun system. One can often tell how thoroughly someone has studied the Sanskrit language by how well he or she is able to use the verbs. The great stylists of Sanskrit composition like Patañjali (2nd cent. BCE),[20] Jayanta Bhaṭṭa (9th cent. CE),[21] Abhinavagupta (9th-10th cents. CE),[22] and Paṇḍitarāja Jagannātha (16th cent. CE),[23] to name just a few, used correctly many verbs in many tenses and moods in their works. Their rich use of verb tenses and moods enlivens both their prose and their poetry. Others, less well grounded in grammar, resorted mostly to passive constructions, featuring verbs turned into nouns or adjectives like past participles with the occasional exception of a present tense or two. Much of later Sanskrit writing, especially in technical treatises and late additions to the Purāṇas ("Ancient Tales and Lore"), is of this nature. Mastering the verbs is difficult and so such mastery became a rarer and rarer achievement.

Here I will give just a brief overview of the verbs with one common example of the conjugation of the verb "to be," from the root $\sqrt{bh\bar{u}}$, in the present system. This should help readers at the very least to identify some of the verbs as they occur in the *mantras* of the Upaniṣad. The verb system has a number of tenses, which refers to the time in which an action is performed, e.i. past, present, or future. It also has moods which are manners of conceiving or expressing action: indicative, imperative, optative, conditional, and subjunctive. Verbs also have voices which indicate the way the subject of the verb is related to the action of the verb: these are active, middle, and passive. These will be discussed more later.

Sanskrit has essentially five tenses: (1) the present (and its moods, that is the indicative [a statement of fact], the imperative [a command] and the optative [an expression of desire or wish or a more gentle command]), (2) the imperfect (an action beginning in the past and not complete in the present), (3) the perfect (an action completed in the remote past and not witnessed by the speaker), (4) the aorist (an action completed in

[20]This is the author of the *Mahābhāṣya* ("The Great Commentary"), the masterful commentary on Pāṇini's grammatical *sūtras*. This Patañjali is not considered the same person as the author of the *Yoga-sūtras*.

[21]Jayanta Bhaṭṭa, a Kaśmiri *brāhmaṇa*, was the author of the masterpiece on Hindu logic called the *Nyāya-mañjarī* ("Bouquet of Logic"). In one part of his work, he makes fun of *brāhmaṇa* priests who demonstrate their ignorance of Sanskrit grammar by using the wrong forms in their ritual recitations.

[22]Abhinavagupta was the great Kaśmiri Śaivite master who wrote on Śaivite *tantra* in his masterpiece, the *Tantrāloka* ("Illumination of Tantra") and on Sanskrit literary criticism through learned commentaries on literary critical texts.

[23]Paṇḍitarāja Jagannātha was the last great representative of *rasa* (aesthetic rapture) school of Sanskrit literary criticism. His unfinished masterpiece was the *Rasa-gaṅgādhara* ("Ocean of Aesthetic Rapture").

[24]The aorist also has an optative mood that is called the benedictive, that is, expressing a blessing or a wish for someone's well-being.

[25]The future tense also has a conditional, a kind of past future. The conditional is kind of combination of the future and the past and is char-

the recent past),[24] (5) the future (actions to be taken in the future).[25] There are also participles for the present, perfect, and future and one infinitive ("to be," "to do," "to speak," etc). In the Vedic language there was a subjunctive mood which has all but disappeared in the later classical Sanskrit language.[26]

As you can see there are three past tenses, each theoretically distinct in meaning from the others, but which in practical use are often found to be interchangeable: the imperfect, perfect, and aorist. There are two forms of the future tense: a simple future and a periphrastic future, which are just different ways of expressing a future action. Then there is the present. There are also three moods: indicative, imperative, optative and conditional. Each verb has three numbers: singular, dual, and plural. The verbs also have three persons: first person ("I ... "), second person ("You ... "), and third person ("he/she/it ... "). Finally, there are three voices: active, middle, and passive. Thus, each tense of a verb has at least eighteen forms and often twenty-seven, because some are found in all the voices: active, middle, and passive.[27]

The traditional grammarians, following Pāṇini, recognize ten verb tenses and moods giving as names for the tenses and moods short, three letter words beginning with the letter "l." Thus, *laṭ* is the name of the present tense, for instance.[28] The "a" and the "ṭ" are indicatory letters called "it" just as we saw before in the identification of the alphabet and noun endings. Here, the "l" itself stands for the ending that are added after the verbal stem. Those endings are:[29]

Active Voice (Parasmaipada)

Person	Singular	Dual	Plural
Third Person	ti	tas	anti
Second Person	si	thas	tha
First Person	mi	vas	mas

Middle Voice (Ātmanepada)

Person	Singular	Dual	Plural
Third Person	te	āte	ante or ate
Second Person	se	āthe	dhve
First Person	e	vahe	mahe

We shall only be concerned here with the present system which consists of the present indicative tense, the imperfect tense, the imperative mood, and the optative mood. What makes these a group is the fact that they construct their forms from a special stem and there are ten ways to make that stem. Thus all the verbs in the Sanskrit language are divided into ten classes or groups. We shall only look at the first class which is called *bhvādi*, or the group beginning with the root $\sqrt{bh\bar{u}}$, "to be or become." This class is the largest of the ten classes of verbs. It constructs its present system forms from the stem *bhava*.

Present Active (Parasmaipada)

Person	Singular	Dual	Plural
Third Person	bhavati (he/she/it is)	bhavataḥ (the two are)	bhavanti (they are)
Second Person	bhavasi (you are)	bhavathaḥ (you two are)	bhavatha (you are)
First Person	bhavāmi (I am)	bhavāvaḥ (we two are)	bhavāmaḥ (we are)

acterized by some as an expression of the "future-in-the-past." The future is: "he will run," and the conditional: "he would run." See Roderick S. Bucknell, *Sanskrit Manual*, 38 and following. (Delhi: Motilal Banarsidass Publishers, 1994)

[26] A subjunctive is the form of a verb which expresses an action or state not as a fact, but only as a conception of the mind still contingent and dependent. Example: "I suggest that he study." Here "study" is a subjunctive form. It differs from the form of the verb that would go with "he" in the present indicative (statement of fact): "he studies."

[27] The distinction between active and middle is often not easy to see. In Sanskrit, this distinction is described with the words *parasmaipada*, "word for another," and *ātmanepada*, "word for oneself." These roughly correspond to "transitive" and "reflexive" voices, that is, the action's object is another or the action's object is oneself.

[28] Pāṇini's aphorism is *vartamāne laṭ* (3.2.123), "laṭ in the present tense." The rest are: *liṭ* = perfect, *luṭ* = periphrastic future, *lṛṭ* = simple future, *leṭ* = subjunctive, *loṭ* = imperative, *laṅ* = imperfect, *liṅ* = optative, *luṅ* = aorist, *lṛṅ* = conditional.

[29] All of these endings, both active and middle, are given in a single aphorism in Pāṇini (3.4.78).

Imperfect Active (Parasmaipada)

Person	Singular	Dual	Plural
Third Person	abhavat (he/she/it was)	abhavatām (the two were)	abhavan (they were)
Second Person	abhavaḥ (you were)	abhavatam (you two were)	abhavata (you were)
First Person	abhavam (I was)	abhavāva (we two were)	abhavāma (we were)

Imperative Active (Parasmaipada)

Person	Singular	Dual	Plural
Third Person	bhavatu (let he/she/it be ...)	bhavatām (let the two were be ...)	bhavantu (let them be ...)
Second Person	bhava (be ...)	bhavatam (let you two be ...)	bhavata (let you be ...)
First Person	bhavāni (let me be ...)	bhavāva (let we two be ...)	bhavāma (let us be ...)

Optative Active (Parasmaipada)

Person	Singular	Dual	Plural
Third Person	bhavet (may he/she/it be ...)	bhavetām (may the two be ...)	bhaveyuḥ (may they be ...)
Second Person	bhaveḥ (may you be ...)	bhavetam (may you two be ...)	bhaveta (may you be ...)
First Person	bhaveyam (may I be ...)	bhaveva (may we two be ...)	bhavema (may we be ...)

This should give you some sense of how the verbs work. Here I have presented only the active voice. The middle and passive voices have not been given here. Those can be found in any of the standard Sanskrit grammar texts listed at the end of this introduction or at various sites online. Many of the verbs in the Upaniṣad are conjugated just like this, or in very similar ways. The ten classes of verbs only apply to the present system illustrated above. In the other tenses like the perfect, the future, the aorist, the verbs are not distinguished on the basis of those ten groups, because the verb stems are constructed in mostly similar ways.

There are a few other things to point out about verbs before turning to other topics. One thing that the verbs do in Sanskrit is they take prefixs called *upasargas*. Sometimes the meaning of the verb does not change much with the addition of such a prefix, but often the meaning changes. As one Sanskrit grammarian (J. Prabhakara Sastri) explained to me once, the prefix does not add any new meaning to the meaning of the verb. Rather, it singles out a meaning already present in the verb and brings it to the forefront. The following are the prefixes of the Sanskrit verbs:[30]

pra — forth
parā — away
apa — away
sam — together
anu — after
ava — down
nis or nir — out
dus or dur — ill
vi — asunder
ā — near
ni — down
adhi — upon
api — on
ati — beyond
su — well
ud — up
abhi — against
prati — towards
pari — around
upa — up to

A striking example of how a prefix can change the meaning of a word is found in the case the root $\sqrt{gam}$, "to go." By adding the prefix "ā" to the root of *gam* (*āgam*) it changes its meaning to "to come." Just to give a sense of how these verbal prefaces affect the meaning of the verb, I will show the variations using one verb, the *gam* "to go." It combines with all of the prefixes:

pragam — to go forwards
parāgam — to go away
apagam — to go away

[30] *Upasargas* are defined by Pāṇini's aphorism 1.4.59: *upasargāḥ kriyāyoge*, "(the items beginning with pra) when added to verbs are called *upasargas*."

saṃgam — to meet
anugam — to go after, follow
avagam — to go down, descend to
nirgam — to go out
durgama — impassable[31]
vigam — to go asunder
āgam — to go near (i.e., to come)
nigam — to settle down upon or near
adhigam — to approach
apigam — to enter
atigam — to pass by or over
sugama — easy to traverse[32]
udgam — to come forth
abhigam — to go near to
pratigam — to go towards
parigam — to go round or about or through
upagam — to go near to

As you can see these prefixes bring about subtle changes in the basic meaning of the verb. The basic verb meaning just indicates "going" or "moving." The prefixes adjust the generic meaning to more specific directions and intents.

Three things remain to be mentioned briefly: participles, gerunds (or absolutives), and infinitives. Participles are parts of speech partaking of the nature of both verb and adjective. Thus they are declined as adjectives to agree with the the nouns they modify, but they convey a verbal meaning. They exist in all three voices: active, middle, and passive, and in the present, perfect and future. I won't go into how the participles are formed. Instead I will give a few examples. In the Fourth Mantra, for instance, we have two present participles in the third line:[33] *dhāvataḥ*, "running," and *tiṣṭhat*, "standing." The first is a present participle of the root √*dhāv* "to run" and is in the accusative plural case because it must agree with the word it modifies *anyān* "others." The second is a present participle of the root √*sthā* "to stand." It is in the nominative singular case because in modifies the pronoun *tat* "it" which refers to the Self. So "it, though standing still, surpasses others who are running."

Adverbs and Indeclinables

A number of important words in Sanskrit are called indeclinables. That is to say they are not changed through the addition of suffixes or prefixes in the ways we have seen verbs or nouns are. The rules of *sandhi* or euphonic combination do apply to them, however. So sometimes they are found combined with the words that precede or follow them. They often function as adverbs, which means they qualify or modify the action of the verb in some way. They may also function in other ways as well such as conjunctives. In just about every one of the *mantras* in this Upaniṣad we find indeclinables present. In the Invocation Mantra (ॐ *pūrṇam adaḥ* ...), we find the indeclinable *eva*. It is a restrictive particle that follows the word it emphasizes. It is often translated: "just," "only," or "exactly." In Mantra One we find three indeclinables: *ca*, *mā*, and *svit*. The first of these means "and," the second one means "do not ... ," and the third is a particle of interrogation, inquiry, or doubt meaning: "do you think?," "perhaps," or "indeed." Combined with the interrogative pronoun *kasya* (whose?) it most commonly means "anyone's." Thus the last quater of that *mantra* means: "Do not take anyone's property."

The following list contains, in alphbetical order, many of the most common indeclinables, most of which can be found in our text:

antar "within." "between"
anyathā "otherwise," "in a manner different from this"
api "likewise," "moreover," "and"
atha "now," "then," "afterwards" introducing something new at the beginning of a sentence
bāhyataḥ "outside of"
ca "and"
ced "if"
eva emphasis, "just," "only," "exactly"
evam "thus," "so,"
hi "for," "because," "to be sure"
iha "here," "now," "in this case"
iti "thus"
iva "like"
kevalam "only"
kila "indeed," "certainly," "to be sure"
kim "what?" "why"
kva "where?"
mā "do not ... "
na "not"
nāma "indeed," "certainly," "to be sure"

[31] This is not a verb form, but an adjective made from the verbal root *gam* joined with the prefix *dur*.
[32] This is not a verb form, but an adjective made from the verbal root *gam* joined with the prefix *su*.
[33] *tad dhāvato'nyān atyeti tiṣṭhat*

punaḥ "again"
saha "(together) with"
svid "do you think?" "perhaps," "indeed"
tathā "thus," "so," "accordingly"
tu "but," "however"
u "and" [an old particle from the Veda]
vā "or"
vai emphasizes the preceding word
vinā "without," "except"
yadi "if"
yathā "as," "like"

Compounds

Compounds are combinations of two or more words into a single word unit. All of the languages belonging to the Indo-European family of languages use compound words. In English, for instance, we have words like roadhouse, roadhog, roadrunner, and so forth. Surely, you can think of more examples. This is an inheritance from English's Indo-European roots. But Sanskrit has carried the practice of forming and using compound words further than most of the other members of the family. This is specially true of the later forms of the language. In the earlier forms, such as the form found in this Upaniṣad, the use of compounds words is not as highly developed or as common as it later becomes. In the later language compound words might be formed from as many as ten or more words. Here compound words contain at most two words joined into one. An example of a compound word in the Īśā Upaniṣad is in Mantra 3: *ātma-hanaḥ*, "killing the self." This compound is formed from two words, *ātman*, "self," and *han*, "killing." In Mantra Six we find another: *sarva-bhūteṣu* "in all beings," made of *sarva*, "all," and *bhūta*, "beings." In Mantra Eight we there is another: *apāpa-viddham* "not pierced by sin," made of *pāpa*, "sin," and *viddha*, "pierced," with the negative prefix *a* added to make the compound negative. Without the *a* it would mean "pierced by sin." Though not as common or as complex in the language of the early Upaniṣads, a brief discussion of compounds in Sanskrit is useful here.

There are three kinds of compound words in Sanskrit. The first kind is called a co-ordinative compound or a *dvandva* ("coupling") compound. It is a coupling compound in the sense that words are joined together in the compound to form a list connected together by the conjunction "and." Thus the compound word *hasty-aśvau* means "an elephant and a horse." The words that are placed earlier in the compound appear in their stem forms which means their forms without any of the case endings we discussed earlier as part of case declintion. The last word in the compound provides the gramatical gender and the number. The same compound above written *hasty-aśvāḥ* with the plural ending instead of the dual ending would mean "elephants and horses." If it were to appear as *hasty-aśvam* with a neuter ending the component words would refer to the categories elephant and horse, not individuals belonging to those categories. One can string together words into long compounds consisting primarily of lists using this co-ordinative compound.

Another kind of compound is called the determinative compound. They are called determinative because the earlier member of the compound determines or qualifies the following or later member. As an example from English take the case of "washcloth." The prior member "wash" determines the kind of cloth the second member is. Of all the different kinds of cloth there are, washcloth refers to the kind used for washing. Thus the first member determines the kind the second member is. In Sanskrit there are two kinds of determinative compounds: dependent determinatives (*tat-puruṣa*) and descriptive determinatives (*karmadhāraya*). A fine example of a dependent determinative is found in the compound *ātma-han* from Mantra Three. The first member *ātman* "self" is the object of the action of the second member *han* "killing." Thus, the case relationship between the members of that compound can understood as accusative ("killing the self") or it could also perhaps be genitve ("killing of the self").

In the descriptive determinative compound, the first member provides an attribute for the second member. A fine example can be found in the English word blackbird. Blackbird refers to a specific kind of bird, not all black birds. Nevertheless, its first member (black) qualifies or adds an attribute to or modifies the second (bird). In our case, a good example of a descriptive determinative is found in Mantra Six, *sarva-bhūteṣu* "in all beings." This first member *sarva* "all" modifies the second member *bhūta* "beings" as an adjective would. One of the main characteristics of descriptive determinatives is that if the members were written separately, that is, not as part of a compound, they would both have the same case endings. And, in fact, in the first half of Mantra Six we find the members of *sarva-bhūta* written separately with the same case endings (*sarvāṇi bhūtāni*, "all beings"). This is the way adjectives behave with respect to the words they modify in Sanskrit, that is, they take on the same case ending as the word they modify. Another example of a descriptive determinative in Mantra Fifteen in the compound *satya-dharmāya*, "for [one who has the] true teaching or character." *Satya* supplies the attribute (true) of *dharma* (teaching or character).

The last kind of compound is called by some the possessive compound[34] and by others the exocentric compound[35] These are adjectival compounds that agree with and modify some other word outside of itself. This other word can be either expressed or left unexpressed. The native grammarian's name for this compound is *bahuvrīhi*, "much rice." As a possessive compound it modifies another noun in the sentence by signifying that that other person or thing "has or possesses much rice." This is, thus, an example of how possessive compounds work. The pot or person that possesses "much rice" is ouside of or exocentric to the compound.

There are a couple of possible examples of the possessive compound in the Īśā. In Mantra Eight, for instance, the word *paryagāt* when understood as a verb meaning "he has become," turns *apāpa-viddham* into a possessive compound in the sense that "he has become [someone] who is not pierced by sin." In other words, he has become someone who possesses the quality of being "unpierced by sin."[36] The noun that *apāpa-viddham* modifies is unexpressed in the verse, but is implied as the substantive of all the adjectives in the first half of the verse (respendent, bodiless, etc.). One might supply *puruṣam*, "person" as the unexpressed substantive for that *mantra*. Thus, "he has become a person who is unpierced by sin, ..."

Another example comes from Mantra Fifteen, in the word *satya-dharmāya*, "for the sake of the true teaching or law." As a possessive pronoun the unexpressed substantive (noun or pronoun) could be understood as *mahyam* "for me," that is, for the author or reciter of the *mantra* who is asking that the golden disc of the sun be removed so that he can see "the face of the truth." Thus, it would read "for me who possesses a truthful nature." One finds a different meaning depending on what kind of compound one, determinative or possessive, one thinks it is.

Another way to understand this compound *satya-dharmāya* is to connect it with the only other word in the verse that is in the dative case, *dṛṣṭaye*, "for a vision." In that case, *satya-dharmāya* would modify *dṛṣṭaye* to give us "for a vision whose character trait is truth."

Compound words in Sanskrit are an important part of Sanskrit grammar. Learning to recognize them and properly interpret them is an important part of learning to read Sanskrit. Even with the short compounds found in the Īśā there is possibility of misconstrual. When the compounds become much longer in Classical Sanskrit the problem of proper construal becomes even more difficult. For more in-depth discussion of Sanskrit compound words, consult some of the reference works given below.

Syntax

Syntax refers to the way a language arranges its words in order to create meaningful units of expression. Each language does this differently. In English we are accustomed to having the subject come first followed by the verb and its adverbs if there are any followed by the object of the verb with its (the object's) modifiers. In Sanskrit word order is different. A sentence in Sanskrit typically begins with the subject preceeded by its adjectives followed by the object preceded by its adjectives followed by the verb preceded by its modifiers or adverbs. This is, of course, the prose order. Since so much of Sanskrit is written in meter, this order is often interrupted by the requirements of the meter. Though this might be a problem in other languages, since Sanskrit is an inflected language, that is, since the various parts of speech are indicated by specific endings, it is not a problem in Sanskrit. The subject will be marked by a nominative or first case-ending (unless it is part of a passive construction).[37] The verb will agree with the subject in terms of number and person, and the object and its modifiers will be in the accusative or second case. Therefore, the order they come in does not really matter that much. One can better see the typical syntactic relationships of Sanskrit in the commentary of Śaṅkara on the Īśā (which we have included here) than one can in the text itself. Nevertheless, knowing something about the operations of standard syntax in Sanskrit and recognizing case agreement between the various parts of

[34]MacDonell, page 175 and following.

[35]Coulson, 117 and following.

[36]As MacDonell says (p. 175 para 189): Every kind of determinative can be turned into a possessive.

[37]In a passive construction the subject is in the instrumental or third case and the object is the nominative or first case: *sā dṛśyate mayā*, "She is seen by me." In other words, "I see her."

Sanskrit sentences help one grasp the properly intended meanings of texts, even if written in verse.

Prosody

Prosody is the study or description of the various meters used in writing versified poetry in different languages. It is an important part of the study of Sanskrit because so much is written in verse in Sanskrit. Huge epics like the *Mahābhārata* and the *Rāmāyaṇa* are written entirely in verse, as is the oldest of the Vedic texts, the *Ṛg-veda Saṃhitā*, the earliest collection of hymns in ancient India (1500-800 BCE). There are hundreds of different meters used in Classical Sanskrit poetry and composition. In Vedic Sanskrit there are far fewer meters among which is the famous *gāyatrī* meter. Nevertheless, the use and elaboration of meter has been an important part of the history of the Sanskrit language. Several works have been composed on the topic of prosody, but since there are only two kinds of verses used in the Īśā, we will only discuss those two. Fortunately, the meters used in this text, *anuṣṭubh* and *triṣṭubh*, were important for the development of later meters in classical Sanskrit, specially *anuṣṭubh*, from which the epic and purāṇic meter called the *śloka* developed. As Coulson puts it: "This is the bread-and-butter metre of Sanskrit verse, comparable in function and importance with the Latin hexameter or the English iambic pentameter."[38] The *triṣṭubh* is the most common meter used in the Ṛg Veda, accounting for about two-fifths of the verses of the text. It is also the source of many of the later classical meters of the longer variety.

Sanskrit meters are measured either by the number of syllables of differing lengths or by the number of *morea*.[39] Most of the meters in Sanskrit are measured by the first method. Syllables have two lengths, which we shall call light (⏑) and heavy (-). Short vowels are usually light, and long vowels and dipthongs are always heavy. Short vowels followed by two or more consonants are heavy. *Visarga* (*ḥ*) and *anusvara* (*ṃ*) are considered full consonants in matters of meter and a short vowel followed by one of them is always considered heavy.

The *anuṣṭubh* is generally divided into four quarters called *pādas*. Each *pāda* has eight syllables producing two half verses with sixteen syllables each, the whole stanza having 32 syllables. Here is the basic rhythm pattern of the meter:

⏓⏓⏓⏓⏑–́–́⏓ / ⏓⏓⏓⏓⏑–́⏑⏓ |

⏓⏓⏓⏓⏑–́–́⏓ / ⏓⏓⏓⏓⏑–́⏑⏓ ||

The first four syllables of each *pāda* can be either light (⏑) or heavy (-). The fifth syllable has to be light and the sixth has to be heavy in each *pāda*. In general *pādas* one and three differ from *pādas* two and four in that the seventh syllable is heavy and the eighth is light while in *pādas* two and four the seventh syllable is light and the eighth is heavy. This creates a syncopated effect between *pādas* one and three and two and four.[40] However, in actual practice, the final syllable of all of the *pādas* may be either light or heavy. Let's look at the Mantra Two (as emended by Ježić) as an example:

kūr vānn ē vē hă kār mā ṇĭ
jĭ jī vĭ ṣēc chă tāṃ să māḥ|
ē vāṃ vĭ dĭ nān yă thē tĭ
nă kār mă līp yă tē nă rē||

As we can see by comparing the rhythms of this verse with the model that *pādas* one and two fit the pattern perfectly. *Pāda* three, however, does not. Instead of ⏑–́–́⏓ for the last four syllables, we get –⏑–⏑. Anomalies like this occur often in Sanskrit meter. As it turns out, the *anuṣṭubh* has two accepted forms. If a verse fits the regular form as given above, it is called *pathyā*, "proper or regular." If it does not, it is called *vipulā*, "broad or wide." *Pāda* three here is one of the accepted *vipulā* forms.

The *triṣṭubh* also has four quarters or *pādas*, but they have eleven syllables each. It is divided into two half verses of twenty-two syllables each. It thus has forty-four syllables in total. The basic pattern of a *triṣṭubh* is as follows:

⏓–⏓–,⏑⏑– /–⏑–⏓ | or

⏓–⏓–⏓,⏑⏑ / –⏑–⏓ ||

The comma marks the *caesura* or word break. It can come after four syllables or after five. Let's see how the first *triṣṭubh* in the Īśā, Mantra 4, matches up to this:

[38]Coulson, 250.

[39]A *mora* is a unit of syllablic weight which determines stress or timing. In general short vowels have one *mora* of weight and long vowels or dipthongs have two *mora*.

[40]Coulson, 250.

ăn ē jăd ē kāṃ, mă nă sō jă vī̄ yō
nāi nād dē vā̄, ā̄p nŭ vān pū̄r văm ār ṣăt|
tād dhā̄ vă tō 'nyā̄n, āt yē tĭ tī ṣṭhăt
tās mīnn ă pō, mā̄ tă rī śvā̄ dă dhā̄ tĭ|| 4||

The first quarter fits the model perfectly. Its *caesura* comes after the fifth syllable and is followed by two light syllables and a heavy syllable. The last four syllables are within the scope of the model. The other *pādas*, however, do not fit as well. The second, for instance, has its *caesura* after the fourth syllable, but instead of two lights and a heavy, it has a heavy, a light, and another heavy. The last four syllables fit the model well, however. In fact, the last four syllables of all the *pādas* fit the model well. The third *pāda*, however, is one syllable short. *Pādas* two and four have exactly the same *caesura* placement and meter. So while there is regularity here, these is also variation. It is apparently common for verses in this meter to have one syllable too many or one too few. One might argue that complete regularity would become boring and may be impossible to achieve.

Apart from experiencing and learning to appreciate the beauty of the rhythms and music of ancient and classical Sanskrit verse, the study of Sanskrit prosody can sometimes tip one off to changes inexpertly made to verses over the course of two and half millennia or so of transmission. We've seen several cases of this in our study of the Īśā. Mantra 2, an *anuṣṭubh*, for instance, did not fit the model for *anuṣṭubhs* because of having an extra syllable in the third *pāda*, prompting the suggestion that *ito'sti* be replaced by a simple indeclinable *iti* removing the extra syllable from the third *pāda*. Similarly, the word *tvayi* ("for you") in the same *pāda* can be replaced by *vidi* ("for one who knows") removing the odd second person address quality of the *mantra* carried through in rest of the *mantra*. Thus, a good understanding of prosody can be a useful tool in interpreting ancient Sanskrit texts like the *Īśopaniṣad*.

Select Bibliography

Aklujkar, Ashok. *Sanskrit: an Easy Introduction to an Enchanting Language*. 3 vols. (Richmand, B.C., Canada: Svādhyāya Publications, 1992)

Bucknell, Roderick S. *Sanskrit Manual: a Quick Reference Guide to the Phonology and Grammar of Classical Sanskrit*. (Delhi: Motilal Banarsidass Publishers, 1994)

Coulson, Michael. *Sanskrit: a Complete Course for Beginners*. (Sevenoaks, Kent, UK: Hodder & Stoughton, 1992)

MacDonell, Arthur A. *A Sanskrit Grammar for Students*. (Oxford: Oxford University Press, [repr.] 1962)

MacDonell, Arthur A. *A Vedic Grammar for Students*. (New Delhi: D.K. Printworld (P) Ltd., [repr.] 1999)

Varadaraja. *Laghukaumudī: a Sanskrit grammar*, trans. James R. Ballantyne. (Delhi: Motilal Banarsidass, [repr.] 1976)

Full Devanāgarī Text (Upaniṣad and Śaṅkara)

पूर्णमदः पूर्णमिदं
पूर्णात्पूर्णमुदच्यते।
पूर्णस्य पूर्णमादाय
पूर्णमेवावशिष्यते॥

॥ॐ शान्तिः शान्तिः शान्तिः ॐ॥

शङ्करः :

श्रीगणेशाय नमः

ईशिता सर्वभूतानां सर्वभूतमयश्च यः।
ईशावास्येन सम्बोध्यमीश्वरं तं नमाम्यहम्॥

ईशावास्यमित्यादयो मन्त्राः कर्मस्वविनियुक्ताः। तेषामकर्मशेषस्यात्मनो आयतिमात्रप्रकाशकत्वात्। आयतिमात्रं चात्मनः शुद्धत्वापापविद्धत्वैकत्वनित्यत्वाशरीरत्वसर्वगतत्वादि वक्ष्यमाणम्। तच्च कर्मणा विरुध्येतेति युक्त एवैषां कर्मस्वविनियोगः।

न ह्येवं लक्षणमात्मनो आयतिमात्रमुत्पाद्यं विकार्यमाप्यं संस्कार्यं कर्तृभोक्तृरूपं वा येन कर्मशेषता स्यात्। सर्वासामुपनिषदामात्मायतिमात्रनिरूपणेनैवोपक्षयात्। गीतानां मोक्षधर्माणां चैवंपरत्वात्। तस्मादात्मनो ऽनेकत्वकर्तृत्वभोक्तृत्वादि चाशुद्धत्वपापविद्धत्वादि चोपादाय लोकबुद्धिसिद्धं कर्माणि विहितानि।

यो हि कर्मफलेनार्थी दृष्टेन ब्रह्मवर्चसादिनादृष्टेन स्वर्गादिना च द्विजातिरहं न काणकुब्जत्वाद्यनधिकारप्रयोजकधर्मवानित्यात्मानं मन्यते सोऽधिक्रियते कर्मस्विति ह्यधिकारविदो वदन्ति ।

तस्मादेते मन्त्रा आत्मनो आयतिमात्रप्रकाशनेनात्मविषयं स्वाभाविकमज्ञानं निवर्तयन्तः शोकमोहादिसंसारधर्मविच्छित्तिसाधनमात्मैकत्वादिविज्ञानमुत्पादयन्ति । इत्येवमुक्ताधिकार्यभिधेयसम्बन्धप्रयोजनान्मन्त्रान्संक्षेपतो व्याख्यास्यामः ॥

ॐ ईशावास्यमिदं सर्वं
यत्किंच जगत्यां जगत्।
तेन त्यक्तेन भुञ्जीथा
मा गृधः कस्य स्विद्धनम्॥ १॥

ईशा ईष्टे इतीट् तेनेशा। ईशिता परमेश्वरः परमात्मा सर्वस्य। स हि सर्वमीष्टे सर्वजन्तूनामात्मा सन् प्रत्यगात्मतया तेन स्वेन रूपेणात्मनेशा वास्यमाच्छादनीयम्।

किम् ? इदं सर्वं यत्किंच यत्किञ्चिज्जगत्यां पृथिव्यां जगत्तत्सर्वं स्वेनात्मनेशेन प्रत्यगात्मतयाऽहमेवेदं सर्वमिति परमार्थसत्यरूपेणानृतमिदं सर्वं चराचरमाच्छादनीयं स्वेन परमात्मना।

यथा चन्दनागर्वादेरुदकादिसम्बन्धजक्लेदादिजमौपाधिकं दौर्गन्ध्यं तत्स्वरूपनिघर्षणेनाच्छाद्यते स्वेन पारमार्थिकेन गन्धेन। तद्वदेव हि स्वात्मन्यध्यस्तं स्वाभाविकं कर्तृत्वभोक्तृत्वादिलक्षणम् जगद्वैतरूपं जगत्यां पृथिव्याम्, जगत्यामिति उपलक्षणार्थत्वात्सर्वमेव नामरूपकर्माख्यं विकारजातं परमार्थसत्यात्मभावनया त्यक्तं स्यात्।

एवमीश्वरात्मभावनया युक्तस्य पुत्राद्येषणात्रयसंन्यास एवाधिकारो न कर्मसु। तेन त्यक्तेन त्यागेनेत्यर्थः। न हि त्यक्तो मृतः पुत्रो वा भृत्यो वा आत्मसम्बन्धिताया अभावादात्मानं पालयत्यतस्त्यागेनेत्ययमेव वेदार्थः। भुञ्जीथाः पालयेथाः।

एवं त्यक्तैषनस्त्वं मा गृधः, गृधिमाकाङ्क्सां मा कार्षीर्धनविषयाम्। कस्यस्विद्धनं कस्यचित्परस्य स्वस्य वा धनं मा काङ्क्षीरित्यर्थः। स्विदित्यनर्थको निपातः।

अथवा मा गृधः। कस्मात् ? कस्यस्विद्धनमित्याक्षेपार्थो न कस्यचिद्धनमस्ति यद्गृध्येत। आत्मैवेदं सर्वमितीश्वरभावनया सर्वं त्यक्तमत आत्मन एवेदं सर्वमात्मैव च सर्वमतो मिथ्याविषयां गृधिं मा कार्षीरित्यर्थः॥ १॥

कुर्वन्नेवेह कर्माणि
जिजीविषेच्छतं समाः।
एवं त्वयि नान्यथेतो ऽस्ति
न कर्म लिप्यते नरे॥ २॥

कुर्वन्नेव इह निर्वर्तयन्नेव कर्माण्यग्निहोत्रादीनि जिजीविषेज्जीवितुमिच्छेत्। शतं शतसङ्ख्याकाः समाः संवत्सरान्। तावद्धि पुरुषस्य परमायुर्निरूपितम्। तथा च प्राप्तानुवादेन यज्जिजीविषेच्छतं वर्षाणि तत्कुर्वन्नेव कर्माणीत्येतद्विधीयते।

एवमेवंप्रकारेण त्वयि जिजीविषति नरे नरमात्राभिमानिनीत एतस्मादग्निहोत्रादीनि कर्माणि कुर्वतो वर्तमानात्प्रकारादन्यथा प्रकारान्तरं नास्ति येन प्रकारेणाशुभं कर्म न लिप्यते कर्मणा न लिप्यत इत्यर्थः। अतः शास्त्रविहितानि कर्माण्यग्निहोत्रादीनि कुर्वन्नेव जिजीविषेत्।

कथं पुनरिदमवगम्यते पूर्वेण मन्त्रेण संन्यासिनो ज्ञाननिष्ठोक्ता द्वितीयेन तदशक्तस्य कर्मनिष्ठेत्युच्यते। ज्ञानकर्मणोर्विरोधं पर्वतवदकम्प्यं यथोक्तं न स्मरसि किम् ? इहाप्युक्तं, यो हि जिजीविषेत्स कर्म कुर्वन्। ईशावास्यमिदं

सर्वं तेन त्यक्तेन भुञ्जीथाः मा गृधः कस्य स्विद्धनमिति च। न जीविते मरणे वा गृधिं कुर्वीतारण्यमियादिति च पदम्। ततो न पुनरियादिति संन्यासशासनात्। उभयोः फलभेदं च वक्ष्यति।

इमौ द्वावेव पन्थानावनुनिष्क्रान्ततरौ भवतः क्रियापथश्चैव पुरस्तात्संन्यासश्चोत्तरेण निवृत्तिमार्गेण एषणात्रयस्य त्यागः। तयोः संन्यासपथ एवातिरेचयति। न्यास एवात्यरेचयदिति च तैत्तिरीयके।

> द्वाविमावथ पन्थानौ यत्र वेदाः प्रतिष्ठिताः।
> प्रवृत्तिलक्षणो धर्मो निवृत्तश्च विभावितः॥ [म. भा. १२.२४१.६] इत्यादि।

पुत्राय विचार्य निश्चितमुक्तं व्यासेन वेदाचार्येण भगवता। विभागं चानयोर्दर्शयिष्यामः॥ २॥

अथेदानीमविद्वन्निन्दार्थोऽयं मन्त्र आरभ्यते—

> असुर्या नाम ते लोका
> अन्धेन तमसावृताः।
> तांस्ते प्रेत्याभिगच्छन्ति
> ये के चात्महनो जनाः॥ ३॥

असुर्याः परमात्मभावमद्वयमपेक्ष्य देवादयोऽप्य् असुराः, तेषां च स्वभूता लोका असुर्या नाम। नामशब्दोऽनर्थको निपातः।

ते लोकाः कर्मफलानि। लोक्यन्ते दृश्यन्ते भुज्यन्त इति जन्मानि। अन्धेनादर्शनात्मकेनाज्ञानेन तमसा आवृताः आच्छादिताः। तान् स्थावरान् तान् प्रेत्य त्यक्त्वेमं देहम् यथाकर्म यथाश्रुतम्।

आत्मानं घ्नन्तीत्यात्महनः। के ते जनाः ? येऽविद्वांसः। कथं ते आत्मानं नित्यं हिंसन्ति ? अविद्यादोषेण विद्यमानस्यात्मनस् तिरस्करणात्। विद्यमानस्य आत्मनो यत्कार्यं फलम् अजरामरत्वादिसंवेदनलक्षणं तद्धतस्येव तिरोभूतं भवतीति प्राकृताविद्वांसो जना आत्महन उच्यन्ते। तेन ह्यात्महननदोषेण संसरन्ति ते॥ ३॥

यस्यात्मनो हननादविद्वांसः संसरन्ति, तद्विपर्ययेण विद्वांसो जना मुच्यन्ते। ते नात्महनः। तत्कीदृशमात्मतत्त्वमित्युच्यते—

> अनेजदेकं मनसो जवीयो
> नैनद्देवा आप्नुवन् पूर्वमर्षत्।
> तद्धावतोऽन्यानत्येति तिष्ठत्
> तस्मिन्नपो मातरिश्वा दधाति॥ ४॥

अनेजन्न एजत्। एजृ कम्पने। कम्पनं चलनं स्वावस्थाप्रच्युतिस्तद्वर्जितं सर्वदैकरूपमित्यर्थः। तच्चैकं सर्वभूतेषु। मनसः सङ्कल्पादिलक्षणाज्जवीयो जववत्तरम्।

कथं विरुद्धमुच्यते ध्रुवं निश्चलमिदं मनसो जवीय इति च ? नैष दोषः। निरुपाध्युपाधिमत्त्वेनोपपत्तेः। तत्र निरुपाधिकेन स्वेन रूपेणोच्यते अनेजदेकमिति। मनसोऽन्तःकरणस्य सङ्कल्पविकल्पलक्षणस्योपाधेरनुवर्तनादिह देहस्थस्य मनसो ब्रह्मलोकादिदूरगमनं सङ्कल्पेन क्षणमात्राद्भवतीत्यतो मनसो जविष्ठत्वं लोके प्रसिद्धम्।

तस्मिन्मनसि ब्रह्मलोकादीन् द्रुतं गच्छति सति प्रथमं प्राप्त इवात्मचैतन्यावभासो गृह्यते ऽतो मनसो जवीय इत्याह। नैनद्देवाः द्योतनाद्देवाश्चक्षुरादीनीन्द्रियाण्येतत्प्रकृतमात्मतत्त्वं नाप्नुवन्न प्राप्तवन्तः। तेभ्यो मनो जवीयः। मनोव्यापारव्यवहितत्वादाभासमात्रमप्यात्मनो नैव देवानां विषयीभवति।

यस्माज्जवनान्मनसो ऽपि पूर्वमर्षत्पूर्वमेव गतं व्योमवद्व्यापित्वात्। सर्वव्यापि तदात्मतत्त्वं सर्वसंसारधर्मवर्जितं स्वेन निरुपाधिकेन स्वरूपेणाविक्रियमेव सदुपाधिकृताः सर्वाः संसारविक्रिया अनुभवतीत्यविवेकिनां मूढानामनेकमिव च प्रतिदेहं प्रत्यवभासत इत्येतदाह तद्धावतो द्रुतं गच्छतोऽन्यानात्मविलक्षणान्मनोवागिन्द्रियप्रभृतीनत्येति अतीत्य गच्छतीव। इवार्थं स्वयमेव दर्शयति तिष्ठदिति। स्वयमविक्रियमेव सदित्यर्थः।

तस्मिन्नात्मतत्त्वे सति नित्यचैतन्यस्वभावे मातरिश्वा मातर्यन्तरिक्षे श्वयति गच्छतीति मातरिश्वा वायुः सर्वप्राणभृत्क्रियात्मको यदाश्रयाणि कार्यकारणजातानि यस्मिन्नोतानि प्रोतानि च यत्सूत्रसंज्ञकं सर्वस्य जगतो विधारयितृ स मातरिश्वा। अपः कर्माणि प्राणिनां चेष्टालक्षणानि अग्न्यादित्यपर्जन्यादीनां ज्वलनदहनप्रकाशाभिवर्षणादिलक्षणानि दधाति कर्तृषु विभजतीत्यर्थः। धारयतीति वा। भीषाऽस्माद्वातः पवते [तै. उ. २.८.१] इत्यादिश्रुतिभ्यः। सर्वा हि कार्यकरणादिविक्रिया नित्यचैतन्यात्मस्वरूपे सर्वास्पदभूते सत्येव भवन्तित्यादि॥ ४॥

न मन्त्राणाम् जामितास्तीति पूर्वमन्त्रोक्तमप्यर्थं पुनराह—

> तदेजति तन्नैजति
> तद्दूरे तद्वन्तिके।
> तदन्तरस्य सर्वस्य
> तदु सर्वस्यास्य बाह्यतः॥ ५॥

तदात्मतत्त्वं यत्प्रकृतं तदेजति चलति तदेव च नैजति स्वतो नैव चलति स्वतो ऽचलमेव सच्चलतीवेत्यर्थः। किंच तद्दूरे वर्षकोटिशतैरप्यविदुषामप्राप्यत्वाद्दूर इव। तद् उ अन्तिक इति च्छेदः। तद्वन्तिके समीपेऽत्यन्तमेव विदुषामात्मत्वान्न केवलं दूरेऽन्तिके च। तदन्तरभ्यन्तरेऽस्य सर्वस्य। य आत्मा सर्वान्तर इति श्रुतेः। अस्य सर्वस्य जगतो नामरूपक्रियात्मकस्य तद्वपि सर्वस्यास्य बाह्यतो व्यापकत्वादाकाशवन्निरतिशयसूक्ष्मत्वादन्तः। प्रज्ञानघन एवेति च शासनान्निरन्तरं च॥ ५॥

यस्तु सर्वाणि भूतानि
आत्मन्येवानुपश्यति।
सर्वभूतेषु चात्मानं
ततो न विजुगुप्सते॥ ६॥

यः परिव्राड्मुमुक्षुः सर्वाणि भूतान्यव्यक्तादीनि स्थावरान्तान्यात्मन्येवानुपश्यत्यात्मव्यतिरिक्तानि न पश्यतीत्यर्थः। सर्वभूतेषु च तेष्वेव चात्मानं तेषामपि भूतानां स्वमात्मानमात्मत्वेन यथास्य देहस्य कार्यकारणसङ्घातस्यात्माऽहं सर्वप्रत्ययसाक्षिभूतश्चेतयिता केवलो निर्गुणोऽनेनैव स्वरूपेणाव्यक्तादीनां स्थावरान्तानामहमेवात्मेति सर्वभूतेषु चात्मानं निर्विशेषं यस्त्वनुपश्यति स ततस्तस्मादेव दर्शनान्न विजुगुप्सते विजुगुप्सां घृणां न करोति। प्राप्तस्यैवानुवादोऽयम्। सर्वा हि घृणा आत्मनोऽन्यद्दुष्टं पश्यतो भवत्यात्मानमेवात्यन्तविशुद्धं निरन्तरं पश्यतो न घृणानिमित्तमर्थान्तरमस्तीति प्राप्तमेव। ततो न विजुगुप्सत इति॥ ६॥

इमम् एव अर्थम् अन्योऽपि मन्त्र आह—

यस्मिन् सर्वाणि भूतान्य्
आत्मैवाभूद्विजानतः।
तत्र को मोहः कः शोक
एकत्वमनुपश्यतः॥ ७॥

यस्मिन् काले यथोक्तात्मनि वा तान्येव भूतानि सर्वाणि परमार्थात्मदर्शनादात्मैवाभूदात्मैव संवृत्तः परमार्थवस्तु विजानतः तत्र तस्मिन् काले तत्रात्मनि वा को मोहः कः शोकः। शोकश्च मोहश्च कामकर्मबीजमजानतो भवति। न त्वात्मैकत्वं विशुद्धं गगनोपमं पश्यतः को मोहः कः शोक इति शोकमोहयोरविद्याकार्ययोराक्षेपेणासम्भवप्रदर्शनात्सकारणस्य संसारस्यात्यन्तमेवोच्छेदः प्रदर्शितो भवति॥ ७॥

योऽयमतीतैर्मन्त्रैरुक्त आत्मा स स्वेन रूपेण किं लक्षण इत्याहायं मन्त्रः—

स पर्यगाच्छुक्रमकायमव्रणम्
अस्नाविरं शुद्धमपापविद्धम्।
कविर्मनीषी परिभूः स्वयम्भू-
र्याथातथ्यतोऽर्थान् व्यदधाच्छाश्वती-
भ्यः समाभ्यः॥ ८॥

स यथोक्त आत्मा पर्यगात्परि समन्तादगाद्गतवानाकाशवद्व्यापी इत्यर्थः। शुक्रं शुद्धं ज्योतिष्मद्दीप्तिमानित्यर्थः। अकायमशरीरो लिङ्गशरीरवर्जित इत्यर्थः। अव्रणमक्षतम्। अस्नाविरं स्नावाः शिरा यस्मिन्न विद्यन्त इत्यस्नाविरम्। अव्रणमस्नाविरमित्याभ्यां स्थूलशरीरप्रतिषेधः। शुद्धं निर्मलमविद्यामलरहितमिति कारणशरीरप्रतिषेधः। अपापविद्धं धर्माधर्मादिपापवर्जितम्। शुक्रमित्यादीनि वचांसि पुल्लिङ्गत्वेन परिणेयानि। स पर्यगादित्युपक्रम्य कविर्मनीषीत्यादिना पुल्लिङ्गत्वेनोपसंहारात्।

कविः क्रान्तदर्शी सर्वादृक्। नान्योऽतोऽस्ति द्रष्टा (बृ.उ. ३.८.११) इत्यादिश्रुतेः। मनीषी मनस ईषिता सर्वज्ञ ईश्वर इत्यर्थः। परिभूः सर्वेषां पर्युपरि भवतीति परिभूः। स्वयम्भूः स्वयमेव भवतीति। येषामुपरि भवति यश्चोपरि भवति स सर्वः स्वयमेव भवतीति स्वयम्भूः।

स नित्यमुक्त ईश्वरो याथातथ्यतः सर्वज्ञत्वाद्यथातथाभावो याथातथ्यं तस्माद्यथाभूतकर्मफलसाधनतोऽर्थान् कर्तव्यपदार्थान् व्यदधाद्विहितवान् यथानुरूपं व्यभजदित्यर्थः, शाश्वतीभ्यो नित्याभ्यः समाभ्यः संवत्सराख्येभ्यः प्रजापतिभ्य इत्यर्थः॥ ८॥

अत्राद्येन मन्त्रेण सर्वैषणापरित्यागेन ज्ञाननिष्ठोक्ता प्रथमो वेदार्थः ईशावास्यमिदं सर्वं . . . मा गृधः कस्यस्विद्धनमिति। अज्ञानां जिजीविषूणां ज्ञाननिष्ठासम्भवे कुर्वन्नेवेह कर्माणि . . . जिजीविषेदिति कर्मनिष्ठोक्ता द्वितीयो वेदार्थः।

अनयोश्च निष्ठयोर्विभागो मन्त्रप्रदर्शितयोर्बृहदारण्यकेऽपि प्रदर्शितः सो ऽकामयत जाया मे स्यात् (बृ.उ. १.४.१७) इत्यादिना अज्ञस्य कामिनः कर्माणीति। मन एवास्यात्मा वाग्जाया (बृ.उ. १.४.१७) इत्यादिवचनादज्ञत्वं कामित्वं च कर्मनिष्ठस्य निश्चितमवगम्यते। तथा च तत्फलं सप्तान्नसर्गस्तेष्वात्मभावेनात्मस्वरूपावस्थानम्।

जायाद्येषणात्रयसंन्यासेन च आत्मविदां कर्मनिष्ठाप्रातिकूल्येनात्मस्वरूपनिष्ठैव दर्शिता किं प्रजया करिष्यामो येषां नोऽयमात्मायं लोकः (बृ.उ. ४.४.२२) इत्यादिना। ये तु ज्ञाननिष्ठाः संन्यासिनस्तेभ्यो सुर्या नाम त इत्यादिना

अविद्वन्निन्दाद्वारेण आत्मनो याथात्म्यं स पर्यगादित्येतदन्तैर्मन्त्रैरुपदिष्टम्। ते ह्यत्राधिकृता न कामिन इति। तथा च श्वेताश्वतराणां मन्त्रोपनिषदि अत्याश्रमिभ्यः परमं पवित्रं प्रोवाच सम्यगृषिसङ्घजुष्टम् (श्वे.उ. ६.२१) इत्यादि विभज्योक्तम्। ये तु कर्मिणः कर्मनिष्ठाः कर्म कुर्वन्त एव जिजीविषवस्तेभ्य इदमुच्यते—

अन्धं तमः प्रविशन्ति
येऽविद्यामुपासते।
ततो भूय इव ते तमो
य उ विद्यायां रताः॥ ९॥

कथं पुनरेवमवगम्यते न तु सर्वेषामिति। उच्यते—अकामिनः साध्यसाधनभेदोपमर्देन यस्मिन् सर्वाणि भूतान्यात्मैवाभूद्विजानतः। तत्र को मोहः कः शोक एकत्वमनुपश्यत इति यदात्मैकत्वविज्ञानमुक्तं तन्न केनचित्कर्मणा ज्ञानान्तरेण वा ह्यमूढः समुच्चिचीषति। इह तु समुच्चिचीषया अविद्वदादिनिन्दा क्रियते। तत्र च यस्य येन समुच्चयः सम्भवति न्यायतः शास्त्रतो वा तदिहोच्यते यद्दैवं वित्तं देवताविषयं ज्ञानं कर्मसम्बन्धित्वेनोपन्यस्तं न परमात्मज्ञानम्। विद्यया देवलोकः (बृ.उ. १.५.१६) इति पृथक्फलश्रवणात्। तयोर्ज्ञानकर्मणोरिह एकैकानुष्ठाननिन्दा समुच्चिचीषया न निन्दापरैव एकैकस्य पृथक्फलश्रवणाद्विद्यया तदारोहन्ति, विद्यया देवलोकः (बृ.उ. १.५.१६) न तत्र दक्षिणा यन्ति, कर्मणा पितृलोकः (बृ.उ. १.५.१६) इति। न हि शास्त्रविहितं किञ्चिदकर्तव्यतामियात्।

तत्र अन्धं तमः अदर्शनात्मकं तमः प्रविशन्ति। के येऽविद्यां विद्याया अन्या अविद्या तां कर्म इत्यर्थः कर्मणो विद्याविरोधित्वात्। तामविद्यामग्निहोत्रादिलक्षणामेव केवलामुपासते तत्पराः सन्तो ऽनुतिष्ठन्तीत्यभिप्रायः। ततस्तस्मादन्धात्मकात्तमसो भूय इव बहुतरमेव ते तमः प्रविशन्ति। के कर्म हित्वा ये उ ये तु विद्यायामेव देवताज्ञान एव रताः अभिरताः। तत्रावान्तरफलभेदं विद्याकर्मणोः समुच्चयकारणमाह। अन्यथा फलवदफलवतोः सन्निहितयोरङ्गाङ्गितैव स्यादित्यर्थः॥ ९॥

अन्यदेवाहुर्विद्ययान्यदाहुरविद्यया।
इति शुश्रुम धीराणां ये नस्तद्विचचक्षिरे॥ १०॥

अन्यत्पृथगेव विद्यया क्रियते फलमित्याहुर्वदन्ति विद्यया देवलोकः (बृ.उ. १.६.१६), कर्मणा क्रियते कर्मणा पितृलोकः (बृ.उ. १.५.१६) इति श्रुतेः। इत्येवं शुश्रुम श्रुतवन्तो वयं धीराणां धीमतां वचनम्। ये आचार्या नोऽस्मभ्यं तत्कर्म च ज्ञानं च विचचक्षिरे व्याख्यातवन्तस्तेषामयमागमः पारम्पर्यागत इत्यर्थः॥ १०॥

विद्यां चाविद्यां च यस्
तद् वेदोभयं सह।
अविद्यया मृत्युं तीर्त्वा
विद्ययामृतमश्नुते॥ ११॥

यत एवमतो विद्यां चाविद्यां च देवताज्ञानं कर्म चेत्यर्थः। यस्तदेतदुभयं सहैकेन पुरुषेण अनुष्ठेयं वेद तस्यैवं समुच्चयकारिण एव एकपुरुषार्थसम्बन्धः क्रमेण स्यादित्युच्यते।

अविद्यया कर्मणा अग्निहोत्रादिना मृत्युं स्वाभाविकं कर्म ज्ञानं च मृत्युशब्दवाच्यमुभयं तीर्त्वा अतिक्रम्य विद्यया देवताज्ञानेनामृतं देवतात्मभावमश्नुते प्राप्नोति। तद्ध्यमृतमुच्यते यद्देवतात्मगमनम्॥ ११॥

अधुना व्याकृताव्याकृतोपासनयोः समुच्चिचीषया प्रत्येकं निन्दोच्यते।

अन्धं तमः प्रविशन्ति
येऽसम्भूतिमुपासते।
ततो भूय इव ते तमो
य उ सम्भूत्यां रताः॥ १२॥

अन्धं तमः प्रविशन्ति येऽसम्भूतिं सम्भवनं सम्भूतिः सा यस्य कार्यस्य सा सम्भूतिः तस्या अन्याऽसम्भूतिः प्रकृतिः कारणमविद्याव्याकृताख्या तामसम्भूतिमव्याकृताख्यां प्रकृतिं कारणमविद्यां कामकर्मबीजभूताम् दर्शनात्मिकामुपासते ये ते तदनुरूपमेवान्धं तमोऽदर्शनात्मकं प्रविशन्ति। ततस्तस्मादपि भूयो बहुतरमिव तमः प्रविशन्ति य उ सम्भूत्यां कार्यब्रह्मणि हिरण्यगर्भाख्ये रताः॥ १२॥

अधुनोभयोरुपासनयोः समुच्चयकारणमवयवफलभेदमाह—

अन्यदेवाहुः संभवाद्
अन्यदाहुरसंभवात्।
इति शुश्रुम धीराणां
ये नस्तद् विचचक्षिरे॥ १३॥

अन्यदेव पृथगेवाहुः फलं सम्भवात्सम्भूतेः कार्यब्रह्मोपासनादणिमाद्यैश्वर्यलक्षणं व्याख्यातवन्त इत्यर्थः।

तथा चान्यदाहुरसम्भवादसम्भूतेरव्याकृतादव्याकृतोपासनाद्यदुक्तमन्धं तमः प्रविशन्तीति प्रकृतिलय इति च पौराणिकैरुच्यत इत्येवं शुश्रुम धीराणां वचनं ये नस्तद्विचचक्षिरे व्याकृताव्याकृतोपासनफलं व्याख्यातवन्त इत्यर्थः॥ १३॥

यत एवमतः समुच्चयः सम्भूत्यसम्भूत्युपासनयोर्युक्त एवैकपुरुषार्थत्वाच्चेत्याह—

संभूतिं च विनाशं च
यस्तद् वेदोभयं सह।
विनाशेन मृत्युं तीर्त्वा
संभूत्यामृतमश्नुते॥ १४॥

सम्भूतिं च विनाशं च यस्तद्वेदोभयं सह विनाशो धर्मो यस्य कार्यस्य स तेन धर्मिणा अभेदेन उच्यते विनाश इति, तेन तदुपासनेनानैश्वर्यमधर्मकामादिदोषजातं च मृत्युं तीर्त्वा—हिरण्यगर्भोपासनेनाप्ति ह्यणिमादिप्राप्तिः फलम्, तेनानैश्वर्यादिमृत्युमतीत्य असम्भूत्या अव्याकृतोपासनया अमृतं प्रकृतिलयलक्षणमश्नुते। सम्भूतिं च विनाशं चेत्यत्रावर्णलोपेन निर्देशो द्रष्टव्यः प्रकृतिलयफलश्रुत्यनुरोधात्॥ १४॥

मानुषदैववित्तसाध्यं फलं शास्त्रलक्षणं प्रकृतिलयान्तम्। एतावती संसारगतिः। अतः परं पूर्वोक्तमात्मैवाभूद्विजानत इति सर्वात्मभाव एव सर्वैषणासंन्यासज्ञाननिष्ठाफलम्। एवं द्विप्रकारः प्रवृत्तिनिवृत्तिलक्षणो वेदार्थो ऽत्र प्रकाशितः। तत्र प्रवृत्तिलक्षणस्य वेदार्थस्य विधिप्रतिषेधलक्षणस्य कृत्स्नस्य प्रकाशने प्रवर्ग्यान्तं ब्राह्मणमुपयुक्तम्। निवृत्तिलक्षणस्य वेदार्थस्य प्रकाशने ऽत ऊर्ध्वं बृहदारण्यकमुपयुक्तम्।

तत्र निषेकादिश्मशानान्तं कर्म कुर्वन् जिजीविषेद्यो विद्यया सहापरब्रह्मविषयया तदुक्तं विद्यां चाविद्यां च यस्तद्वेदोभयं सह। अविद्यया मृत्युं तीर्त्वा विद्ययामृतमश्नुते इति।

तत्र केन मार्गेणामृतत्वमश्नुत इत्युच्यते। तद्यत्तत्सत्यमसौ स आदित्यो य एष एतस्मिन्मण्डले पुरुषो यश्चायं दक्षिणे ऽक्षन्पुरुष एतदुभयं सत्यम्। ब्रह्मोपासीनो यथोक्तकर्मकृच्च यः सो ऽन्तकाले प्राप्ते सत्यात्मानमात्मनः प्राप्तिद्वारं याचते हिरण्मयेन पात्रेण इति।

हिरण्मयेन पात्रेण
सत्यस्यापिहितं मुखम्।
तत्त्वं पूषन्नपावृणु
सत्यधर्माय दृष्टये॥ १५॥

हिरण्मयमिव हिरण्मयं ज्योतिर्मयमित्येतत्। तेन पात्रेणैवापिधानभूतेन सत्यस्यैवादित्यमण्डलस्थस्य ब्रह्मणो ऽपिहितमाच्छादितं मुखं द्वारम्। तत्त्वं हे पूषन्नपावृणवपसारय सत्यस्योपासनात्सत्यं धर्मो यस्य मम सो ऽहं सत्यधर्मा तस्मै मह्यमथवा यथाभूतस्य धर्मस्यानुष्ठात्रे दृष्टये तव सत्यआत्मन उपलब्धये॥ १५॥

पूषन्नेकर्षे यम सूर्य प्राजापत्य
व्यूह रश्मीन् समूह तेजः।
यत्ते रूपं कल्याणतमं तत्ते पश्यामि
यो ऽसावसौ पुरुषः सो ऽहमस्मि॥ १६॥

हे पूषन् जगतः पोषणात्पूषा रविस्तथैक एव ऋषति गच्छति इत्येकर्षिः—हे एकर्षे तथा सर्वस्य संयमनाद्यमः—हे यम तथा रश्मीनां प्राणानां रसानाञ्च स्वीकरणात् सूर्यः—हे सूर्य प्रजापतेरपत्यं प्राजापत्यः—हे प्राजापत्य व्यूह विगमय रश्मीन्स्वान्। समूह एकीकुरु उपसंहरते तेजस्तापकं ज्योतिः।

यत्ते तव रूपं कल्याणतममत्यन्तशोभनं तत्ते तवात्मनः प्रसादात्पश्यामि। किञ्चाहं न तु त्वां भृत्यवद्याचे यो ऽसावादित्यमण्डलस्थो व्याहृत्यवयवः पुरुषः पुरुषाकारत्वात्पूर्णं वानेन प्राणबुद्ध्यात्मना जगत्समस्तमिति पुरुषः पुरि शयनाद्वा पुरुषः सो ऽहमस्मि भवामि॥ १६॥

वायुरनिलममृतम्
अथेदं भस्मान्तं शरीरम्।
ओं क्रतो स्मर कृतं स्मर
क्रतो स्मर कृतं स्मर॥ १७॥

अथेदानी मम मरिष्यतो वायुः प्राणो ऽध्यात्मपरिच्छेदं हित्वा अधिदैवतात्मानं सर्वात्मकमनिलममृतं सूत्रात्मानं प्रतिपद्यतामिति वाक्यशेषः। लिङ्गं चेदं ज्ञानकर्मसंस्कृतमुत्क्रामत्विति द्रष्टव्यं मार्गयाचनसामर्थ्यात्। अथेदं शरीरमग्नौ हुतं भस्मान्तं भूयात्। ओमिति यथोपासनमोंप्रतीकात्मकत्वात्सत्यात्मकमग्न्याख्यं ब्रह्माभेदेनोच्यते। हे क्रतो सङ्कल्पात्मक स्मर यन्मम स्मर्तव्यं तस्य कालो ऽयं प्रत्युपस्थितो ऽतः स्मर। एतावन्तं कालं भावितं कृतमग्ने स्मर यन्मया बाल्यप्रभृत्यनुष्ठितं कर्म तच्च स्मर। क्रतो स्मर कृतं स्मर इति पुनर्वचनमादरार्थम्॥ १७॥

पुनरन्येन मन्त्रेण मार्गं याचते—

अग्ने नय सुपथा राये अस्मान्
विश्वानि देव वयुनानि विद्वान्।
युयोध्यस्मज्जुहुराणम् एनो
भूयिष्ठां ते नम उक्तिं विधेम॥ १८॥

हे अग्ने नय गमय सुपथा शोभनेन मार्गेण। सुपथेति विशेषणं दक्षिणमार्गनिवृत्त्यर्थम्। निर्विण्णो ऽहं दक्षिणेन मार्गेण गतागतलक्षणेनातो याचे त्वां पुनः पुनर्गमनागमनवर्जितेन शोभनेन पथा नय। राये धनाय कर्मफलभोगायेत्यर्थः, अस्मान्यथोक्तधर्मफलविशिष्टान् विश्वानि सर्वाणि हे देव वयुनानि कर्माणि प्रज्ञानानि वा विद्वाञ्ज्ञानन्।

किञ्च युयोधि वियोजय विनाशय अस्मदस्मत्तो जुहुराणं कुटिलं वञ्चनात्मकमेनः पापम्। ततो वयं विशुद्धाः सन्त इष्टं प्राप्स्याम इत्यभिप्रायः। किन्तु वयमिदानीं ते न शक्नुमः परिचर्यां कर्तुम्। भूयिष्ठां बहुतरां ते तुभ्यं नम उक्तिं नमस्कारवचनं विधेम नमस्कारेण परिचरेम इत्यर्थः।

अविद्यया मृत्युं तीर्त्वा
विद्ययामृतमश्नुते। (ई.उ.११)
विनाशेन मृत्युं तीर्त्वा-
सम्भूत्यामृतमश्नुते। (ई.उ.१४)

इति श्रुत्वा केचित्संशयं कुर्वन्ति। अतस्तन्निराकरणार्थं संक्षेपतो विचारणां करिष्यामः।

तत्र तावत्किं निमित्तः संशय इत्युच्यते।

विद्याशब्देन मुख्या परमात्मविद्यैव कस्मान्न गृह्यते ऽमृतत्वं च। ननूक्तायाः परमात्मविद्यायाः कर्मणश्च विरोधात्समुच्चयानुपपत्तिः।

सत्यम्। विरोधस्तु नावगम्यते विरोधाविरोधयोः शास्त्रप्रमाणकत्वात्। यथाविद्यानुष्ठानं विद्योपासनञ्च शास्त्रप्रमाणकं तथा तद्विरोधाविरोधावपि। यथा च न हिंस्यात्सर्वा भूतानीति शास्त्रादवगतं पुनः शास्त्रेणैव बाध्यते ऽध्वरे पशुं हिंस्यादिति। एवं विद्याविद्ययोरपि स्यात्। विद्याकर्मणोश्च समुच्चयः।

न,

दूरमेते विपरीते विषूची
अविद्या या च विद्या (क.उ.१.२.४) इति श्रुतेः।

विद्यां चाविद्यां चेति वचनादविरोध इति चेन्न हेतुस्वरूपफलविरोधात्।

विद्याविद्याविरोधाविरोधयोर्विकल्पासम्भवात् समुच्चयविधानादविरोध एवेति चेन्न सहसम्भवानुपपत्तेः।

क्रमेणैकाश्रये स्यातां विद्याविद्ये इति चेन्न विद्योत्पत्तौ अविद्याया ह्यास्तत्वात्तदाश्रये ऽविद्यानुपपत्तेः। न ह्यग्निरुष्णः प्रकाशश्चेति विज्ञानोत्पत्तौ यस्मिन्नाश्रये तदुत्पन्नं तस्मिन्नेवाश्रये शीतो ऽग्निरप्रकाशो वेत्यविद्याया उत्पत्तिर्नापि संशयो ऽज्ञानं वा :

यस्मिन् सर्वाणि भूतान्य-
आत्मैवाभूद्विजानतः।
तत्र को मोहः कः शोक
एकत्वमनुपश्यतः (ई.उ. ७) इति

शोकमोहाद्यसम्भवश्रुतेः। अविद्यासम्भवात्तदुपादानस्य कर्मणो ऽप्यनुपपत्तिम् अवोचाम।

अमृतमश्नुत इत्यापेक्षिकम् अमृतम्। विद्याशब्देन परमात्मविद्याग्रहणे हिरण्मयेनेत्यादिना द्वारमार्गादियाचनमनुपपन्नं स्यात्। तस्मादुपासनया समुच्चयो न परमात्मविज्ञानेनेति यथास्माभिर्व्याख्यात एव मन्त्राणामर्थ इत्युपरम्यते॥ १८॥

इति श्रीमत्परमहंसपरिव्राजकाचार्यस्य श्रीशङ्करभगवतः कृतावीशावास्योपनिषद्भाष्यं सम्पूर्णम्।

Full Devanāgarī Text (Upaniṣad and Madhva)

पूर्णमदः पूर्णमिदं
पूर्णात्पूर्णमुदच्यते।
पूर्णस्य पूर्णमादाय
पूर्णमेवावशिष्यते॥

॥ॐ शान्तिः शान्तिः शान्तिः ॐ॥

ॐ ईशावास्यमिदं सर्वं
यत्किंच जगत्यां जगत्।
तेन त्यक्तेन भुञ्जीथा
मा गृधः कस्य स्विद्धनम्॥ १॥

नित्यानित्यजगद्धात्रे नित्याय ज्ञानमूर्तये।
पूर्णानन्दाय हरये सर्वयज्ञभुजे नमः॥
यस्माद्ब्रह्मेन्द्ररुद्रादिदेवतानां श्रियोऽपि च।
ज्ञानस्फूर्तिः सदा तस्मै हरये गुरवे नमः॥

स्वायम्भुवो मनुरेतैर्मन्त्रैर्भगवन्तमाकूतिसूनुं यज्ञनामानं विष्णुं तुष्टाव

स्वायम्भुवः स्वदौहित्रं विष्णुं यज्ञाभिधं मनुः।
ईशावास्यादिभिर्मन्त्रैस्तुष्टावावहितात्मना॥
रक्षोभिरुग्रैः सम्प्राप्तः खादितुं मोचितस्तदा।
स्तोत्रं श्रुत्वैव यज्ञेन तान् हत्वाऽवध्यतां गतान्॥
प्रादाद्धि भगवांस्तेषामवध्यत्वं हरः प्रभुः।
तैर्वध्यत्वं तथाऽन्येषामतः कोऽन्यो हरेः प्रभुः॥
इति ब्रह्माण्डे।

भागवते चायमेवार्थ उक्तः। ईशस्याऽऽवासयोग्यमीशावास्यम्। जगत्यां प्रकृतौ। तेनेशेन त्यक्तेन दत्तेन भुञ्जीथाः।

स्वतः प्रवृत्त्यशक्तत्वादीशावास्यमिदं जगत्।
प्रवृत्तये प्रकृतिगं यस्मात्स प्रकृतीश्वरः॥
तदधीनप्रवृत्तित्वात्तदीयं सर्वमेव यत्।
तद्दत्तेन भुञ्जीथा अतो नान्यं प्रयाचयेत्॥ इति ब्रह्माण्डे॥ २॥

कुर्वन्नेवेह कर्माणि
जिजीविषेच्छतं समाः।
एवं त्वयि नान्यथेतो ऽस्ति
न कर्म लिप्यते नरे॥ २॥

अकुर्वतः कर्म न लिप्यते इति नास्ति।

अज्ञस्य कर्म लिप्येत कृष्णोपास्तिमकुर्वतः।
ज्ञानिनोऽपि यतो ह्रास आनन्दस्य भवेद् ध्रुवम्।
अतोऽलेपेऽपि लेपः स्यादतः कार्यैव सा सदा॥
इति नारदीये॥ २॥

असुर्या नाम ते लोका
अन्धेन तमसावृताः।
तांस्ते प्रेत्याभिगच्छन्ति
ये के चात्महनो जनाः॥ ३॥

सुष्ठु रमणविरुद्धत्वादसुराणां प्राप्यत्वाच्चासुर्याः। न च रमन्त्यहो असदुपासनयाऽऽत्महन इत्युक्तत्वात्।

महादुःखहेतुत्वात् प्राप्यत्वादसुरैस्तथा।
असुर्या नाम ते लोकास्तान् यान्ति विमुखा हरौ॥ इति वामने॥

ये के चेत्यनेन नियम उक्तः। नियमेन तमो यान्ति सर्वेऽपि विमुखा हरौ इति च॥ ३॥

अनेजदेकं मनसो जवीयो
नैनद्देवा आप्नुवन् पूर्वमर्षत्।
तद्धावतोऽन्यानत्येति तिष्ठत्
तस्मिन्नपो मातरिश्वा दधाति॥ ४॥

अनेजन्निर्भयत्वात्तदेकं प्राधान्यतस्तथा।
सम्यग्ज्ञातुमशक्यत्वादगम्यं तत्सुरैरपि॥
स्वरं तु सर्वानगमत्पूर्वमेव स्वभावतः।
अचिन्त्यशक्तितश्चैव सर्वगत्वाच्च तत्परम्॥
द्रवतोऽत्येति सन्तिष्ठंस्तस्मिन् कर्माण्यधान्मरुत्।
मारुत्येव यतश्चेष्टा सर्वा तां हरयेऽर्पयेत्॥ इति ब्रह्माण्डे

ऋष ज्ञाने॥ ४॥

तदेजति तन्नैजति
तद्दूरे तद्वन्तिके।
तदन्तरस्य सर्वस्य
तदु सर्वस्यास्य बाह्यतः॥ ५॥

तदेजति तत एव एजत्यन्यत्। तत् स्वयं नैजति।

ततो बिभेति सर्वोऽपि न बिभेति हरिः स्वयम्।
सर्वगत्वात्स दूरे च बाह्येऽन्तश्च समीपगः॥
इति तत्त्वसंहितायाम्॥ ५॥

यस्तु सर्वाणि भूतानि
आत्मन्येवानुपश्यति।
सर्वभूतेषु चात्मानं
ततो न विजुगुप्सते॥ ६॥

सर्वगं परमात्मानं सर्वं च परमात्मनि।
यः पश्येत्स भयाभावान्नाऽऽत्मानं गोप्तुमि-
च्छति॥ इति सौकरायणश्रुतिः॥ ६॥

यस्मिन् सर्वाणि भूतान्य्
आत्मैवाभूद्विजानतः।
तत्र को मोहः कः शोक
एकत्वमनुपश्यतः॥ ७॥

यस्मिन् परमात्मनि सर्वभूतानि स परमात्मैव तत्र सर्वभूतेष्वभूत्। एवं सर्वभूतेष्वेकत्वेन परमात्मानं विजानतः को मोहः ?

यस्मिन् सर्वाणि भूतानि स आत्मा सर्वभूतगः।
एवं सर्वत्र यो विष्णुं पश्येत्तस्य विजानतः॥
को मोहः कोऽथवा शोकः स विष्णुं पर्यगाद्यतः॥
इति पिप्पलादशाखायाम्।

पूर्वोक्तानुवादेन शोकमोहाभावोऽपि विजानतश्चात्रोच्यते।
अभ्यासश्च सर्वगत्वस्य तात्पर्यद्योतनार्थः॥ ७॥

स पर्यगाच्छुक्रमकायमव्रणम्
अस्नाविरं शुद्धमपापविद्धम्।
कविर्मनीषी परिभूः स्वयम्भू-
र्याथातथ्यतोऽर्थान् व्यदधाच्छाश्वती-
भ्यः समाभ्यः॥ ८॥

शुक्रं तच्छोकराहित्यादव्रणं नित्यपूर्णतः।
पावनत्वादसदा शुद्धमकायं लिङ्गवर्जनात्।
स्थूलदेहस्य राहित्यादस्नाविरमुदाहृतम्॥
एवम्भूतोऽपि सार्वज्ञात् कविरित्येव शब्द्यते।
ब्रह्मादिसर्वमनसां प्रकृतेर्मनसोऽपि च॥

ईशितृत्वान्मनीषी स परिभूस्सर्वतो वरः।
सदाऽनन्याश्रयत्वाच्च स्वयम्भूः परिकीर्तितः॥
स सत्यं जगदेतादृङ्नित्यमेव प्रवाहतः।
अनाद्यनन्तकालेषु प्रवाहैकप्रकारतः॥
नियमेनैव ससृजे भगवान् पुरुषोत्तमः।
संज्ञानन्दशीर्षोऽसौ संज्ञानन्दबाहुकः।
संज्ञानन्ददेहश्च संज्ञानन्दपादवान्॥
एवम्भूतो महाविष्णुर्यथार्थं जगदीदृशम्।
अनाद्यनन्तकालीनं ससर्जात्मेच्छया प्रभुः॥
इति वाराहे॥ ८॥

अन्धं तमः प्रविशन्ति
येऽविद्यामुपासते।
ततो भूय इव ते तमो
य उ विद्यायां रताः॥ ९॥

अन्यदेवाहुर्विद्ययान्यदाहुरविद्यया।
इति शुश्रुम धीराणां ये नस्तद्विचच-
क्षिरे॥ १०॥

अन्यथोपासका ये तु तमोऽन्धं यान्त्यसंशयम्।
ततोऽधिकमिव व्यक्तं यान्ति तेषामनिन्दकाः॥
तस्माद्यथास्वरूपं तु नारायणमनामयम्।
अयथार्थस्य निन्दां च ... ॥ ९॥ १०॥

विद्यां चाविद्यां च यस्
तद् वेदोभयं सह।
अविद्यया मृत्युं तीर्त्वा
विद्ययामृतमश्नुते॥ ११॥

... ये विदुः सह सज्जनाः।
ते निन्दयाऽयथार्थस्य दुःखाज्ञानादिरूपिणः।
दुःखाज्ञानादिसन्तीर्णाः सुखज्ञानादिरूपिणः॥
यथार्थस्य परिज्ञानात्सुखज्ञानादिरूपताम्।
यान्त्येवं ... ॥ ११॥

अन्धं तमः प्रविशन्ति
येऽसम्भूतिमुपासते।
ततो भूय इव ते तमो
य उ सम्भूत्यां रताः॥ १२॥

अन्यदेवाहुः संभवाद्
अन्यदाहुरसंभवात्।
इति शुश्रुम धीराणां
ये नस्तद् विचचक्षिरे॥ १३॥

... सृष्टिकर्तृत्वं
नाङ्गीकुर्वन्ति ये हरेः॥
तेऽपि यान्ति तमो घोरं
तथा संहारकर्तृताम्।
नाङ्गीकुर्वन्ति तेऽप्येवं
तस्मात्सर्वगुणात्मकम्॥
सर्वकर्तारमीशेशं
सर्वसंहारकारकम्॥ १२, १३॥

संभूतिं च विनाशं च
यस्तद् वेदोभयं सह।
विनाशेन मृत्युं तीर्त्वा
संभूत्यामृतमश्नुते॥ १४॥

यो वेद संहृतिज्ञानाद्
देहबन्धाद्विमुच्यते।
सुखज्ञानादिकर्तृत्व-
ज्ञानात्तद्भक्तिमाव्रजेत्॥
सर्वदोषविनिर्मुक्तं
गुणरूपं जनार्दनम्।
जानीयान्न गुणानां च
भागहानिं प्रकल्पयेत्॥
न मुक्तानामपि हरेः
साम्यं विष्णोरभिन्नताम्।
नैव प्रचिन्तयेत्तस्माद्
ब्रह्मादेः साम्यमेव वा॥
मानुषादिविरिञ्चान्तं
तारतम्यं विमुक्तिगम्।
ततो विष्णोः परोत्कर्षं
सम्यग्ज्ञात्वा विमुच्यते॥ इति कौर्मे॥

हिरणमयेन पात्रेण
सत्यस्यापिहितं मुखम्।
तत्त्वं पूषन्नपावृणु
सत्यधर्माय दृष्टये॥ १५॥

पात्रं हिरणमयं सूर्य-
मण्डलं समुदाहृतं।
विष्णोः सत्यस्य तेनैव
सर्वदाऽपिहितं मुखं॥
तत्तु पूर्णत्वतः पूषा
विष्णुर्दर्शयति स्वयम्।
सत्यधर्माय भक्ताय ... ॥ १५॥

पूषन्नेकर्षे यम सूर्य
प्राजापत्य व्यूह रश्मीन्।
समूह तेजः यत्ते रूपं
कल्याणतमं तत्ते पश्यामि॥ १६॥

... प्रधानज्ञानरूपतः।
विष्णुरेकऋषिर्ज्ञेयो यमो नियमनाद्धरिः।
सूर्यः स सूरिगम्यत्वात् प्राजापत्य प्रजापतेः।
विशेषेणैव गम्यत्वात् ... ॥ १६॥

यो ऽसावसौ पुरुषः सो ऽहमस्मि॥ १७॥

... अहं चासावहेयतः।
अस्मि नित्यास्तितामानात्सर्वजीवेषु सं-
स्थितः।
स्वयं तु सर्वजीवेभ्यो व्यतिरिक्तः परो हरिः।
स क्रतुर्ज्ञानरूपत्वादग्निरङ्गप्रणेतृतः॥ इति ब्र-
ह्माण्डे॥ १७॥

वायुरनिलममृतम्
अथेदं भस्मान्तं शरीरम्॥ १८॥

ओं क्रतो स्मर कृतं स्मर
क्रतो स्मर कृतं स्मर॥ १९॥

यस्मिन्नयं स्थितः सोऽप्यमृतं, किमु परः ? ः ब्रह्मैव निलयनं यस्य वायोः सोऽनिलम्।

अतिरोहितविज्ञानाद्वायुरप्यमृतः स्मृतः।
मुख्यामृतः स्वयं रामः परमात्मा सनातनः॥
इति रामसंहितायाम्॥ १८॥

भक्तानां स्मरणं विष्णोर्नित्यज्ञप्तिस्वरूपतः।
अनुग्रहोन्मुखत्वं तु नैवान्यत्क्वचिदिष्यते॥
इति ब्रह्मतर्के॥ १९॥

अग्ने नय सुपथा राये अस्मान्

विश्वानि देव वयुनानि विद्वान्।
युयोध्यस्मज्जुहुराणम् एनो
भूयिष्ठां ते नम उक्तिं विधेम॥ २०॥

वयुनं ज्ञानम्। त्वद्दत्तया वयुनयेदमचष्ट विश्वमिति वचनाद्। जुहुराणं अस्मानल्पीकुर्वत्। युयोधि वियोजय।

यदस्मान् कुरुतेऽत्यल्पांस्तदेनोऽस्मद्वि-
योजय।
नय नो मोक्षवित्तायेत्यस्तौद्यज्ञं मनुः स्वराड्॥
इति स्कन्दे॥

युयु वियोगे इति धातुः। भक्तिज्ञानाभ्यां भूयिष्ठां नम उक्तिं विधेम॥ २०॥

पूर्णशक्तिचिदानन्दश्रीतेजःस्पष्टमूर्तये।
ममाभ्यधिकमित्राय नमो नारायणाय ते॥

इति श्रीमदानन्दतीर्थभगवत्पादाचार्यविरचितमीशावास्योपनिषद्भाष्यं सम्पूर्णम्॥

Bibliography

Āgāse, Bālaśāstrī, editor. *Īśāvāsyopaniṣat saṭīkaśāṅkarabhāṣyoketā*. Puṇyākhyapattana [Pune]: Ānandāśrama, 1827 śakābda [1905], 2nd edition. In Sanskrit. Edited with the commentaries of Śaṅkara and Ānandagiri.

Bādarāyaṇa. *The Vedānta Sūtras of Bādarāyaṇa*. New York, NY: Dover Publications Inc., 1962, 1st edition. In English. Translated by George Thibaut with the comm. of Śaṅkara.

Brahma, Nalinīkānta, editor. *Śrīmadbhagavadgītā*. Kalikātā, India: Navabhārata Pābliśārsa, 1986, 1st edition. In Sanskrit (Bengali script) with the comm. of Madhusūdana Sarasvatī with Bengali translation of text and comm. Originally edited and translated by Bhūtanātha Saptatīrtha.

Brereton, Joel P. "The Particle iva in Vedic Prose." *Journal of the American Oriental Society* 102, 3: (1982) 443–450.

———. *Eastern canons: approaches to the Asian classics*, New York: Columbian University Press, 1990, chapter The Upaniṣads, 115–135. 1st edition.

———. "The Race of Mudgala and Mudgalānī." *Journal of the American Oriental Society* 122, 2: (2002) 224–234. Indic and Iranian Studies in Honor of Stanley Insler on his Sixty-fifth Birthday.

———. "The Composition of the Maitreyi Dialogue in the *Bṛhadāraṇyaka Upaniṣad*." *Journal of the American Oriental Society* 126, 3: (2006) 323–345.

van Buitenen, J. A. B. *The Bhagavadgītā in the Mahābhārata: a Bilingual Edition*. Chicago: University of Chicago, 1981, 1st edition. In Sanskrit (translit.) and English. Trans. by J. A. B. van Buitenen.

Deutsch, Eliot. *The Bhagavad Gita*. New York, Chicago, San Francisco: Holt, Rinehart and Winston, 1968, 1st edition. In English. Introd. and trans. by Eliot Deutsch.

Edgerton, Franklin. *The beginnings of Indian philosophy; selections from the Rig Veda, Atharva Veda, Upanisads, and Mahābhārata*. UNESCO collection of representative works. Indian series. Cambridge: Harvard University Press, 1965, 1st edition. In English. Translated from the Sanskrit with and introd., notes, and glossarial index. Includes bibliographies and index.

———. *The Bhagavad Gītā*. Cambridge, Mass.: Harvard University Press, 1972, 1st edition. Fourth Printing. In English. Introd. and trans. by Franklin Edgerton.

Forsthoefe, Thomas A. *Knowing Beyond Knowledge: Epistemologies of Religious Experience in Classical and Modern Advaita*. Ashgate World Philosophy Series. Alderhot, England & Burlington, VT.: Ashgate, 2002, 1st edition. Includes bibliographical references (183-195) and index.

Gambhirananda, Swami. *Eight Upaniṣads*, volume 1-2. Calcutta, India: Advaita Ashrama, 1977, 4th repr. edition. In English and Sanskrit with the commentary of Śaṅkara (English). Translation by Swami Gambhirananda.

———. *Upaniṣad-granthāvalī*, volume 1-3. Kalikātā: Udbodhana Kāryālaya, 1992, 12th edition. In Sanskrit (Bengali script) and Bengali. Translation by Swami Gambhirananda.

Ghate, V. S. *The Vedānta.* Poona, India: The Bhandarkar Oriental Research Institute, 1960, 2nd edition. In English. "A study of the *Brahma-sūtras* with the *bhāṣyas* of Śaṅkara, Rāmānuja, Nimbārka, Madhva and Vallabha.".

Hacker, Paul. *Philology and Confrontation: Paul Hacker on Traditional and Modern Vedanta.* Albany, New York: State University of New York Press, 1995, 1st edition. Translated from the German by Wilhelm Halbfass.

Hume, Robert Ernest. *The Thirteen Principal Upanishads.* London, Oxford, New York: Oxford University Press, [1921] 1977, repr. edition. In English. Introduction and translation by Robert Ernest Hume.

Ježić, Mislav. *The Proceedings of the Fourth International Vedic Workshop,* Società Editrice Fiorentina and Primus Books, forthcoming, chapter Īśā-Upaniṣad: History of the Text in the Light of the Upaniṣadic Parallels. 1st edition.

Jones, Richard H. "Vidyā and Avidyā in the Īśa Upaniṣad." *Philosophy East and West* 31, 1: (1981 (Jan.)) 79–87.

Kale, M. R. *A Higher Sanskrit Grammar.* Delhi, India: Motilal Banarsidass, 1984, repr. edition.

Krishnamurti, Sharma. B. N. *Philosophy of Śrī Madhvacarya.* Delhi, India.: Motilal Banarsidass, 1991 [1986], revised ed. edition.

Leggett, Trevor. *The Chapter of the Self.* London.: Routledge & Kegan Paul, 1978, 1st edition. Includes Leggett's trans. of the Chapter of the Self from the *Āpastambha-dharma-sūtra* with Śaṅkara's comm.

MacDonell, Arthur. *A Vedic Grammar for Students.* New Delhi, India: D. K. Printworld, [1916] 1999, repr. edition.

———. *A Sanskrit Grammar for Students.* Oxford: Oxford University Press, 1927, 3rd edition.

Madhva. *Upaniṣad-bhāsyam.* Bangalore, India: Poornaprajna Samshodhana Mandiram, 1997, 1st edition. In Sanskrit. Includes the comms. of Jayatīrtha, Vādirājatīrtha, and Rāghavendratīrtha on seven Upaniṣads (Īśā, Kena, Kaṭha, Ṣaṭpraśna, Ātharvana, Māṇḍūkya, and Taittirīya).

Nakamura, Hajime. *A history of early Vedānta philosophy,* volume 1-2. Delhi, India: Motilal Banarsidass, 1983-2004, 1st edition. In English. Translation of: *Shoki no Vēdānta tetsugaku.* Thesis (doctoral)—Univesity of Tokyo, 1942. Vol. 2: translated into English by Hajime Nakamura, Trevor Legget, and others; edited by Sengaku Mayeda. Vol. 2: lacks series statement. Includes bibliographical references and index.

Olivelle, Patrick, editor. *Upaniṣads: a new translation.* Oxford and New York: Oxford University Press, 1996, 1st edition. In English. Introd. and trans. by Patrick Olivelle.

———. *Dharmasūtras: the Law Codes of Ancient India.* Oxford and New York: Oxford University Press, 1999, 1st edition. In English. Trans. by Patrick Olivelle.

Potter, Karl H. *Presuppositions of India's philosophies.* Delhi, India: Motilal Banarsidass Publishers, 1991, 1st edition. First Indian edition.

———. *Advaita Vedānta up to Śaṅkara and his Pupils.* Encyclopedia of Indian Philosophies (vol. 3). Delhi, India.: Motilal Banarsidass, 2008, repr. edition. Includes index (613-35).

Puruṣottama. *Vedāntaratnamañjuṣā.* Benares, India: Chowkhamba Sanskrit Book Depot, 1908, 1st edition. In Sanskrit (Devanāgarī). This is a commentary by Puruṣottama on the *Daśaślokī* of Nimbārka.

Radhakrishnam, S. *The Principal Upaniṣads.* New Delhi, India: Indus [HarperCollins *Publishers* India], [1953] 1994, 1st edition. In English with Sanskrit text (translit.). Trans. by S. Radhakrishnan.

Rambachan, Anantanand. *Accomplishing the accomplished: the Vedas as a source of valid knowledge in Śaṅkara.* Monograph ... of the Society for Asian and Comparative Philosophy; no. 10. Honolulu: University of Hawaii Press, 1991, 1st edition. Includes bibliographical references (p. [159]-165) and index.

Rāmānuja. *Vedārtha-saṅgraha of Śrī Rāmānujācārya.* Mysore, India: Sri Ramakrishna Ashrama, 1968, 2nd edition. In Sanskrit (Devanāgarī) with English translation and introduction by S. S. Raghavachar, MA.

Śaṅkara. *Upadeshasāhasrī of Śaṅkarāchārya*. Mylapore, Madras: Sri Ramakrishna Math, 1949, 1st edition. In Sanskrit (Devanāgarī). English trans. with notes by Swāmī Jagadānanda. Based on the commentary of Rāmatīrtha.

———. *A Thousand Teachings: the Upadeśasāhasrī of Śaṅkara*. Albany, New York: State University of New York Press, 1992, 1st edition. English translation with introduction by Sengaku Mayeda.

Sargeant, Winthrop. *The Bhagavad Gita*, volume In Sanskrit (Devanāgarī and transliteration) and English. Introduction and translations by Winthrop Sargeant. Albany, New York: State University of New York Press, 1994, 1st edition. In Sanskrit (Devanāgarī and transliteration) and English.

Sarma, Deepak. *An Introduction to Madhva Vedanta*. Aldershot, Hampshire, England; Burlington, VT: Ashgate Pub. Ltd., 2003.

Sharma, Arvind. *The Experiential Dimension of Advaita Vedānta*. Delhi, India.: Motilal Banarsidass, 1993, 1st edition. Includes bibliographical references (111-112) and index.

———. *The Rope and the Snake*. New Delh, India: Manohar Publishers & Distributors, 1997, 1st edition. Includes bibliographical references (p. [147]-149) and index.

Sharma, B. N. Krishnamurti. *History of the Dvaita school of Vedānta and its literature: from the earliest beginnings to our own time*. Delhi, India.: Motilal Banarsidass, 1981, 2nd rev. ed. edition.

Smith, R. Morton. "On the White Yajurveda Vaṃśa." *East and West* 16, 1: (1966) 112–125.

———. "Re-meaning Philosophy." *Annals of the Bhandarkar Oriental Research Institute* 48/49: (1968) 123–136. Golden Jubilee Volume 1917-1967.

Staal, Frits. *Discovering the Vedas: Origins, Mantras, Rituals, Insights*. Gurgaon, India.: Penguin Books (India), 2008, 1st edition. Includes index (403-19).

Stcherbatsky, Th. *The Conception of Buddhist Nirvāṇa*. The Hague: Mouton & Co., 1965, 2nd edition. Indo-Iranian Reprints. Indo-Iranian Journal, VI. Originally published by the Academy of Sciences of the USSR, Leningrad, 1927.

Tarkabhūṣaṇa, Pramathanātha, editor. *Śrīmadbhagavadgītā*. Kalikātā, India: Deva Sāhitya Kuṭīra Prāibheṭa Limiṭiḍa, 2001, 7th edition. In Sanskrit (Bengali script) with the comms. of Śaṅkara and Ānandagiri with Bengali translations of the text and Śaṅkara's comm. by Pramathanātha Tarkabhūṣaṇa.

Thieme, P. "Īśopaniṣad (= Vājasaneyi-saṃhitā 40) 1-14." *Journal of the American Oriental Society* 85, 1: (1965) 89–99.

Vedavyāsa. *Viṣṇupurāṇam*. Dilli, India: Parimala Pablikeśansa, 1986, 1st edition. In Sanskrit (Devanāgarī) with the comm. of Śrīdhara Svāmin.

Vidyābhūṣaṇa, Baladeva. *Prameya-ratnāvalī*. Kirksville, MO, USA: Blazing Sapphire Press, 2006, 1st edition. In *The Fundaments of Vedānta: Vedāntic Texts for Beginners*, ed. and trans. by Neal Delmonico.

Yogīndra, Sadānanda. *Vedānta-sāra*. Kirksville, MO, USA: Blazing Sapphire Press, 2006, 1st edition. In *The Fundaments of Vedānta: Vedāntic Texts for Beginners*, ed. and trans. by Neal Delmonico.

Śāstrī, Dinesh Chandra Bhattacharya. *The Fundamentals of Vedānta: Vedāntic Texts for Beginners*, Kirksville, MO, USA: Blazing Sapphire Press, 2006, chapter A Brief Overview of Advatia Vedānta, 225–245. 1st edition. Translated by Neal Delmonico from the Bengali essay "Advaitavedānter Digdarśana" in *Bhāratīya Darśana Kośa*, edited by Srimohan Bhattacharya and Dinesh Chandra Bhattacharya Śāstrī (Calcutta: Sanskrit College, 1981), vol. 3, part 1, 159-190.

Index

CPSIA information can be obtained
at www.ICGtesting.com
Printed in the USA
FSOW04n1740150417
33051FS

9 781936 135097